THE SCHOLAR'S LIBRARY
*General Editor :*—Guy Boas, M.A.

SHORTER POEMS

OF

JOHN MILTON

# SHORTER POEMS

OF

# JOHN MILTON

Edited by

## B. A. WRIGHT

FORMERLY PROFESSOR OF ENGLISH,
UNIVERSITY OF SOUTHAMPTON

LONDON

MACMILLAN & CO LTD

NEW YORK · ST MARTIN'S PRESS

1961

MACMILLAN AND COMPANY LIMITED
*London Bombay Calcutta Madras Melbourne*

THE MACMILLAN COMPANY OF CANADA LIMITED
*Toronto*

ST MARTIN'S PRESS INC
*New York*

PRINTED IN GREAT BRITAIN

# CONTENTS

| | PAGE |
|---|---|
| Life and Introduction | vii |
| Chronology of Milton's Life | xli |
| The Text | xliii |

Poems :—

| | |
|---|---|
| *Paraphrase on Psalm 114* | 1 |
| *Psalm 136* | 2 |
| *On the Death of a Fair Infant* | 5 |
| *At a Vacation Exercise* | 9 |
| *Song on May Morning* | 11 |
| *The Fifth Ode of Horace* | 12 |
| *On the Morning of Christ's Nativity* | 14 |
| *The Passion* | 24 |
| *Upon the Circumcision* | 27 |
| *On Time* | 28 |
| *At a Solemn Music* | 29 |
| *On Shakespear* | 30 |
| *On the University Carrier* | 31 |
| *Another on the Same* | 32 |
| *An Epitaph on the Marchioness of Winchester* | 34 |
| *L'Allegro* | 37 |
| *Il Penseroso* | 42 |
| *Arcades* | 47 |
| *Comus* | 51 |

# CONTENTS

| | PAGE |
|---|---|
| *Lycidas* | 85 |
| *Sonnets I–XIX* | 91 |
| Introductions and Notes to Poems | 103 |
| Appendix | |
| Milton's Cosmology | 207 |
| Questions | 209 |

# LIFE AND INTRODUCTION

THE chief original sources for the life of Milton are :
the biography by his nephew, Edward Phillips ; an
anonymous biography, perhaps written by the younger
nephew, John Phillips ; the biographical notes of
John Aubrey, who was acquainted with Milton and
collected what information he could from Milton's
relations and friends after his death ; and, prior to
all these in date and authenticity, the numerous and
often lengthy passages in Milton's writings which
constitute a fairly complete autobiography.

John Milton was born in Bread Street, Cheapside,
London, on December 9, 1608, at a house, which was
also his father's place of business, called *The Spread
Eagle*. His father, who came originally from Oxford-
shire, was a scrivener or notary ; he prospered in
business, and, in Aubrey's words, got a plentiful
estate. But the father, besides being successful in
business, was also a man of culture. In particular
he was an accomplished musician and a composer of
some celebrity in a time that has been called the
golden age of English music. In a collection of
madrigals published in 1601 and in a book of songs
published in 1614 his compositions were printed
together with those of Byrd, Orlando Gibbons, and
*Training in* other leading musicians of the day. He
*Music* instructed and interested his son in music ;
Aubrey says the poet " had a delicate tuneable voice
and had good skill : his father instructed him : he had
an organ in his house : he played on that most."

vii

Milton more than once acknowledges what he owed to his father, and not the least of his debts was this early training in music. He himself assigns a specific place to music in the *Tractate of Education* ; and his poems are full of references to music that show not only his delight in the art but, what is rarer among poets, his exact knowledge. It was his musical knowledge and training, as much as his study and practice of Latin and Italian poetry, that enabled him to become the greatest technician in English verse. One particular effect of his musical training, pointed out by Hanford,* is worth remark. All his father's known compositions are settings to words, and he must have instructed his son in those points of versification of which the musician is most keenly aware ; consequently Milton learned to write not only lyrics to be read but songs to be sung. Some of the most charming of Milton's early verse, such as the songs in *Arcades* and *Comus*, were written to be set to music. His technical interest in the relation of the two arts is revealed in the sonnet to his friend Lawes, who composed the music for those songs.

The greatest care was bestowed on Milton's early education, and his father, as Tillyard observes, " was *Renaissance* as anxious to instil learning into his son *Education* as Lord Chesterfield to inculcate the social graces." In the *Second Defence* Milton says, " My father directed me as a child to literature and learning, which I applied myself to so eagerly that from twelve years of age I hardly ever retired to bed from my studies before midnight." He was first put under the charge of a tutor, a Scotch presbyterian divine, and then sent at the age of twelve to St. Paul's school. It is important to understand the form and character of this early

* In this Introduction I have made constant use of Professor J. H. Hanford's *Youth of Milton*.

education. St. Paul's was a grammar school, one of the schools founded during the sixteenth century to give instruction chiefly through the rediscovered classical literature. To renaissance Europe the classics offered not only a perfected literature but a philosophy and way of life, a civilisation to be admired and imitated in every respect ; the study of the classics, therefore, together with instruction in the Bible and the Christian religion, provided a complete education. This meant in effect that renaissance education was essentially a literary education, a training in language and all its uses given through the classics. Latin was of course the chief means of instruction, and Latin composition in verse and prose was a prominent part of the school curriculum. In the *Tractate of Education* Milton was to describe these exercises as " a preposterous exaction, forcing the empty wits of children to compose themes, verses, and orations, which are the acts of ripest judgment and the final work of a head filled by long reading and observation " ; here he was joining with the educational reformers of the time who, influenced by the new scientific philosophy, criticised the literary character of the prevalent system and contended that a knowledge of " things " rather than of " words " should be the controlling purpose of education. However that may be, this literary education produced its proper effect during the sixteenth and seventeenth centuries in an eloquence such as the English tongue has never since achieved.

English composition took its natural place in the schools as an accompaniment to Latin composition. At Westminster school the writing of English verse was a regular part of the curriculum, and it was probably so at St. Paul's. Milton's own early versifying, of which he and his biographers speak, was nothing out of the way and would probably be done in the ordinary course of school work, even though with more than ordinary zest and accomplishment for a schoolboy. The two verse paraphrases from the Psalms, for instance, written during his schooldays, are not to be explained as the precocious efforts of a boy brought up in a puritan home ; they are, as Hanford has pointed out, literary exercises as much in accordance with the renaissance cultural tradition as the writing of Latin verse. We see these early productions of Milton's in their right connection if we remember that Sir Thomas Wyatt, the first of our renaissance poets, produced his metrical versions of the Psalms alongside his imitations of Italian love lyrics, and the Scottish humanist Buchanan his Latin versions of the Psalms alongside his imitations of the love poetry of Ovid. Buchanan's Latin versions were in fact school texts which Milton almost certainly used at St. Paul's ; there are several places in his own renderings where the turn of phrase obviously derives from Buchanan's Latin.

This close association of the Bible with the classics and the general intermingling of pagan and Christian thought was a mental habit of the age which it is important to take account of in the study of Milton. From the beginning of the Renaissance in Italy, humanist writers, imitating their admired classical authors in every point, had used pagan forms to embody Christian ideas, sentiments, and beliefs ; Jove or Pan signified more often than not the Christian God, Olympus the Christian heaven. Such use of pagan mythology aptly illustrates the way in which classical literature penetrates and controls all the thinking of the age, religious or secular. Nor was it otherwise in those Protestant countries which, like England, had only felt the full effects of the Renaissance at the time of the Reformation ; for the religious revival was intimately connected with the revival of letters, and the religious reformers were many of them good humanists also. The rediscovery of classical literature, interesting men in the beliefs and opinions of the ancient world, releasing their minds from the authoritative teaching of the Church, had been one of the main forces behind the religious revolt ; and the two movements had much in common both as to means and ends. Just as classical scholars found inspiration in the dignity and enlightenment of the ancient world, so the religious reformers went back beyond what they regarded as the monkish ignorance and superstition of the Middle Ages to the purity of ritual and belief in the early Church ; and the critical methods of the new scholarship were necessary for the historical research involved in this appeal to primitive Christianity. The new scholarship was also necessary to Protestants in their task of retranslating the Bible ; it was typical humanists like Erasmus, intent on scholarship rather than on religious change, who made the translation of the Bible into the modern tongues possible. So classical and biblical scholarship progressed together, the Bible took its place in the humanistic scheme, the literary forms of the Bible were compared with those of classical literature, and the large infusion of Greek and Roman thought present from the beginning in Christian theology was recognised afresh and made the starting-point for re-interpretations of Christian doctrine.

Such was the cultural tradition in which Milton was trained and which never ceased to exercise its influence over his mind. His literary standards remained always classical, and when he extols the Bible as literature he does so by comparison with that of Greece and Rome. *Paradise Lost* itself illustrates this double allegiance to Christianity and classical paganism ; for it was inspired by the ambition, common to the renaissance poets of Europe, to

write an epic on a Christian theme that might vie
with the poems of Homer and Vergil. Again, his
ethical and religious ideas owe at least as much to
classical authors as to Christian teaching or the
Scriptures ; just as his political and social doctrines
owe as much to the same source as to the affairs of
the day and his political connections.

In 1625, at the age of seventeen, Milton entered
at Christ's College, Cambridge ; he remained in
*Cambridge* residence for the full period of seven years
then required for the degree of M.A. The
universities throughout Europe had so far been but
little influenced in their formal instruction by the
intellectual changes that had been taking place in
the outside world, and the system of education
Milton found in force at Cambridge was still that of
the Middle Ages. The first four years of study required for the B.A. degree were mainly devoted to
rhetoric, logic, and metaphysics in the scholastic
tradition. This meant that the student was chiefly
trained in dialectics ; he had to learn to handle
the mass of scholastic learning, to thread his way
through the subtleties of scholastic logic, and to
dispute on the nice problems of scholastic philosophy.
Periodically he was required to take part in public
Disputations, the mediaeval form of examination,
delivering a Latin speech either for or against the
thesis set for debate. Some of Milton's own
*Prolusions*, academical orations of this kind which he
had preserved, were published towards the end of
his life ; besides enabling us to appreciate the mental
discipline provided by this system of education, they
frequently illustrate the development of Milton's ideas.
(See Tillyard : *Milton's Private Correspondence and
Academic Exercises*.)

Milton, in the usual way, profited from these studies
at the same time that he derided them. In after

years he was to accuse the universities of being " not yet well recovered from the scholastic grossness of barbarous ages," and to complain of the undergraduates being " mocked and deluded all this while with ragged notions and babblements, while they expected worthy and delightful knowledge." He did not, however, wait until he had left the university to declare his opinion of the curriculum. In the *Prolusions* (written, we must remember, and publicly delivered as academical exercises in pursuance of his degrees) he never misses an opportunity of expressing his contempt for the studies he is forced to pursue ; the *Third Prolusion*, in particular, is a direct attack on the scholastic philosophy and an enthusiastic appeal for a more humanistic learning. This antipathy to the university curriculum must have manifested itself early ; for Milton got at loggerheads with his tutor during his first year at Cambridge and was rusticated for a term. The matter seems to have been amicably settled, however, by changing the tutor, and in time Milton came to be both popular and respected in the college. Despite his opinion of the official studies he certainly made the best of them ; " was a very hard student in the University," says Aubrey, " and performed all his exercises there with good applause." And the effect of these seven years' training in traditional mediaeval knowledge is fully apparent in his writings. The truth is that Milton, like all the writers and scholars of this age of transition, derived much of his thought and learning from that scholastic literature he professed to despise ; and there consequently arise what appear to us mental contradictions similar to that between his Christian faith and his pagan forms of expression. Thus, many of the theological ideas and beliefs of this " Puritan " poet come direct from the scholastic system of thought ; although interested in the new science, particularly the new astronomy, he naturally thinks in terms of mediaeval physics ; in the main he is a rationalist, trusting in the sovereign power of Reason, yet he finds no difficulty in writing convincingly of astrology, alchemy, magic, fairies, and witchcraft. In all these respects he was typical of the age.

Milton's chief grievance against the educational discipline of the University was that it did not favour the cultivation of the muses ; yet it was during his second year at Cambridge that he entered on his first productive period as a poet. Most of this early verse, previous to the *Nativity Ode*, is in Latin ; but Milton's Latin poems are an integral part of his work and have to be taken into account in tracing the growth of his ideas, the literary influences behind his English writings, and the development of his English style ; and frequently they reveal his personality and his interests in a more intimate manner than his English poems. Of the seven poems probably written in 1626 one is the English elegy *On the Death of a Fair Infant* and the other six are Latin poems. All are imitative in manner and have something of the air of literary exercises : in the English poem he too obviously follows certain contemporary fashions in verse, whilst the Latin poems are modelled on Ovid and Horace. And yet to say that they are exercises and imitative is not to say that they are insincere or entirely un-original ; it is simply that Milton like other poets had to find his own style by practice on chosen models. Part of the interest in studying the early poems is to watch the emergence of his individual style, as well as his first handling of characteristic themes and motives. Many of the traits of the later Miltonic manner obviously derive from his practice of Latin verse : the use of words in their Latin sense and of Latin constructions and idioms ; the control of the

*Latin Poetry*

LIFE AND INTRODUCTION

long metrical paragraph ; the ready allusion to
classical myth and fable.

Three of the Latin poems written during the first
four years at Cambridge give an insight into Milton's
emotional life at this time and reveal one of the
sources of his creative activity. In *Elegy I* (1626),
*Elegy VII* (1628), and *Elegy V* (1629) he writes on the
theme of feminine beauty and the influence of love
in an entirely sensuous and pagan manner, imitating
the love poetry of Ovid and other Latin elegists. In
the sense already indicated these poems too are
literary exercises. Latin love poetry was admired and
imitated as a branch of classical literature ; and
Milton was only following the example of other
eminent and respectable humanists in desiring to
show his skill in it. The skill lay in expressing himself exactly in the manner of his models : and if the
classical elegists dwelt solely on the sensuous side of
love, Milton must do likewise. It does not follow
that he failed to put his own moral interpretation on
the poetry (as we shall see that he claims to have
done), any more than his constant use of classical
mythology proves him to have been devoid of
Christian sentiments and beliefs. Yet, although the
classical tradition explains how Milton came to write
poems he would never have written in English, it
does not explain away their significance. They reveal
a side of his nature which, because of his moral
earnestness and because his English poetry does not
express it so simply and frankly, we are apt to ignore
or undervalue. His susceptibility to " female charm "
is equally evident in the English poetry but is there
usually associated with moral issues, with the condemnation of vice or the praise of virtue ; the Latin
elegies represent this side of his mind isolated, as it
were, by a literary convention from the moral con-
siderations that in reality, then as later, controlled it.

xv

In the *Apology for Smectymnuus*, a tract written in 1642, Milton has given his own account of this stage in his mental and literary development. He is replying in the tract to certain defamatory statements of his controversial opponent, who among other things had accused him of loose living ; Milton meets this in a characteristic way by relating the development of his personal ideal of chastity, an ideal that found final poetic expression in *Comus*. With this as main theme he proceeds to write his literary biography, something corresponding in prose to Wordsworth's poetical history of " The Growth of a Poet's Mind." It is a document of the utmost value for the whole of the first period of Milton's life, and especially for the interpretation of *Comus*. He begins with the time of emotional and imaginative awakening represented by the Latin elegies, with which he definitely connects the first strong impulse of his own poetic activity. In his classical reading he was attracted, he says, both by the harmonious style and by the matter of " the smooth elegiac poets " (chief among whom would be Ovid). " Whence having observed them to account it the chief glory of their wit in that they were able to judge, to praise, and by that could esteem themselves worthiest to love those high perfections which under one or other name they took to celebrate ; I thought with myself . . . that what emboldened them to this task might with such diligence as they used embolden me." In other words, this love poetry " in praise of ladies dead " appealed to his youthful emotions and incited him to try his poetic talent on similar themes. It is not a new story of poetic initiation. But Milton adds that he considered his own abilities would best appear " by how much more wisely and with more love of virtue I should choose (let rude ears be absent) the object of not unlike praises "—celebrate the lady of his choice, that is, in verse more chaste but not inferior to that of the Latin poets.

Critics are dubious of the interpretation Milton put on this Ovidian phase and the motives he imputed to himself some thirteen years after the event. They point out that the Latin elegies he wrote under the immediate inspiration of the Roman elegists betray no signs of any such higher moral purpose, except in avoiding indecencies. But this is to ignore the other love poems written at this time, of which Milton was also thinking and which justify his words. These other poems were written in direct imitation of Italian poetry, and the difference in tone reveals to what an extent the character and tone of his Latin elegies were due to the literary convention in which he was working.

The Italian influence in Milton's work is second in importance only to that of the classics, with which *Italian* indeed it is closely connected ; for Italy, *Poetry* where the revival of learning began, was for long the centre of humanistic studies, it was the source of all the artistic and intellectual movements of the Renaissance, and it was the first country to produce a modern literature that might be put in comparison with that of Greece and Rome. The writers of all countries admired and studied and imitated Italian literature as they did the classics ; " but Milton," says Smart, " who was the last great poet of the age which looked to Italy for inspiration, was also its most complete and accomplished scholar." The effects are discernible in his thought and his poetic forms, his prosody, and his style. Dr. Johnson observed that one of the sources of Milton's style was " his familiarity with the Tuscan poets : the disposition of his words is, I think, frequently Italian." His study and practice of Italian verse reinforced the effects of his study and practice

of Latin verse ; he learnt much from the Italians of
the ways in which a writer in a modern tongue might
reproduce the art of classical poets.

The first of these poems revealing the new influence
is the sonnet *To a Nightingale*, which is considered to
have been composed about the same time as the fifth
Latin elegy, in the spring of 1629 ; the theme is the
same (the immemorial theme of the renewal of love
and the poetic impulse with the return of spring) and
the opening lines of the sonnet are a direct translation
from the elegy : yet the tone and sentiment are quite
different. The poems, however, that especially concern
us are a series of Italian love sonnets in Petrarchan
form, which were probably composed during this same
year ; for it is these sonnets that justify Milton's words
in the *Apology*. What he writes there suggests poems
in honour of a particular person ; the Latin elegies
do not answer to this description and the only poems
that can possibly be meant are the Italian sonnets
addressed to someone named Emilia, who appears
to have been a lady of Italian descent living in
England. Some critics suppose " the object of his
praises " to be an imaginary ideal, but Smart is
almost certainly right in concluding that we have
here a genuine " record of his first love."

Turning again to the *Apology for Smectymnuus* we find
our interpretation fits precisely with what Milton
goes on to say. He asks his readers not to blame him
for seeking " in those years " the reward to be won
by the poet in extolling feminine beauty, " whereof
not to be sensible when good and fair in one person
meet argues both a gross and shallow judgment,
and withal an ungentle and swainish breast." He
then adds : " If I found those authors (*i.e.* the Roman
elegists) anywhere speaking unworthy things of themselves or unchaste of those names they had extolled,
this effect it wrought on me, from that time forward

their art I still applauded but the men I deplored ; and above them all preferred the two famous renowners of Beatrice and Laura (*i.e.* Dante and Petrarch), who never write but honour of them to whom they devote their verse, displaying sublime and pure thoughts without transgression." Since Milton's Italian studies go back many years (his skill in Italian verse would alone prove that), it is evident that the Latin and Italian influences referred to in this passage were simultaneous : throughout these years he applauded the art of the classical poets while preferring the purer sentiments and thoughts of the Italians.

Milton here draws attention to the main distinction between ancient and modern love poetry. The Petrarchan tradition he followed in his Italian sonnets expressed a romantic view of the relationship of the sexes which reversed that of the classical world and may be reckoned the most original contribution of mediaeval chivalry to our modern civilisation : it exalted woman as the embodiment of all perfections, representing her as an object of worship and man as her humble and reverential servant. For Milton this religion of love could be no more than a passing phase ; by temperament he inclines to the classical and puritan view of woman as belonging to the inferior sex, the view put with admirable brevity in *Paradise Lost* :—

" He for God only, she for God in him."

Nevertheless, romantic love with its chivalric ideal of womanhood is an element in his early poetry, and, in association with the Platonic view of love and beauty with which it naturally assimilates, was given mature expression in *Comus*.

So far Milton has been working in various literary forms and conventions, none of which could fully

reveal his individual genius ; but at Christmas
of this same year of 1629 he composed the ode *On
the Morning of Christ's Nativity*, the first truly
Miltonic poem. The ode, an astonish-
ing performance at the age of twenty-one, was the
outcome of his first clear vision of the true power
of poetry and of the kind of poet he should be.
Not only did he know now the heroic themes on
which he would write, but, what was even more
important, he had come to realise the long years of
training and experience that would be needed to
prepare him for his task. Mere literary accomplishment would not be enough ; he must make himself
both intellectually and morally fit for such poetry as
he intended to write. His aim was not to be restricted, like Pope's, to becoming the most " correct "
of poets, to acquiring skill to produce faultless verse
on any subject that happened to present itself ; nor to
contriving by verbal craft and intellectual ingenuity
to write plausibly on great matters. The poet, he had
come to see, must be the equal of his poetry in
character as well as in mind ; there must be no
pretence in the thought and sentiment any more than
in the art ; he must speak the truth out of his own
knowledge and worth : in a word, he must first *be*
his poem. The famous passage in which Milton
expresses this characteristic view follows immediately
on that last quoted from the *Apology*:—

*The Poetic Vocation*

" And long it was not after when I was confirmed
in this opinion, that he who would not be frustrate of
his hope to write well hereafter in laudable things
ought himself to *be* a true poem, that is a composition
and pattern of the best and honourablest things ; not
presuming to sing high praises of heroic men or
famous cities, unless he have in himself the experience
and practice of all that which is praiseworthy."

The reason for referring this statement to the close of 1629 and for believing that the Nativity Ode was inspired by this first clear vision of the poetic life is that the sixth Latin elegy, which is addressed to his friend Diodati and in which Milton mentions that he is writing the ode, expresses the same view that the validity of poetry depends on the personal integrity of the poet : the heroic or epic poet is a kind of prophet, speaking the truth revealed by the gods to one who has kept himself pure as a priest at their altars and dedicated himself to their service.

The remainder of Milton's life, even when he seemed to turn aside from his purpose, was dominated by this resolution to dedicate himself to the service of poetry. He had gone to Cambridge with a view to entering the Church ; not only did he abandon this intention, but he declined to take to any of the professions his university training qualified him for. On leaving Cambridge in 1632 he settled with his parents at Horton, a village near Windsor, where his father had retired from business some years earlier ; and here for another five years he continued much the same course of life as he had led at Cambridge. Relations and friends were naturally critical of what seemed an aimless way of life ; but Milton knew what he was about, and held to his course. The decision not to make his way in the world by the ordinary paths would never have been taken by one of so active and purposeful a nature unless he had been confident of winning power and fame by other means ; the ambition that governed his conduct was to be stated later in the *Reason of Church Government*, " that by labour and intent study (which I take to be my portion in life) joined with the strong propensity of nature, I might perhaps leave something so written to aftertimes as they should not willingly let it die." On settling at Horton he laid his plans to this end ; and to see the

Horton period in proper perspective as a stage in
Milton's life one must realise that he was mainly
engaged during these years, not in writing the poems
of the period, but in systematic study and preparation
for the greater poetic task ahead. The poems are
occasional poems, and three of the more important—
*Arcades*, *Comus*, and *Lycidas*—were in fact written on
request. These facts have nothing, of course, to do
with their poetic value ; as completed works of art
they are independent of origins and conditions of
production ; but to realise that they are the inter-
mittent work of a mind intent on a greater purpose
helps us to appreciate the moods in which they were
composed, to understand certain peculiarities of
thought, and to avoid misinterpretations.

The course of systematic studies now undertaken
to equip himself for his future work was on a truly
*Studies at* Miltonic scale, and was to be pursued with
*Horton* characteristic thoroughness not only
throughout the years at Horton, but right up to
the time of his blindness. Much of it—his wide
and continuous reading in ancient and modern
literatures, in philosophy and theology—was an ex-
tension of studies already embarked on at Cambridge ;
but the comprehensive study of world history he
now began was a new departure and will serve to
illustrate the thoroughness of his methods. He started
with Greek and Roman history, studying the chief
original authorities ; proceeded next to the history
of the early church as recorded in the first Christian
historians and the writings of the Fathers ; then to
the history of the Eastern Empire down to the fall
of Constantinople in the fifteenth century, and of
the Western Empire from the fall of Rome through
the Middle Ages ; this brought him to the period of
the European Renaissance and from this point, which
he had reached at the time of writing *Lycidas*, he

proposed to go on to study the histories of the various Italian cities separately.

One of the chief sources of our detailed knowledge of these studies, more particularly the historical studies, is Milton's Commonplace Book, discovered in 1874. This book, which he commenced to keep during the Horton period, consists of extracts from certain parts of his reading arranged so as to illustrate his opinions on current questions of ecclesiastical and civil government and of social morality ; and it reveals a deeper purpose in his studies than the mere acquisition of knowledge. Milton believed that the poet should instruct men in true living ; that his office was analogous to that of the prophets of Israel and the orators of Greece and Rome. He believed that poetry should deal with all the problems of life, whether public or private, and be " of power, beside the office of a pulpit, to imbreed and cherish in a great people the seeds of virtue and public civility." It was therefore necessary that the poet should have considered the principles of a rightly organised society, that he should have a political philosophy ; and this was one of the chief purposes of his historical studies.

The entries in the Commonplace Book reveal that already during the quiet days at Horton he was forming the opinions that were to be applied to affairs of the day in his prose tracts : his republican principles, his views on divorce, his conviction that Church and State should be separate in their functions, his general doctrine of liberty as it affects the whole life of the citizen, all are clearly indicated. There is every reason to believe that even though Milton had not devoted the middle years of his life to the political struggle, his political views would have been the same, equally definite and equally important to him, and would have found their place in his epic.

In this general history of Milton's development *Comus* is the one poem of the Horton period to which *Chivalric Romance* special attention must be paid ; for *Comus* not only reveals his youthful mind most completely, but illustrates the last two formative influences recorded by Milton in the *Apology for Smectymnuus* :—

" Next . . . I betook me among those lofty fables and romances which recount in solemn cantos the deeds of knighthood founded by our victorious kings, and from hence had in renown over all Christendom. There I read it in the oath of every knight that he should defend to the expence of his best blood, or his life if it so befell him, the honour and chastity of virgin or matron. . . . And if I found in the story afterward any of them by word or deed breaking that oath, I judged it the same fault of the poet as that which is attributed to Homer, to have written undecent things of the gods."

The general terms in which Milton speaks would apply to the whole vast field of mediaeval Arthurian romance ; and certainly he was well read in this literature. But " solemn cantos " suggests that he is referring more especially to the renaissance epic of chivalric romance, the form in which the modern poets had attempted to rival the poems of Homer and Vergil ; and the Arthurian legend was indeed to be Milton's own first choice of subject for his epic. The epic of romance had been developed in Italy during the sixteenth century by Boiardo, Ariosto, and Tasso, with whose works Milton was later if not already acquainted ; of all the poems in this class, however, he was probably referring chiefly to the *Faerie Queene* of Spenser, who had himself been inspired by his Italian predecessors. That Milton had been studying the *Faerie Queene* some time before writing *Comus* is suggested by the allusion in *Il Penseroso*, but it is in *Comus* that we see the full effects of the influence. The allegory of chastity in the third book of the *Faerie Queene* was Milton's chief poetic model, so far as he followed one, in treating the same theme ; besides resemblances in thought, incident, and phraseology, there is the direct tribute paid to Spenser under the name of Meliboeus,

" The soothest shepherd that ere pip'd on plains."

The epithet " soothest " indicates Milton's regard for Spenser as a teacher, a speaker of truth such as he himself meant to be ; the same praise is given in the *Areopagitica*, where he writes of " our sage and serious Spenser, whom I dare be known to think a better teacher than Scotus or Aquinas." When Milton told Dryden that Spenser was his " original," *i.e.* his poetical father, he meant above all that as a poetic teacher he had carried on the Spenserian tradition.

It was as the poet of platonism that Spenser especially interested and attracted Milton ; and this *Platonism* brings us to a consideration of the second of the formative influences during this period. Renaissance platonism was a strange amalgam (the main elements are explained in the note to *Il Penseroso*, ll. 87-96) and it assumed many forms ; the particular form that concerns us at the moment is what was known as Platonic Love. In order to understand what Spenser and Milton in turn made of this ruling idea of the age it is necessary first to understand Plato's doctrine of Ideas, which is the key to his philosophy. By Ideas Plato means the realities which constitute the true nature and plan of the universe, and alone give meaning and purpose to life. Reality is clearly not to be found in the world known to the senses, the material world of change and decay, of contradictory good and evil ; behind this confused show of life there must be a permanent and self-consistent, a logical world. Since it is only in abstract thought that such a world can be conceived, it must be a world of mind or pure intelligence ; and this is Plato's world of Ideas, of perfect truth and goodness and beauty, the other world of spiritual existence. This is the world in which our souls existed before entering the body, and to which they will return. Whilst the soul, however, is a prisoner in the body it forgets the real world to which it belongs, being made subject to sensual desires and earthly interests ; yet it is possible even in this life to regain something of that true knowledge by exercise of the reason, the supreme faculty of the soul that enables us to escape from the world of the senses and of false appearance and to see things as they really are. Those who practise this way of life, whom we call Philosophers or Lovers of Wisdom, are the truly virtuous souls ; for no one who sees what is really good will be so foolish as to act contrary to it. Plato accordingly identifies virtue with knowledge and vice with ignorance. In a famous passage of the *Phaedrus* he represents the nature of the soul under the figure of a charioteer driving two winged steeds. The steeds represent our irrational impulses, the one all such passions of the heart as indignation and anger and self-will, the other the appetites of the flesh ; the charioteer is the reason, which should curb and control these passions and direct them to the pursuit of the knowledge that is virtue.

Now this myth of the *Phaedrus* is used by Plato in expounding his theory of love and beauty, as one aspect of his general doctrine of Ideas. There is an Idea of beauty, just as there are Ideas of truth and goodness, because it is known in our experience as an integral part of reality ; and love is the passion for this Idea of beauty, which we seek in this world as we seek for goodness and truth. Plato's theory of love and beauty is therefore a part of his theory of knowledge and of his attempt to provide a rational interpretation of existence : renaissance platonists adapted it to Christian doctrine and the romantic view of love. The results can be studied in Spenser's poetry, particularly in the *Hymns in Honour of Love and Beauty* and in the *Faerie Queene*. The Platonic Idea of beauty is there used to interpret the chivalric ideal of womanhood. Feminine beauty is regarded as a reflection of the Ideal Beauty, as truth and goodness made visible, the expression of an inward perfection ; it is the beautiful soul that fashions for itself a beautiful body. Woman's beauty is therefore a symbol of moral and spiritual power, exercising its influence on the spirit of man ; and love is an act of worship, a religious discipline, an ascent from earthly to heavenly love. In the *Faerie Queene* this sexual idealism is used allegorically to represent the Christian virtues ; in *Book I* Una, for instance, represents Christian Truth, which reveals itself in a surpassing beauty able to unmask fraud and to subdue the most savage breast. But the inevitable effect of this symbolism is that whatever virtue Spenser's heroines are meant to embody reduces itself in action to the particular female virtue of chastity. Chastity is definitely presented in the story of Britomart ; but the stories of Una and Belphoebe and Amoret are exactly similar in type—all are virgins who meet with misadventures, but whose beauty can dash

" brute violence
With sudden adoration and blank awe."

The fact is that the Christian and chivalric ideal of

chastity was the representative virtue of this particular form of renaissance platonism ; and the mystic doctrine of chastity became one of the ruling ideas of the time, to be met with not only in every branch of imaginative literature but in such a practical affair as the national adoration of Elizabeth as the Virgin Queen.

In *Comus* Milton makes full poetic use of these traditional ideas and sentiments : the idea that the soul fashions the body, that feminine beauty expresses moral and spiritual grace, the identification of virtue with chastity, and the half-superstitious belief in the magic power of chastity. But *Comus* is more than a rehandling of a familiar literary theme under the influence of Spenserian platonism. For years Milton had been a diligent student of Plato and he understood the relation of the neoplatonic ideas of his time to Plato's own teaching. *Comus* is a platonic poem in a more original and genuine sense. The main argument, as announced in the opening and closing lines of the poem, is the free immortal life that awaits the virtuous soul ; and since these opening lines are a summary of Plato's *Phaedo*, Milton presumably interpreted virtue in the true platonic sense, identifying it with the rule of reason and with knowledge. Chastity is only introduced later as the motive of the story that is to illustrate this larger theme of virtue as knowledge and of vice as ignorance. The evidence for this reading of the poem will be found in the notes ; but there is also the evidence of Milton's statement in the *Apology*. Having spoken of Spenser and the poets of romance, he next says :—

" Thus from the laureate fraternity of poets riper years and the ceaseless round of study and reading led me to the shady spaces of philosophy, but chiefly to the divine volumes of Plato and his equal Xeno-

phon : where if I should tell ye what I learnt of
chastity and love, I mean that which is truly so, whose
charming cup is only virtue which she bears in her
hand to those who are worthy (the rest are cheated
with a thick intoxicating potion which a certain
sorceress, the abuser of love's name, carries about)
and how the first and chiefest office of love begins
and ends in the soul, producing those happy twins of
her divine generation, knowledge and virtue—with
such abstracted sublimities as these it might be worth
your listening, readers."

This passage remains the best comment on the
inspiration and purpose of *Comus*.

In the *Second Defence* Milton tells us that after five
years spent at Horton and a year after his mother's
*Continental* death, " being eager to visit foreign
*Tour* countries, and above all Italy, I obtained
my father's consent and left home with one servant."
To visit the country he knew so well through its
literature, both ancient and modern, had been a
long cherished desire and he made the most of his
opportunity now that it had come. It was probably about the middle of April, soon after receiving
the letter from Sir Henry Wotton prefixed to the
1645 edition of *Comus*, that he set out, travelling
by way of Paris and Nice to Florence. At Florence,
the cultural centre of Italy, he remained two
months, being well received by Florentine society
and their literary academies, and forming several
lasting friendships. " There it was," says Milton in
the *Areopagitica*, " that I found and visited the famous
Galileo, grown old, a prisoner to the Inquisition for
thinking in astronomy otherwise than the Franciscan
and Dominican licensers thought." From Florence
he went on to Rome, " where I was retained another
two months by the antiquities and ancient renown

of that city, and enjoyed the accomplished society of Lucas Holstenius (Keeper of the Vatican Library) and of many other learned and talented men." Proceeding next to Naples he received an introduction to Manso, Marquis of Villa, who had been the friend and patron of Tasso ; Manso showed him many courteous attentions, and Milton on leaving addressed to him a Latin poem in which he speaks for the first time of writing an English epic on the Arthurian wars. Milton was now preparing to cross over to Sicily and afterwards to Greece when, about the end of 1638, he received news of impending civil war in England, " and I thought it shameful to be travelling quietly for the improvement of my mind while my fellow countrymen were fighting for liberty at home." The civil war referred to was the First Bishops' War, brought about by the King's attempt in the summer of 1637 to enforce the episcopal system in the Scottish Church ; actual hostilities did not commence until March 1639, but Milton had heard how both sides were already arming and that war was now inevitable. Although he could not with an easy conscience go farther afield, he evidently felt no call, so long as he was in touch with home events, to hurry back. He spent another two months at Rome and another two at Florence, where he found himself as welcome, he says, as if it had been his native country ; then crossed the Apennines to Venice, staying there a month and shipping home the books collected in Italy ; then crossed the Alps to Geneva, where he passed some weeks ; and finally arrived back in England in July or August 1639.

Soon after his return Milton settled in London, taking apartments in St. Bride's Churchyard, Fleet *London :* Street, where " he first undertook the *First Tracts* education and instruction of his sister's sons," Edward and John Phillips. It was probably now that he wrote the *Epitaphium Damonis*, the best of all his Latin poems, in which he commemorates his friend Diodati, who had died while Milton was abroad ; as a pastoral elegy on one who was nearer and dearer than Edward King, it is instructive to compare its carefully wrought effects with those of *Lycidas*. After a few months Milton hired a " pretty garden-house in Aldersgate Street," and here, he tells us, " I returned happily to my interrupted studies, trusting the issue of public affairs to God and to those to whom the people had committed that charge." However, he was not long to remain aloof from the political controversies of the day. The Long Parliament met in November 1640 and it soon appeared that the question on which there was most difference of opinion was the reform of the English Church. " As soon as liberty of speech was no longer subject to control," writes Milton in the *Second Defence*, " all mouths were opened against the bishops. . . . This awakened all my zeal and attention. I saw that a way was opening for the establishment of real liberty ; that the foundation was laying for the deliverance of man from the yoke of slavery and superstition . . . and as I had from my youth studied the distinctions between religious and civil rights, I perceived that if ever I wished to be of use I ought at least not to be wanting to the church and to my fellow Christians in a crisis of so much danger. I therefore determined to relinquish the other pursuits in which I was engaged and to transfer the whole force of my talents and industry to this one important object." The result was his first pamphlet, *Of Reformation Touching Church Discipline*, published in the summer of 1641, which argues the case for the abolition of episcopacy and the setting up of a truly " reformed " church on the model of the Scottish Presbyterian system. When this had been partially accomplished Milton was to find that Presbyterianism could be as tyrannical and intolerant as Anglicanism, and that " New Presbyter was but old Priest writ large."

Milton was acting with full deliberation when he laid aside his literary studies and designs for the pamphleteering and political work that was to occupy the whole middle period of his life.  He was devoting himself to the cause of liberty on his own principle that " he who would not be frustrate of his hope to write well hereafter in laudable things ought himself to *be* a true poem . . . not presuming to sing high praises of heroic men or famous cities unless he have in himself the experience and the practice of all that which is praiseworthy."  In the *Reason of Church Government*, written early in 1642, he speaks at large of his poetic ambitions, " hereby to make it manifest with what small willingness I endure to interrupt the pursuit of no less hopes than these, and leave a calm and pleasing solitariness, fed with cheerful and confident thoughts, to embark in a troubled sea of noises and harsh disputes."  Yet if he were to shirk playing his part in the national struggle, " I foresee what stories I should hear within myself, all my life after, of discourage and reproach. . . . Thou hast the diligence, the parts, the language of a man, if a vain subject were to be adorned or beautified, but when the cause of God and His Church was to be pleaded, for which purpose that tongue was given thee which thou hast, God listened if He could hear thy voice among His zealous servants but thou wert dumb as a beast ; from hence forward be that which thine own brutish silence hath made thee. . . . Whatever thou dost now talk, or write, or look is the alms of other men's active prudence and zeal.  Dare not now to say or do anything better than thy former sloth and infancy . . . what before was thy sin is now thy duty, to be abject and worthless. These and such like lessons as these, I know would have been my matins daily, and my evensong." It was, then, in order that he might not lose his self-respect and know himself unworthy of heroic poetry that Milton sacrificed to politics those twenty years which a certain sort of literary critic never ceases lamenting : the poet these critics would have had Milton be could never have written *Paradise Lost*.

Between June 1641 and March 1642 Milton turned out in rapid succession five pamphlets on this question of church reform, which are known as the anti-prelatical tracts and make the first group of his prose writings. In May 1642, " he took a *First Marriage* journey into the country," says Edward Phillips, " nobody about him certainly knowing the reason why," and a month later returned a married man. His wife was Mary Powell, eldest daughter of Richard Powell, a Justice of the Peace, of Forest Hill, six miles from Oxford. Mary was seventeen years old and did not, according to Phillips, take kindly to " a philosophical life (after having been used to a great house, and much company and joviality). Her friends, possibly incited by her own desire, made earnest suit by letter to have her company the remaining part of the summer." Her husband consenting, Mary went home about the end of July, promising to be back by the end of September. In the meantime King and Parliament had begun to collect their forces for the coming struggle, and there was much marching and counter-marching of troops in and around Oxford ; in these circumstances neither Mary nor her family thought that she should rejoin her Parliamentarian husband who, when September had passed, began sending letters and finally sent a foot-messenger urging her return. On October 29, after the battle of Edgehill, the King entered Oxford, which was to be his headquarters for the rest of the war ; Forest Hill was in the area controlled by the Royalist forces in Oxford and Richard Powell necessarily threw in his lot with the King's party. The Powells, says Phillips, now " began to repent them of having matched the eldest daughter of the family to a person so contrary to them in opinion ; and thought it would be a blot in their escutcheon, whenever that Court should come to flourish again." After the battle of Naseby in June 1645, which finally broke the Royalist army and settled the issue of the civil war, the Powells, now ruined, decided that Mary should return to her husband. Milton forgave and took her back. After the fall of Oxford in June 1646 the remainder of the Powell family joined her at Milton's house for several months, " her father and mother, and several of her brothers and sisters, which were in all pretty numerous."

A year after his wife deserted him Milton published his first divorce tract, *The Doctrine and Discipline of Divorce,* which was issued in an enlarged form the next year and followed up by three other tracts on the same subject. No doubt his own unfortunate marriage was the immediate occasion prompting him to write these tracts ; but divorce was a much debated question in Protestant countries and one in which Milton had interested himself as long ago as the Horton days. His main thesis is, that to grant divorce only on the ground of adultery is to degrade the whole idea and purpose of marriage, in which intellectual and spiritual companionship should be a primary consideration ; accordingly he advocates the granting of divorce on application to those who find themselves unsuited to each other in mind and character.

*Second Group of Tracts*

On June 14, 1643, Parliament had passed a new Ordinance for Printing, putting an end to the freedom enjoyed by the press since the Court of the Star Chamber, which had previously exercised a rigid control of the press under Laud, was abolished in the first year of the Long Parliament : all publications were now once more required to be licensed by an official censor. The Act expressed the determination of the Presbyterian party, now in control in Parliament, to impose a new uniformity in religious practice and belief ; Milton recognised it as a revival of the recent tyranny of Charles I and his ministers, and promptly proceeded to defy the authorities. His first divorce tract, published a few weeks after the ordinance came into force, was unlicensed and unregistered like its predecessors ; the second edition appeared also without licence and was addressed, by way of open challenge, to the Parliament and the Assembly of Divines. Milton's conduct was aggravated by the fact that his views on divorce definitely placed him among those free-thinkers against whom the ordinance was especially directed. The tract was denounced in a sermon preached before Parliament ; and in reply to a petition of the Stationers' Company (whose commercial rights were injured by unauthorised publications) Parliament ordered the Printing Committee to inquire out the author. So far as we know the matter went no further ; but the affair roused Milton to address to Parliament his public protest in what is the best known of all his prose works, *Areopagitica : A Speech for the Liberty of Unlicensed Printing.* He also made his poetic comment in *Sonnets VI, VII,* and *X.*

These tracts together with the *Tractate of Education* all belong to the years 1643–1645, and form the second group of Milton's prose works ; their public as distinct from any private purpose is clearly and honestly expressed in the passage from the *Second Defence* quoted in the notes to *Sonnet VII.* For the

1645-9.

next four years Milton retired from public controversy and occupied himself with three works of scholarship : one was the *History of Britain*, the result of studies undertaken originally with a view to writing his epic on the early and legendary history of the nation ; another was the *Christian Doctrine*, a complete system of theology based on Scripture that was to provide the intellectual framework of *Paradise Lost* ; and the third was a new Latin dictionary. At the same time he was watching public events as closely as ever, and the course of his opinions may be followed in the sonnets composed during this period of 1645-1649. The Presbyterian influence in Parliament was declining and the Independents, in alliance with Cromwell's army, were coming into control. Originally the Independents were those who held that each religious congregation should be autonomous, free from all external jurisdiction ; and it was they who had resisted the attempt of the Presbyterians, both in Parliament and in the Assembly of Divines, to establish a rigid ecclesiastical system in England. The party naturally attracted to itself all who objected to being priest-ridden, all who desired toleration for either religious or secular opinions, and all who entertained liberal or revolutionary views of any kind. In all respects Milton was a thoroughgoing Independent. Moreover, he was in sympathy with the increasing republican sentiment of the party. An early entry in the Commonplace Book shows that he had inclined towards republican views long before the civil war ; and now, as it became more and more apparent that the King could not be trusted to make a lasting and satisfactory settlement with the nation, Milton was entirely in agreement with the Independent leaders in Parliament and Army that the King must be got rid of and a republic set up. After the second civil

1648.

war, which Milton commemorates in his sonnet to

Fairfax, Charles was brought to trial and executed in February 1649 ; two weeks later Milton published his pamphlet, *Of the Tenure of Kings and Magistrates,* in which, although he does not mention Charles, he argues the general thesis that subjects, being free men, have the right to depose or to put to death a tyrant or wicked king.

The new government was quick to secure Milton's talents for its official service : in March 1649 he was *Official Work* appointed Secretary for Foreign Tongues *under the* to the Council of State. His duties con-*Commonwealth* sisted in translating foreign documents, drafting the Latin correspondence with foreign powers, and composing replies in Latin or English to any publications at home or abroad calculated to influence public opinion and sentiment against the Commonwealth. We need take account only of his writings under the last head, in which he appeared as the literary champion of the revolutionary government and the principles on which it was founded. During its first year the greatest danger to the security of the new government was the horror felt throughout the nation at the execution of the King, which had produced a reaction in favour of monarchy and disposed people to regard Charles as a royal martyr. This sentiment had been fostered by the publication, immediately after the execution, of the *Eikon Basilike* (Royal Image), *the portraiture of his sacred majesty in his solitude and sufferings* ; purporting to be an authentic copy of the King's prayers and meditations during his last years up to the hour of his death, it had obtained an enormous circulation. The Council, alarmed at its effect on public opinion, ordered Milton to deal with it. As Milton saw it, his duty was to check the spread of a pernicious political sentiment by striking at its root, and he did not spare his blows ; the *Eikonoklastes* (Image-

Breaker) is a merciless criticism of both the dead King and his book.

The horror and indignation felt throughout Europe at the act of the English regicides also threatened the prestige and safety of the Commonwealth. Charles II, an exile in France, had engaged Salmasius, one of the foremost European scholars, to write an elaborate Latin treatise vindicating the dead King and holding up to public execration the men guilty of his blood and of usurping the sovereign power. It appeared in the autumn of 1649 and, on account of its author's renown, the English Government could not afford to ignore it ; the Council accordingly ordered that " Mr. Milton do prepare something in answer to the book of Salmasius." Milton's *Defence of the English People Against Salmasius* occupied him throughout the year 1650, and was completed in face of the warning of his physicians that it would probably cost him his eyesight. His theme, as in the *Tenure of Kings*, is that political power derives from the people, to whom the temporary holders of it are accountable. But, as in the *Eikonoklastes*, his main object is to destroy the credit of his antagonist, and the tract is therefore full of vituperation and personal ridicule ; he achieved his purpose, for Salmasius was considered on the Continent to have been annihilated by the English scholar. The tract indeed created such a stir abroad that Milton's name, as Masson says, was better known on the Continent than that of any Englishman except Cromwell ; and Milton himself tells that soon after its publication he received the congratulations of all the foreign ambassadors in London.

In 1652 Milton became totally blind. The same year his first wife died, leaving him the charge of three *The Years* young children. It may be that he came *of Blindness* near to despair at this time. He made no attempt to answer several continental royalists who had entered the lists against him, and he delayed the specific task laid on him by the Council of answering one anonymous tract, abler than the rest, which appeared in 1652 under the title of *Regii Sanguinis Clamor* (The Cry of the King's Blood). Finally Milton roused himself and his *Second Defence of the English People* appeared in the spring of 1654. He attributes the *Regii Sanguinis Clamor* to Alexander More, whom he castigates unsparingly. More repudiated the authorship and retorted Milton's insults. Milton replied once again in 1655 with the *Pro Se Defensio*, which terminated the controversy.

When Milton became blind an assistant Latin Secretary had been appointed to do most of the routine work ; his own salary was at the same time reduced, and in 1655 was commuted to a life pension. After the conclusion of the Salmasius controversy, therefore, he found himself comparatively free from official duties and able to take up again his private literary tasks. He now resumed work on his Latin dictionary, the *History of Britain*, and the *Christian Doctrine*, which were practically completed between 1655 and 1660. And it may have been during these same years, or it may not have been until after the Restoration, that at last he began the composition of *Paradise Lost*. At the Restoration his life was in danger. The Commons voted that he be taken in charge and prosecuted on account of *Eikonoklastes* and the *First Defence*, all copies of which were ordered to be burnt by the common hangman. But when the Act of Oblivion came out in August 1660, Milton's name was not among those excepted from the royal mercy. In 1667 *Paradise Lost* was published, and in 1671 *Paradise Regained* and *Samson Agonistes*—the most marvellous aftermath in literary history. On November 8, 1674, Milton died, and was buried in St. Giles' Church, Cripplegate.

# CHRONOLOGY OF MILTON'S LIFE

1608, December 9.   Born in Bread Street, Cheapside, London.

1620.   Entered St. Paul's School.

1625, February 12.   Matriculated at Christ's College, Cambridge.

1629, March.   Took B.A. degree.

1629, December.   *On the Morning of Christ's Nativity.*

1632, July.   Took M.A. degree.

1632, July–1638, April.   Lived at Horton.

1634, September 29.   *Comus* performed at Ludlow.

1637, November.   *Lycidas.*

1638, April–1639, August.   Continental tour.

1639–1640.   Settled in London.

1641–1642.   Begins pamphleteering.   Five anti-prelatical tracts : *Of Reformation in England ; Of Prelatical Episcopacy ; Animadversions upon the Remonstrant's Defence ; The Reason of Church Government ; Apology for Smectymnuus.*

1642, May–June.   Married Mary Powell, who left him about a month later.

1643–1645.   *The Doctrine and Discipline of Divorce ; Of Education ; The Judgement of Martin Bucer Concerning Divorce ; Areopagitica ; Tetrachordon ; Colasterion.*

1645.   Milton's wife returns.   Collected minor poems published.

1649.   *The Tenure of Kings and Magistrates* (February). Appointed Secretary for Foreign Tongues to the Council of State (March). *Eikonoklastes* (October).

1651. *Defensio pro Populo Anglicano.*

1652. Milton totally blind. Death of his first wife.

1654. *Defensio Secunda.*

1655. *Defensio Pro Se.*

1656, November. Married Katherine Woodcock.

1658, February. Death of Katherine Woodcock.

1660, March. *The Ready and Easy Way to Establish a Free Commonwealth.*

1663, February. Married Elizabeth Minshull.

1667. *Paradise Lost* published.

1671. *Paradise Regained* and *Samson Agonistes* published.

1673. Second edition of minor poems.

1674. Second edition of *Paradise Lost.*

1674, November 8. Death.

# THE TEXT

THIS volume contains all Milton's English poems
written previous to *Paradise Lost*, except the latter
part of *At a Vacation Exercise* and the translations of
the Psalms done in 1648 and 1653. The chief sources
for the text are Milton's two editions of 1645 and
1673, and the Milton manuscripts in the library of
Trinity College, Cambridge (referred to hereafter as
the *Trinity MS.*). Milton's spelling has been modern-
ised unless it indicates an important difference in
pronunciation, as in a rhyme, or a distinct variant
of a word ; the elisions of the original texts have
been retained except when they represent the normal
modern pronunciation.

It will be found that the text is less heavily punctu-
ated than in most modern editions, which continue
to reproduce the excessive grammatical pointing imposed on Milton's poems by eighteenth and nineteenth century editors. In well constructed verse the
metre enables us to read with the right emphasis and
pauses, and so to catch the meaning as we go ;
grammatical pointing is not only less necessary than
in prose but will frequently interfere with the natural
rhythm of the lines. The punctuation in Milton's
own editions is what is known as rhetorical punctuation, which means that it is directed to showing how
the lines should be read rather than how they should
be grammatically analysed. For instance, the opening line of the speech of the Genius of the Wood in

*Arcades* is printed in the original editions

" Stay gentle Swains, for though in this disguise ".

This appears in most modern editions as

" Stay, gentle Swains, for, though in this disguise,"

which does not bring out the sense any more clearly, but succeeds in murdering the rhythm.   Or take these lines from *Il Penseroso* :—

" Thee chauntress oft the woods among,
    I woo to hear thy even-song ;
    And missing thee, I walk unseen,"

which in modern editions appear as

" Thee, chauntress, oft the woods among
    I woo, to hear thy even-song ;
    And, missing thee, I walk unseen."

Note particularly the false emphasis thrown on *And* at the beginning of the last line, which is typical of the results produced by grammatical pointing.   In removing this grit from Milton's text I have observed certain simple rules : the original punctuation is retained where it is a guide to the rhythm and not likely to mislead a modern reader as to the syntax ; no punctuation is introduced where it might suggest a pause or stress for which there is no warrant in the original versions ;  and punctuation in general has been used as sparingly as possible, in order to leave the verse free to produce its own effects.

# A PARAPHRASE ON PSALM 114

*This and the following Psalm were done by the Author at fifteen years old*

WHEN the blest seed of Terah's faithful son
After long toil their liberty had won,
And pass'd from Pharian fields to Canaan land,
Led by the strength of the Almighty's hand,
Jehovah's wonders were in Israel shown,
His praise and glory was in Israel known.
That saw the troubled sea, and shivering fled,
And sought to hide his froth-becurled head
Low in the earth ; Jordan's clear streams recoil,
As a faint host that hath receiv'd the foil.        10
The high huge-bellied mountains skip like rams
Amongst their ewes, the little hills like lambs.
Why fled the ocean ? and why skipp'd the mountains ?
Why turned Jordan toward his crystal fountains ?
Shake, Earth, and at the presence be agast
Of Him that ever was and aye shall last,
That glassy floods from rugged rocks can crush,
And make soft rills from fiery flint-stones gush.

## PSALM 136

LET us with a gladsome mind
Praise the Lord, for he is kind ;
    For his mercies aye endure,
    Ever faithful, ever sure.

Let us blaze his name abroad,
For of gods he is the God.
    For his, etc.

O let us his praises tell,
Who doth the wrathful tyrants quell ;
    For his, etc.         10

Who with his miracles doth make
Amazed heaven and earth to shake ;
    For his, etc.

Who by his wisdom did create
The painted heavens so full of state ;
    For his, etc.

Who did the solid earth ordain
To rise above the watery plain ;
    For his, etc.

Who by his all-commanding might    20
Did fill the new-made world with light,
    For his, etc.

And caus'd the golden-tressed sun
All the day long his course to run ;
    For his, etc.


The horned moon to shine by night
Amongst her spangled sisters bright.
    For his, etc.


He with his thunder-clasping hand
Smote the first-born of Egypt land ;    30
    For his, etc.


And in despite of Pharao fell
He brought from thence his Israel ;
    For his, etc.


The ruddy waves he cleft in twain
Of the Erythraean main ;
    For his, etc.


The floods stood still like walls of glass
While the Hebrew bands did pass,
    For his, etc.    40


But full soon they did devour
The tawny king with all his power.
    For his, etc.


His chosen people he did bless
In the wasteful wilderness ;
    For his, etc.


In bloody battle he brought down
Kings of prowess and renown ;
    For his, etc.

3

He foil'd bold Seon and his host,      50
That rul'd the Amorrean coast,
    For his, etc.

And large-limb'd Og he did subdue,
With all his over-hardy crew ;
    For his, etc.

And to his servant Israel
He gave their land, therein to dwell.
    For his, etc.

He hath with a piteous eye
Beheld us in our misery,      60
    For his, etc.

And freed us from the slavery
Of the invading enemy.
    For his, etc.

All living creatures he doth feed,
And with full hand supplies their need.
    For his, etc.

Let us therefore warble forth
His mighty majesty and worth,
    For his, etc.      70

That his mansion hath on high
Above the reach of mortal eye.
    For his mercies aye endure,
    Ever faithful, ever sure.

# ON THE DEATH OF A FAIR INFANT
## DYING OF A COUGH

*(Anno aetatis 17)*

### I

O FAIREST flower no sooner blown but blasted,
Soft silken primrose fading timelessly,
Summer's chief honour if thou hadst outlasted
Bleak Winter's force that made thy blossom dry ;
For he, being amorous on that lovely dye
 That did thy cheek envermeil, thought to kiss
But kill'd alas, and then bewail'd his fatal bliss.

### II

For since grim Aquilo, his charioteer,
By boisterous rape the Athenian damsel got,
He thought it touch'd his deity full near    10
If likewise he some fair one wedded not,
Thereby to wipe away th' infamous blot
 Of long-uncoupled bed and childless eld,
Which 'mongst the wanton gods a foul reproach was
  held.

### III

So, mounting up in icy-pearled car,
Through middle empire of the freezing air

5

He wander'd long, till thee he spied from far ;
There ended was his quest, there ceas'd his care :
Down he descended from his snow-soft chair,
    But all unwares with his cold-kind embrace    20
Unhous'd thy virgin soul from her fair biding-place.


### IV

Yet art thou not inglorious in thy fate ;
For so Apollo with unweeting hand
Whilome did slay his dearly-loved mate,
Young Hyacinth, born on Eurotas' strand,
Young Hyacinth, the pride of Spartan land—
    But then transform'd him to a purple flower :
Alack that so to change thee, Winter had no power !


### V

Yet can I not persuade me thou art dead,
Or that thy corse corrupts in earth's dark womb,    30
Or that thy beauties lie in wormy bed,
Hid from the world in a low-delved tomb ;
Could Heaven for pity thee so strictly doom ?
    Oh no ! for something in thy face did shine
Above mortality, that shew'd thou wast divine.


### VI

Resolve me then, O Soul most surely blest
(If so it be that thou these plaints dost hear),
Tell me, bright Spirit, where'er thou hoverest,
Whether above that high first-moving sphere
Or in the Elysian fields (if such there were),    40
    Oh say me true if thou wert mortal wight
And why from us so quickly thou didst take thy flight.

VII

Wert thou some star which from the ruin'd roof
Of shak'd Olympus by mischance didst fall,
Which careful Jove in nature's true behoof
Took up and in fit place did reinstall ?
Or did of late Earth's sons besiege the wall
    Of sheeny Heaven, and thou some goddess fled
Amongst us here below to hide thy nectar'd head ?


VIII

Or wert thou that just maid who once before       50
Forsook the hated earth (oh tell me sooth)
And cam'st again to visit us once more ?
Or wert thou [Mercy], that sweet smiling youth ?
Or that crown'd matron, sage white-robed Truth ?
    Or any other of that heavenly brood
Let down in cloudy throne to do the world some good ?


IX

Or wert thou of the golden-winged host,
Who having clad thyself in human weed
To earth from thy prefixed seat didst post,
And after short abode fly back with speed,          60
As if to shew what creatures Heaven doth breed ;
    Thereby to set the hearts of men on fire
To scorn the sordid world, and unto Heaven aspire ?


X

But oh why didst thou not stay here below
To bless us with thy heaven-lov'd innocence,
To slake his wrath whom sin hath made our foe,
To turn swift-rushing black perdition hence

Or drive away the slaughtering pestilence,
  To stand 'twixt us and our deserved smart?
But thou canst best perform that office where thou
    art.

### XI

Then thou, the mother of so sweet a child,
Her false-imagin'd loss cease to lament,
And wisely learn to curb thy sorrows wild;
Think what a present thou to God hast sent,
And render him with patience what he lent:
  This if thou do, he will an offspring give
That till the world's last-end shall make thy name to
    live.

# AT A VACATION EXERCISE IN THE COLLEGE, PART LATIN, PART ENGLISH

*(Anno aetatis 19)*

*The Latin Speeches ended, the English thus began :—*

HAIL, Native Language, that by sinews weak
Didst move my first endeavouring tongue to speak,
And mad'st imperfect words with childish trips,
Half unpronounc'd, slide through my infant lips,
Driving dumb Silence from the portal door
Where he had mutely sat two years before :
Here I salute thee, and thy pardon ask
That now I use thee in my latter task :
Small loss it is that thence can come unto thee,
I know my tongue but little grace can do thee :         10
Thou need'st not be ambitious to be first,
Believe me I have thither pack'd the worst :
And if it happen as I did forecast
The daintiest dishes shall be served up last.
I pray thee then deny me not thy aid
For this same small neglect that I have made ;
But haste thee straight to do me once a pleasure,
And from thy wardrope bring thy chiefest treasure—
Not those new-fangled toys, and trimming slight
Which takes our late fantastics with delight,         20
But cull those richest robes and gay'st attire
Which deepest spirits and choicest wits desire.
I have some naked thoughts that rove about
And loudly knock to have their passage out,

And weary of their place do only stay
Till thou hast deck'd them in thy best array,
That so they may without suspect or fears
Fly swiftly to this fair assembly's ears.
Yet I had rather, if I were to choose,
Thy service in some graver subject use,                    30
Such as may make thee search thy coffers round
Before thou clothe my fancy in fit sound :
Such where the deep transported mind may soar
Above the wheeling poles, and at Heaven's door
Look in, and see each blissful deity
How he before the thunderous throne doth lie,
Listening to what unshorn Apollo sings
To th' touch of golden wires, while Hebe brings
Immortal nectar to her kingly sire ;
Then passing through the spheres of watchful fire, 40
And misty regions of wide air next under,
And hills of snow and lofts of piled thunder,
May tell at length how green-ey'd Neptune raves,
In Heaven's defiance mustering all his waves ;
Then sing of secret things that came to pass
When beldam Nature in her cradle was ;
And last of kings and queens and heroes old,
Such as the wise Demodocus once told
In solemn songs at king Alcinous' feast,
While sad Ulysses' soul and all the rest            50
Are held with his melodious harmony
In willing chains and sweet captivity.
But fie, my wandering Muse, how thou dost stray !

# SONG ON MAY MORNING

Now the bright morning star, day's harbinger,
Comes dancing from the east, and leads with her
The flowery May, who from her green lap throws
The yellow cowslip and the pale primrose.
 Hail bounteous May that dost inspire
 Mirth and youth and warm desire,
 Woods and groves are of thy dressing,
 Hill and dale doth boast thy blessing.
Thus we salute thee with our early song,
And welcome thee, and wish thee long.  10

# THE FIFTH ODE OF HORACE, LIB. I

*(Quis multa gracilis te puer in rosa)*

*Rendered almost word for word, without rhyme, according to the
Latin measure, as near as the language will permit*

WHAT slender youth bedew'd with liquid odours
Courts thee on roses in some pleasant cave,
    Pyrrha, for whom bind'st thou
    In wreaths thy golden hair,

Plain in thy neatness ?  O how oft shall he
On faith and changed gods complain, and seas
    Rough with black winds and storms
    Unwonted shall admire,

Who now enjoys thee credulous, all gold ;
Who always vacant, always amiable          10
    Hopes thee, of flattering gales
    Unmindful.   Hapless they

To whom thou untried seem'st fair !  Me, in my
    vow'd
Picture, the sacred wall declares to have hung
    My dank and dropping weeds
    To the stern God of Sea.

## AD PYRRHAM.  ODE V

*(Horatius ex Pyrrhae illecebris tanquam e naufragio enataverat, cujus*
*amore irretitos affirmat esse miseros)*

Quis multa gracilis te puer in rosa
Perfusus liquidis urget odoribus
    Grato, Pyrrha, sub antro ?
        Cui flavam religas comam

Simplex munditiis !   Heu, quoties fidem
Mutatosque Deos flebit, et aspera
    Nigris aequora ventis
        Emirabitur insolens,

Qui nunc te fruitur credulus aurea ;
Qui semper vacuam, semper amabilem,
    Sperat, nescius aurae
        Fallacis !   Miseri quibus

Intentata nites.   Me tabula sacer
Votiva paries indicat uvida
    Suspendisse potenti
        Vestimenta maris Deo.

# ON THE MORNING OF CHRIST'S NATIVITY

## (*Composed 1629*)

### I

THIS is the month and this the happy morn
Wherein the Son of Heaven's eternal King,
Of wedded Maid and Virgin Mother born,
Our great redemption from above did bring ;
For so the holy Sages once did sing
   That he our deadly forfeit should release
And with his Father work us a perpetual peace.

### II

That glorious form, that light unsufferable,
And that far-beaming blaze of majesty,
Wherewith he wont at Heaven's high council-table   10
To sit the midst of Trinal Unity,
He laid aside ; and here with us to be,
   Forsook the courts of everlasting day
And chose with us a darksome house of mortal clay.

### III

Say Heavenly Muse, shall not thy sacred vein
Afford a present to the Infant God ?
Hast thou no verse, no hymn or solemn strain,
To welcome him to this his new abode,

Now while the heaven, by the sun's team untrod,
  Hath took no print of the approaching light,    20
And all the spangled host keep watch in squadrons
    bright ?

### IV

See how from far upon the eastern road
The star-led Wisards haste with odours sweet !
O run, prevent them with thy humble ode,
And lay it lowly at his blessed feet ;
Have thou the honour first thy Lord to greet,
  And join thy voice unto the angel quire,
From out his secret altar touch'd with hallow'd fire.

## THE HYMN

### I

It was the winter wild,
While the Heaven-born child    30
  All meanly wrapt in the rude manger lies ;
Nature in awe to him
Had doff'd her gaudy trim,
  With her great Master so to sympathize :
It was no season then for her
To wanton with the sun, her lusty paramour.

### II

Only with speeches fair
She woos the gentle air
  To hide her guilty front with innocent snow,
And on her naked shame,    40
Pollute with sinful blame,
  The saintly veil of maiden white to throw :
Confounded, that her Maker's eyes
Should look so near upon her foul deformities.

III

But he, her fears to cease,
Sent down the meek-ey'd Peace ;
  She, crown'd with olive green, came softly sliding
Down through the turning sphere,
His ready harbinger,
  With turtle wing the amorous clouds dividing ;  50
And waving wide her myrtle wand
She strikes a universal peace through sea and land.


IV

No war or battle's sound
Was heard the world around :
  The idle spear and shield were high uphung,
The hooked chariot stood
Unstain'd with hostile blood,
  The trumpet spake not to the armed throng,
And kings sat still with awful eye
As if they surely knew their sovran Lord was by.  60


V

But peaceful was the night
Wherein the Prince of Light
  His reign of peace upon the earth began :
The winds with wonder whist
Smoothly the waters kiss'd,
  Whispering new joys to the mild ocean,
Who now hath quite forgot to rave,
While birds of calm sit brooding on the charmed wave.


VI

The stars with deep amaze
Stand fix'd in steadfast gaze,
  Bending one way their precious influence,   70

And will not take their flight
For all the morning light
 Or Lucifer that often warn'd them thence ;
But in their glimmering orbs did glow
Until their Lord himself bespake, and bid them go.

### VII

And though the shady gloom
Had given day her room,
 The sun himself withheld his wonted speed,
And hid his head for shame      80
As his inferior flame
 The new-enlighten'd world no more should need ;
He saw a greater sun appear
Than his bright throne or burning axletree could bear.

### VIII

The shepherds on the lawn,
Or ere the point of dawn,
 Sate simply chatting in a rustic row ;
Full little thought they than
That the mighty Pan
 Was kindly come to live with them below ;  90
Perhaps their loves, or else their sheep,
Was all that did their silly thoughts so busy keep.

### IX

When such music sweet
Their hearts and ears did greet
 As never was by mortal finger strook,
Divinely-warbled voice
Answering the stringed noise,
 As all their souls in blissful rapture took :

The air, such pleasure loth to lose,
With thousand echoes still prolongs each heavenly
    close.                 100

### X

Nature that heard such sound
Beneath the hollow round
    Of Cynthia's seat, the airy region thrilling,
Now was almost won
To think her part was done
    And that her reign had here its last fulfilling ;
She knew such harmony alone
Could hold all Heaven and Earth in happier union.

### XI

At last surrounds their sight
A globe of circular light,           110
    That with long beams the shamefac'd night array'd ;
The helmed Cherubim
And sworded Seraphim
    Are seen in glittering ranks with wings display'd,
Harping in loud and solemn quire
With unexpressive notes to Heaven's new-born Heir.

### XII

Such music (as 'tis said)
Before was never made
    But when of old the Sons of Morning sung,
While the Creator great          120
His constellations set
    And the well-balanc'd world on hinges hung,
And cast the dark foundations deep,
And bid the weltering waves their oozy channel keep.

### XIII

Ring out, ye crystal spheres,
Once bless our humane ears
   (If ye have power to touch our senses so),
And let your silver chime
Move in melodious time,
   And let the bass of heaven's deep organ blow,   130
And with your ninefold harmony
Make up full consort to th' angelic symphony.

### XIV

For if such holy song
Enwrap our fancy long
   Time will run back and fetch the Age of Gold,
And speckled Vanity
Will sicken soon and die,
   And leprous Sin will melt from earthly mould,
And Hell itself will pass away
And leave her dolorous mansions to the peering day.

          140

### XV

Yea, Truth and Justice then
Will down return to men,
   Orb'd in a rainbow ; and like glories wearing
Mercy will sit between
Thron'd in celestial sheen,
   With radiant feet the tissued clouds down steering ;
And Heaven as at some festival
Will open wide the gates of her high palace hall.

### XVI

But wisest Fate says No,
This must not yet be so ;         150
   The Babe lies yet in smiling infancy

That on the bitter cross
Must redeem our loss,
  So both himself and us to glorify :
Yet first to those ychain'd in sleep
The wakeful trump of doom must thunder through
    the deep,

### XVII

With such a horrid clang
As on Mount Sinai rang
  While the red fire and smouldering clouds out brake:
The aged Earth agast           160
With terror of that blast
  Shall from the surface to the centre shake,
When at the world's last session
The dreadful Judge in middle air shall spread his
    throne.

### XVIII

And then at last our bliss
Full and perfect is,
  But now begins ; for from this happy day
Th' old Dragon under ground
In straiter limits bound
  Not half so far casts his usurped sway,     170
And wroth to see his kingdom fail
Swindges the scaly horror of his folded tail.

### XIX

The oracles are dumb ;
No voice or hideous hum
  Runs through the arched roof in words deceiving.
Apollo from his shrine
Can no more divine,
  With hollow shriek the steep of Delphos leaving.
No nightly trance or breathed spell     [180
Inspires the pale-ey'd priest from the prophetic cell.

20

XX

The lonely mountains o'er
And the resounding shore
    A voice of weeping heard and loud lament ;
From haunted spring, and dale
Edg'd with poplar pale,
    The parting Genius is with sighing sent ;
With flower-inwoven tresses torn
The Nymphs in twilight shade of tangled thickets
    mourn.

XXI

In consecrated earth
And on the holy hearth
    The Lars and Lemures moan with midnight plaint ;   190
In urns and altars round
A drear and dying sound
    Affrights the Flamens at their service quaint ;
And the chill marble seems to sweat
While each peculiar power forgoes his wonted seat.

XXII

Peor and Baälim
Forsake their temples dim,
    With that twice-batter'd god of Palestine ;
And mooned Ashtaroth,                                  200
Heaven's queen and mother both,
    Now sits not girt with tapers' holy shine ;
The Libyc Hammon shrinks his horn ;
In vain the Tyrian maids their wounded Thammuz
    mourn.

XXIII

And sullen Moloch, fled,
Hath left in shadows dread
    His burning idol all of blackest hue ;

In vain with cymbals' ring
They call the grisly king,
   In dismal dance about the furnace blue.    210
The brutish gods of Nile as fast,
Isis and Orus and the dog Anubis, haste.


### XXIV

Nor is Osiris seen
In Memphian grove or green,
   Trampling the unshower'd grass with lowings loud ;
Nor can he be at rest
Within his sacred chest,
   Nought but profoundest Hell can be his shroud ;
In vain with timbrel'd anthems dark
The sable-stoled sorcerers bear his worshipp'd ark :
                                 220


### XXV

   He feels from Juda's land
   The dreaded Infant's hand,
The rays of Bethlehem blind his dusky eyn.
   Nor all the gods beside
   Longer dare abide,
Not Typhon huge ending in snaky twine :
Our Babe, to shew his Godhead true,
Can in his swaddling bands control the damned crew.


### XXVI

   So when the sun in bed,
   Curtain'd with cloudy red,    230
Pillows his chin upon an orient wave,
   The flocking shadows pale
   Troop to the infernal jail,
Each fetter'd ghost slips to his several grave,

And the yellow-skirted fays
Fly after the night-steeds, leaving their Moon-lov'd
    maze.

### XXVII

    But see, the Virgin blest
    Hath laid her Babe to rest.
Time is our tedious song should here have ending :
    Heaven's youngest-teemed star       240
    Hath fix'd her polish'd car,
Her sleeping Lord with handmaid lamp attending :
And all about the courtly stable
Bright-harness'd angels sit in order serviceable.

# THE PASSION

## I

EREWHILE of music and ethereal mirth,
Wherewith the stage of Air and Earth did ring,
And joyous news of Heavenly Infant's birth,
My muse with Angels did divide to sing ;
But headlong joy is ever on the wing,
In wintry solstice like the shorten'd light
Soon swallow'd up in dark and long out-living night.

## II

For now to sorrow must I tune my song
And set my harp to notes of saddest woe,
Which on our dearest Lord did seize ere long,      10
Dangers and snares and wrongs and worse than so,
Which he for us did freely undergo :
Most perfect Hero, tried in heaviest plight
Of labours huge and hard, too hard for human wight.

## III

He, sovran Priest, stooping his regal head
That dropt with odorous oil down his fair eyes,
Poor fleshly tabernacle entered,
His starry front low-roof'd beneath the skies :
O what a mask was there, what a disguise !
Yet more : the stroke of death he must abide,      20
Then lies him meekly down fast by his brethren's side.

24

## IV

These latest scenes confine my roving verse,
To this horizon is my Phoebus bound,
His godlike acts; and his temptations fierce
And former sufferings, otherwhere are found;
Loud o'er the rest Cremona's trump doth sound:
  Me softer airs befit, and softer strings
Of lute or viol still, more apt for mournful things.

## V

Befriend me Night, best patroness of grief,
Over the pole thy thickest mantle throw            30
And work my flatter'd fancy to belief
That heaven and earth are colour'd with my woe;
My sorrows are too dark for day to know:
  The leaves should all be black whereon I write,
And letters, where my tears have wash'd, a wannish
    white.

## VI

See, see the chariot and those rushing wheels
That whirl'd the prophet up at Chebar flood,
My spirit some transporting cherub feels
To bear me where the towers of Salem stood,
Once glorious towers, now sunk in guiltless blood;  40
  There doth my soul in holy vision sit,
In pensive trance and anguish and ecstatic fit.

## VII

Mine eye hath found that sad sepulchral rock
That was the casket of Heaven's richest store,
And here, though grief my feeble hands uplock,
Yet on the soften'd quarry would I score
My plaining verse as lively as before;

For sure so well instructed are my tears
That they would fitly fall in order'd characters.

### VIII

Or should I thence, hurried on viewless wing,  50
Take up a weeping on the mountains wild,
The gentle neighbourhood of grove and spring
Would soon unbosom all their echoes mild,
And I (for grief is easily beguil'd)
    Might think the infection of my sorrows loud
Had got a race of mourners on some pregnant cloud.

*This Subject the Author finding to be above the years he had when
    he wrote it, and nothing satisfied with what was begun, left it
    unfinished*

# UPON THE CIRCUMCISION

YE flaming Powers and winged Warriors bright
That erst with music and triumphant song,
First heard by happy watchful shepherds' ear,
So sweetly sung your joy the clouds along
Through the soft silence of the listening night,
Now mourn ; and if sad share with us to bear
Your fiery essence can distil no tear,
Burn in your sighs and borrow
Seas wept from our deep sorrow.
He, who with all Heaven's heraldry whilere            10
Enter'd the world, now bleeds to give us ease.
Alas, how soon our sin
  Sore doth begin
    His infancy to seize !

O more exceeding love, or law more just ?
Just law indeed, but more exceeding love !
For we by rightful doom remediless
Were lost in death, till he that dwelt above,
High-thron'd in secret bliss, for us frail dust
Emptied his glory, even to nakedness ;            20
And that great covenant which we still transgress
Entirely satisfied,
And the full wrath beside
Of vengeful justice bore for our excess,
And seals obedience first with wounding smart
This day ; but oh ! ere long
  Huge pangs and strong
    Will pierce more near his heart.

# ON TIME

Fly, envious Time, till thou run out thy race,
Call on the lazy leaden-stepping hours
Whose speed is but the heavy plummet's pace ;
And glut thyself with what thy womb devours,
Which is no more than what is false and vain
And merely mortal dross ;
So little is our loss,
So little is thy gain.
For when as each thing bad thou hast entomb'd,
And last of all thy greedy self consum'd,                    10
Then long Eternity shall greet our bliss
With an individual kiss ;
And Joy shall overtake us as a flood,
When every thing that is sincerely good
And perfectly divine,
With Truth and Peace and Love shall ever shine
About the súpreme throne
Of him, t' whose happy-making sight alone
When once our heavenly-guided soul shall climb,
Then all this earthy grossness quit,                          20
Attir'd with stars, we shall for ever sit,
    Triumphing over Death, and Chance, and thee O
        Time.

# AT A SOLEMN MUSIC

Blest pair of Sirens, pledges of Heaven's joy,    *offspring*
Sphere-born harmonious sisters, Voice and Verse,
Wed your divine sounds and mix'd power employ,
Dead things with inbreath'd sense able to pierce ;    *Orpheus.*
And to our high-rais'd phantasy present
That undisturbed song of pure concent,    *harmony.*
Aye sung before the sapphire-colour'd throne
To him that sits thereon,
With saintly shout and solemn jubilee,    *loud rejoicing.*
Where the bright Seraphim in burning row    10
Their loud uplifted angel-trumpets blow,
And the Cherubic host in thousand quires
Touch their immortal harps of golden wires,
With those just Spirits that wear victorious palms,
Hymns devout and holy psalms
Singing everlastingly :
That we on Earth with undiscording voice
May rightly answer that melodious noise ;    *music.*
As once we did, till disproportion'd sin
Jarr'd against nature's chime and with harsh din    20
Broke the fair music that all creatures made
To their great Lord, whose love their motion sway'd
In perfect diapason, whilst they stood    *see 122.*
In first obedience and their state of good.
O may we soon again renew that song,
And keep in tune with Heaven, till God ere long
To his celestial consort us unite,    *choir*
To live with him and sing in endless morn of light.

# ON SHAKESPEAR

WHAT needs my Shakespear for his honour'd bones
The labour of an age in piled stones,
Or that his hallow'd reliques should be hid
Under a star-ypointing pyramid ?
Dear son of memory, great heir of fame,
What need'st thou such weak witness of thy name ?
Thou in our wonder and astonishment
Hast built thyself a livelong monument :
For whilst to the shame of slow-endeavouring art
Thy easy numbers flow, and that each heart      10
Hath from the leaves of thy unvalued book
Those Delphic lines with deep impression took,
Then thou, our fancy of itself bereaving,
Dost make us marble with too much conceiving ;
And so sepulchred in such pomp doth lie
That kings for such a tomb would wish to die.

# ON THE UNIVERSITY CARRIER,

*who sickened in the time of his Vacancy, being forbid to go to London
by reason of the Plague*

HERE lies old Hobson.   Death hath broke his girt,
And here, alas, hath laid him in the dirt ;
Or else the ways being foul, twenty to one,
He's here stuck in a slough and overthrown.
'Twas such a shifter that, if truth were known,
Death was half glad when he had got him down ;
For he had any time this ten years full
Dodg'd with him betwixt Cambridge and *The Bull*.
And surely, Death could never have prevail'd,
Had not his weekly course of carriage fail'd ;     10
But lately, finding him so long at home,
And thinking now his journey's end was come,
And that he had ta'en up his latest inn,
In the kind office of a chamberlin
Shew'd him his room where he must lodge that night,
Pull'd off his boots, and took away the light.
If any ask for him, it shall be said,
' Hobson has supp'd, and's newly gone to bed.'

# ANOTHER ON THE SAME

HERE lieth one who did most truly prove
That he could never die while he could move ;
So hung his destiny, never to rot
While he might still jog on and keep his trot ;
Made of sphere-metal, never to decay
Until his revolution was at stay.
Time numbers motion, yet (without a crime
'Gainst old truth) motion number'd out his time ;
And like an engine mov'd with wheel and weight,
His principles being ceas'd he ended straight.          10
Rest that gives all men life gave him his death,
And too much breathing put him out of breath ;
Nor were it contradiction to affirm
Too long vacation hasten'd on his term.
Merely to drive the time away he sicken'd,
Fainted, and died, nor would with ale be quicken'd.
' Nay,' quoth he, on his swooning bed outstretch'd,
' If I may not carry, sure I'll ne'er be fetch'd,
But vow, though the cross Doctors all stood hearers,
For one carrier put down to make six bearers.'          20
Ease was his chief disease and, to judge right,
He died for heaviness that his cart went light ;
His leisure told him that his time was come,
And lack of load made his life burdensome,
That even to his last breath (there be that say't)
As he were press'd to death, he cried ' More weight ! '
But had his doings lasted as they were,
He had been an immortal carrier.

# ANOTHER ON THE SAME

Obedient to the moon he spent his date
In course reciprocal, and had his fate                    30
Link'd to the mutual flowing of the seas ;
Yet (strange to think) his wain was his increase.
His letters are deliver'd all and gone,
Only remains this superscription.

ANOTHER ON THE SAME

# AN EPITAPH ON THE MARCHIONESS
## OF WINCHESTER

THIS rich marble doth inter
The honour'd wife of Winchester,
A Viscount's daughter, an Earl's heir,
Besides what her virtues fair
Added to her noble birth,
More than she could own from Earth.
Summers three times eight save one
She had told, alas too soon
After so short time of breath
To house with darkness and with death.      10
Yet had the number of her days
Been as complete as was her praise,
Nature and Fate had had no strife
In giving limit to her life.
Her high birth and her graces sweet
Quickly found a lover meet ;
The virgin quire for her request
The god that sits at marriage feast ;
He at their invoking came,
But with a scarce well-lighted flame ;      20
And in his garland, as he stood,
Ye might discern a cypress bud.
Once had the early matrons run
To greet her of a lovely son,
And now with second hope she goes,
And calls Lucina to her throes ;
But whether by mischance or blame
Atropos for Lucina came,

And with remorseless cruelty
Spoil'd at once both fruit and tree.                    30
The hapless babe before his birth
Had burial, yet not laid in earth ;
And the languish'd mother's womb
Was not long a living tomb.
So have I seen some tender slip,
Sav'd with care from winter's nip,
The pride of her carnation train,
Pluck'd up by some unheedy swain
Who only thought to crop the flower
New shot up from vernal shower ;                        40
But the fair blossom hangs the head
Sideways as on a dying bed,
And those pearls of dew she wears
Prove to be presaging tears
Which the sad morn had let fall
On her hastening funeral.
Gentle Lady, may thy grave
Peace and quiet ever have ;
After this thy travail sore
Sweet rest seize thee evermore,                         50
That to give the world increase
Shorten'd hast thy own life's lease.
Here, besides the sorrowing
That thy noble house doth bring,
Here be tears of perfect moan
Weept for thee in Helicon ;
And some flowers and some bays
For thy hearse to strew the ways,
Sent thee from the banks of Came,
Devoted to thy virtuous name ;                          60
Whilst thou, bright Saint, high sitt'st in glory
Next her much like to thee in story,
That fair Syrian shepherdess
Who after years of barrenness
The highly-favour'd Joseph bore

35

To him that serv'd for her before,
And at her next birth, much like thee,
Through pangs fled to felicity
Far within the bosom bright
Of blazing Majesty and Light :        70
There with thee, new welcome Saint,
Like fortunes may her soul acquaint,
With thee there clad in radiant sheen,
No Marchioness, but now a Queen.

# L'ALLEGRO — The cheerful Man.

Hence, loathed Melancholy,
  Of Cerberus and blackest Midnight born
  In Stygian cave forlorn
'Mongst horrid shapes and shrieks and sights unholy!
Find out some uncouth cell
  Where brooding Darkness spreads his jealous wings
And the night-raven sings ;
  There under ebon shades and low-brow'd rocks,
As ragged as thy locks,
  In dark Cimmerian desert ever dwell.                    10
But come thou Goddess fair and free,
In Heaven yclep'd Euphrosyne
And, by men, heart-easing Mirth ;
Whom lovely Venus at a birth
With two sister Graces more
To ivy-crowned Bacchus bore :
Or whether (as some sager sing)
The frolic wind that breathes the spring,
Zephyr, with Aurora playing
As he met her once a-maying,                              20
There on beds of violets blue
And fresh-blown roses wash'd in dew
Fill'd her with thee, a daughter fair,
So buxom, blithe and debonair.
Haste thee, Nymph, and bring with thee
Jest and youthful Jollity,
Quips and Cranks, and wanton Wiles,
Nods and Becks, and wreathed Smiles
Such as hang on Hebe's cheek

37

And love to live in dimple sleek ;　　　　　　30
Sport that wrinkled Care derides,
And Laughter holding both his sides.
Come, and trip it as you go
On the light fantastic toe,
And in thy right hand lead with thee
The mountain nymph, sweet Liberty ;
And if I give thee honour due,
Mirth, admit me of thy crew,
To live with her and live with thee
In unreproved pleasures free ;　　　　　　40
To hear the lark begin his flight
And singing startle the dull night
From his watch-tower in the skies,
Till the dappled dawn doth rise ;
Then to come in spite of sorrow
And at my window bid good-morrow
Through the sweet-briar or the vine
Or the twisted eglantine.
While the cock with lively din
Scatters the rear of Darkness thin　　　　　50
And to the stack or the barn door
Stoutly struts his dames before,
Oft listening how the hounds and horn
Cheerly rouse the slumbering Morn,
From the side of some hoar hill
Through the high wood echoing shrill.
Sometime walking not unseen
By hedgerow elms, on hillocks green,
Right against the eastern gate
Where the great sun begins his state　　　60
Rob'd in flames and amber light,
The clouds in thousand liveries dight ;
While the ploughman near at hand
Whistles o'er the furrow'd land,
And the milkmaid singeth blithe,
And the mower whets his sithe,

And every shepherd tells his tale
Under the hawthorn in the dale.
Straight mine eye hath caught new pleasures
Whilst the lantskip round it measures :                70
Russet lawns and fallows gray
Where the nibbling flocks do stray,
Mountains on whose barren breast
The labouring clouds do often rest ;
Meadows trim with daisies pied,
Shallow brooks and rivers wide.
Towers and battlements it sees
Bosom'd high in tufted trees,
Where perhaps some beauty lies,
The cynosure of neighbouring eyes.                     80
Hard by, a cottage chimney smokes
From betwixt two aged oaks,
Where Corydon and Thyrsis met
Are at their savoury dinner set
Of herbs and other country messes
Which the neat-handed Phillis dresses ;
And then in haste her bower she leaves
With Thestylis to bind the sheaves,
Or if the earlier season lead
To the tann'd haycock in the mead.                     90
Sometimes with secure delight
The upland hamlets will invite,
When the merry bells ring round
And the jocund rebecks sound
To many a youth and many a maid
Dancing in the chequer'd shade ;
And young and old come forth to play
On a sunshine holiday,
Till the livelong daylight fail.
Then to the spicy nut-brown ale,                       100
With stories told of many a feat :
How fairy Mab the junkets eat ;
She was pinch'd and pull'd, she said,

And by the Friar's Lanthorn led ;
Tells how the drudging goblin sweat
To earn his cream-bowl duly set,
When in one night, ere glimpse of morn,
His shadowy flail hath thresh'd the corn
That ten day-labourers could not end,
Then lies him down the lubbar fiend,     110
And stretch'd out all the chimney's length
Basks at the fire his hairy strength,
And crop-full out of doors he flings
Ere the first cock his matin rings.
Thus done the tales, to bed they creep,
By whispering winds soon lull'd asleep.
Tower'd cities please us then,
And the busy hum of men,
Where throngs of knights and barons bold
In weeds of peace high triumphs hold,     120
With store of ladies whose bright eyes
Rain influence and judge the prize
Of wit or arms, while both contend
To win her grace whom all commend.
There let Hymen oft appear
In saffron robe, with taper clear,
And pomp, and feast, and revelry,
With masque and antique pageantry ;
Such sights as youthful poets dream
On summer eves by haunted stream.     130
Then to the well-trod stage anon,
If Jonson's learned sock be on,
Or sweetest Shakespeare, Fancy's child,
Warble his native wood-notes wild.
And ever against eating cares
Lap me in soft Lydian airs,
Married to immortal verse
Such as the meeting soul may pierce
In notes, with many a winding bout
Of linked sweetness long drawn out,     140

With wanton heed and giddy cunning,
The melting voice through mazes running,
Untwisting all the chains that tie
The hidden soul of harmony ;
That Orpheus' self may heave his head
From golden slumber on a bed
Of heap'd Elysian flowers, and hear
Such strains as would have won the ear
Of Pluto, to have quite set free
His half-regain'd Eurydice.                    150
These delights if thou canst give,
Mirth with *thee* I mean to live.

# IL PENSEROSO

HENCE, vain deluding joys,
    The brood of folly without father bred,
How little you bested,
    Or fill the fixed mind with all your toys ;
Dwell in some idle brain,
    And fancies fond with gaudy shapes possess,
As thick and numberless
    As the gay motes that people the sunbeams,
Or likest hovering dreams,
    The fickle pensioners of Morpheus' train.    10
But hail thou Goddess sage and holy,
Hail divinest Melancholy,
Whose saintly visage is too bright
To hit the sense of human sight,
And therefore to our weaker view
O'erlaid with black, staid Wisdom's hue ;
Black, but such as in esteem
Prince Memnon's sister might beseem,
Or that starr'd Ethiope queen that strove
To set her beauty's praise above    20
The sea nymphs, and their powers offended.
Yet thou art higher far descended :
Thee bright-hair'd Vesta long of yore
To solitary Saturn bore ;
His daughter she (in Saturn's reign
Such mixture was not held a stain).
Oft in glimmering bowers and glades
He met her, and in secret shades
Of woody Ida's inmost grove,

Whilst yet there was no fear of Jove.                30
Come pensive Nun, devout and pure,
Sober, stedfast and demure,
All in a robe of darkest grain
Flowing with majestic train,
And sable stole of cypress lawn
Over thy decent shoulders drawn.
Come, but keep thy wonted state,
With even step and musing gait
And looks commercing with the skies,
Thy rapt soul sitting in thine eyes :        40
There held in holy passion still,
Forget thyself to marble, till
With a sad leaden downward cast
Thou fix them on the earth as fast.
And join with thee calm Peace and Quiet,
Spare Fast, that oft with gods doth diet,
And hears the Muses in a ring
Aye round about Jove's altar sing.
And add to these retired Leisure,
That in trim gardens takes his pleasure ;        50
But first, and chiefest, with thee bring
Him that yon soars on golden wing,
Guiding the fiery-wheeled throne,
The Cherub Contemplation ;
And the mute Silence hist along,
'Less Philomel will deign a song,
In her sweetest saddest plight,
Smoothing the rugged brow of Night,
While Cynthia checks her dragon yoke
Gently o'er the accustom'd oak ;        60
Sweet bird that shunn'st the noise of folly,
Most musical, most melancholy !
Thee, chauntress, oft the woods among
I woo, to hear thy even-song ;
And missing thee, I walk unseen
On the dry smooth-shaven green,

To behold the wandering moon
Riding near her highest noon,
Like one that had been led astray
Through the Heaven's wide pathless way,  70
And oft, as if her head she bow'd,
Stooping through a fleecy cloud.
Oft on a plat of rising ground
I hear the far-off curfew sound,
Over some wide-water'd shore
Swinging slow with sullen roar ;
Or if the air will not permit,
Some still removed place will fit,
Where glowing embers through the room
Teach light to counterfeit a gloom,  80
Far from all resort of mirth
Save the cricket on the hearth
Or the bellman's drowsy charm
To bless the doors from nightly harm.
Or let my lamp at midnight hour
Be seen in some high lonely tower,
Where I may oft outwatch the Bear,
With thrice great Hermes, or unsphere
The spirit of Plato to unfold
What worlds or what vast regions hold  90
The immortal mind that hath forsook
Her mansion in this fleshly nook,
And of those daemons that are found
In fire, air, flood, or under ground,
Whose power hath a true consent
With planet or with element.
Sometime let gorgeous Tragedy
In sceptred pall come sweeping by,
Presenting Thebes, or Pelops' line,
Or the tale of Troy divine,  100
Or what (though rare) of later age
Ennobled hath the buskin'd stage.
But, O sad Virgin, that thy power

Might raise Musaeus from his bower,
Or bid the soul of Orpheus sing
Such notes as warbled to the string
Drew iron tears down Pluto's cheek
And made Hell grant what Love did seek.
Or call up him that left half told
The story of Cambuscan bold,                                    110
Of Camball, and of Algarsife,
And who had Canace to wife,
That own'd the virtuous ring and glass,
And of the wondrous horse of brass
On which the Tartar king did ride ;
And if aught else great bards beside
In sage and solemn tunes have sung,
Of turneys, and of trophies hung,
Of forests, and enchantments drear,
Where more is meant than meets the ear.              120
Thus Night, oft see me in thy pale career
Till civil-suited Morn appear,
Not trick'd and frounc'd as she was wont
With the Attic boy to hunt,
But kerchieft in a comely cloud,
While rocking winds are piping loud,
Or usher'd with a shower still,
When the gust hath blown his fill,
Ending on the rustling leaves
With minute-drops from off the eaves.                   130
And when the sun begins to fling
His flaring beams, me, Goddess, bring
To arched walks of twilight groves,
And shadows brown that Silvan loves
Of pine or monumental oak,
Where the rude axe with heaved stroke
Was never heard the nymphs to daunt
Or fright them from their hallow'd haunt.
There in close covert by some brook,
Where no profaner eye may look,                             140

Hide me from Day's garish eye,
While the bee with honied thigh,
That at her flowery work doth sing,
And the waters murmuring
With such consort as they keep,
Entice the dewy-feather'd Sleep ;
And let some strange mysterious dream
Wave at his wings, in airy stream
Of lively portraiture display'd,
Softly on my eyelids laid ;                         150
And as I wake, sweet music breathe
Above, about or underneath,
Sent by some Spirit to mortals good,
Or the unseen Genius of the wood.
But let my due feet never fail
To walk the studious cloister's pale,
And love the high embowed roof
With antic pillars massy proof,
And storied windows richly dight
Casting a dim religious light ;                     160
There let the pealing organ blow
To the full-voic'd quire below
In service high and anthems clear,
As may with sweetness through mine ear
Dissolve me into ecstasies
And bring all Heaven before mine eyes.
And may at last my weary age
Find out the peaceful hermitage,
The hairy gown and mossy cell,
Where I may sit and rightly spell                   170
Of every star that Heaven doth shew,
And every herb that sips the dew ;
Till old experience do attain
To something like prophetic strain.
These pleasures, Melancholy, give
And I with thee will choose to live.

46

# ARCADES

*Part of an Entertainment presented to the Countess Dowager of Derby at Harefield by some Noble Persons of her Family, who appear on the Scene in pastoral habit, moving toward the seat of state, with this song :—*

## I. Song

Look Nymphs, and Shepherds look,
What sudden blaze of majesty
Is that which we from hence descry,
Too divine to be mistook :
　　This this is she
To whom our vows and wishes bend,
Here our solemn search hath end.
Fame, that her high worth to raise
Seem'd erst so lavish and profuse,
We may justly now accuse　　　　　　　　　10
Of detraction from her praise ;
　　Less than half we find express'd,
　　Envy bid conceal the rest.

Mark what radiant state she spreads
In circle round her shining throne,
Shooting her beams like silver threads :
This this is she alone,
　　Sitting like a goddess bright
　　In the centre of her light.
Might she the wise Latona be　　　　　　　20
Or the tow'red Cybele,

47

Mother of a hundred gods ;
Juno dares not give her odds ;
   Who had thought this clime had held
   A deity so unparallel'd ?

*As they come forward,* The Genius of the Wood *appears
and turning toward them, speaks*

  *Gen.* Stay, gentle Swains, for though in this dis-
     guise
I see bright honour sparkle through your eyes ;
Of famous Arcady ye are, and sprung
Of that renowned flood, so often sung,
Divine Alpheus, who by secret sluice        30
Stole under seas to meet his Arethuse ;
And ye, the breathing roses of the wood,
Fair silver-buskin'd Nymphs, as great and good.
I know this quest of yours and free intent
Was all in honour and devotion meant
To the great mistress of yon princely shrine,
Whom with low reverence I adore as mine,
And with all helpful service will comply
To further this night's glad solemnity,
And lead ye where ye may more near behold    40
What shallow-searching Fame hath left untold ;
Which I full oft amidst these shades alone
Have sat to wonder at, and gaze upon.
For know, by lot from Jove, I am the Power
Of this fair wood, and live in oaken bower,
To nurse the saplings tall, and curl the grove
With ringlets quaint and wanton windings wove ;
And all my plants I save from nightly ill
Of noisome winds and blasting vapours chill,
And from the boughs brush off the evil dew,    50
And heal the harms of thwarting thunder blue
Or what the cross dire-looking planet smites
Or hurtful worm with canker'd venom bites.

When evening grey doth rise, I fetch my round
Over the mount and all this hallow'd ground ;
And early, ere the odorous breath of morn
Awakes the slumbering leaves, or tassell'd horn
Shakes the high thicket, haste I all about,
Number my ranks, and visit every sprout
With puissant words and murmurs made to bless.  60
But else in deep of night, when drowsiness
Hath lock'd up mortal sense, then listen I
To the celestial Sirens' harmony,
That sit upon the nine infolded spheres
And sing to those that hold the vital shears
And turn the adamantine spindle round
On which the fate of gods and men is wound.
Such sweet compulsion doth in music lie,
To lull the daughters of Necessity,
And keep unsteady Nature to her law,        70
And the low world in measur'd motion draw
After the heavenly tune, which none can hear
Of human mould with gross unpurged ear ;
And yet such music worthiest were to blaze
The peerless height of her immortal praise
Whose lustre leads us, and for her most fit,
If my inferior hand or voice could hit
Inimitable sounds.   Yet as we go,
Whate'er the skill of lesser gods can show
I will assay, her worth to celebrate,        80
And so attend ye toward her glittering state ;
Where ye may all that are of noble stem
Approach, and kiss her sacred vesture's hem.


## II. Song

O'er the smooth enamell'd green
Where no print of step hath been,
  Follow me as I sing
  And touch the warbled string :

Under the shady roof
Of branching elm star-proof
    Follow me.                90
I will bring you where she sits
Clad in splendour as befits
    Her deity.
Such a rural Queen
All Arcadia hath not seen.


## III. Song

Nymphs and Shepherds, dance no more
  By sandy Ladon's lilied banks,
On old Lycaeus or Cyllene hoar
  Trip no more in twilight ranks ;
Though Erymanth your loss deplore    100
  A better soil shall give ye thanks.
From the stony Maenalus
Bring your flocks and live with us ;
Here ye shall have greater grace,
To serve the Lady of this place.
Though Syrinx your Pan's mistress were,
Yet Syrinx well might wait on her.
  Such a rural Queen
  All Arcadia hath not seen.

# COMUS

## A Masque presented at Ludlow Castle, 1634

*To the Right Honourable John, Lord Viscount Brackley, son and heir-apparent to the Earl of Bridgewater, etc.*

My Lord,

       This Poem, which received its first occasion of birth from yourself and others of your noble family, and much honour from your own person in the performance, now returns again to make a final dedication of itself to you. Although not openly acknowledged by the Author, yet it is a legitimate offspring, so lovely and so much desired that the often copying of it hath tired my pen to give my several friends satisfaction, and brought me to a necessity of producing it to the public view, and now to offer it up, in all rightful devotion, to those fair hopes and rare endowments of your much-promising youth, which give a full assurance to all that know you of a future excellence. Live, sweet Lord, to be the honour of your name ; and receive this as your own from the hands of him who hath by many favours been long obliged to your most honoured Parents, and, as in this representation your attendant *Thyrsis*, so now in all real expression

Your faithful and most humble Servant,

H. LAWES*

* This Dedication first appeared in the edition of 1637. It was reprinted in 1645, but omitted in 1673.

*The Copy of a Letter written by Sir Henry Wotton to the Author upon the following Poem*

From the College, this 13 of April, 1638

SIR,

It was a special favour when you lately bestowed upon me here the first taste of your acquaintance, though no longer than to make me know that I wanted more time to value it and to enjoy it rightly ; and, in truth, if I could then have imagined your farther stay in these parts, which I understood afterwards by Mr. H., I would have been bold, in our vulgar phrase, to mend my draught (for you left me with an extreme thirst), and to have begged your conversation again, jointly with your said learned friend, at a poor meal or two, that we might have banded together some good Authors of the ancient time ; among which I observed you to have been familiar.

Since your going, you have charged me with new obligations, both for a very kind letter from you dated the 6th of this month, and for a dainty piece of entertainment which came therewith. Wherein I should much commend the tragical part, if the lyrical did not ravish me with a certain Doric delicacy in your Songs and Odes, whereunto I must plainly confess to have seen yet nothing parallel in our language : *Ipsa mollities.* But I must not omit to tell you that I now only owe you thanks for intimating unto me (how modestly soever) the true artificer. For the work itself I had viewed some good while before with singular delight ; having received it from our common friend Mr. R., in the very close of the late R.'s Poems, printed at Oxford : whereunto it was added (as I now suppose) that the accessory might help out the principal, according to the art of Stationers, and to leave the reader *con la bocca dolce.*

Now, Sir, concerning your travels ; wherein I may challenge a little more privilege of discourse with you. I suppose you will not blanch Paris in your way : therefore I have been bold to trouble you with a few lines to Mr. M. B., whom you shall easily find attending the young Lord S. as his governor ; and you may surely receive from him good directions for the shaping of your farther journey into Italy, where he did reside, by my choice, some time for the King, after mine own recess from Venice.

I should think that your best line will be through the whole length of France to Marseilles, and thence by sea to Genoa ; whence the passage into Tuscany is as diurnal as a

Gravesend barge. I hasten, as you do, to Florence or Siena, the rather to tell you a short story, from the interest you have given me in your safety.

At Siena I was tabled in the house of one Alberto Scipioni, an old Roman courtier in dangerous times ; having been steward to the Duca di Pagliano, who with all his family were strangled, save this only man that escaped by foresight of the tempest. With him I had often much chat of those affairs, into which he took pleasure to look back from his native harbour ; and, at my departure toward Rome (which had been the centre of his experience), I had won confidence enough to beg his advice how I might carry myself securely there without offence of others or of mine own conscience. " *Signor Arrigo mio*," says he, " *i pensieri stretti ed il viso sciolto* will go safely over the whole world." Of which Delphian oracle (for so I have found it) your judgment doth need no commentary ; and therefore, Sir, I will commit you with it to the best of all securities, God's dear love, remaining

Your friend, as much at command as any of longer date,

HENRY WOTTON

### Postscript

Sir : I have expressly sent this my footboy to prevent your departure without some acknowledgment from me of the receipt of your obliging letter ; having myself through some business, I know not how, neglected the ordinary conveyance. In any part where I shall understand you fixed, I shall be glad and diligent to entertain you with home-novelties, even for some fomentation of our friendship, too soon interrupted in the cradle.

---

### THE PERSONS

*The Attendant Spirit*, afterwards in the habit of *Thyrsis*.
*Comus*, with his Crew.
*The Lady*.
*First Brother*.
*Second Brother*.
*Sabrina*, the Nymph.

The Chief Persons which presented were :—

The Lord Brackley ;
Mr. Thomas Egerton, his Brother ;
The Lady Alice Egerton.

## COMUS

*The first Scene discovers a wild wood*

*The* Attendant Spirit *descends or enters.*

BEFORE the starry threshold of Jove's court
My mansion is, where those immortal shapes
Of bright aerial spirits live inspher'd
In regions mild of calm and serene air,
Above the smoke and stir of this dim spot
Which men call Earth and with low-thoughted care,
Confin'd and pester'd in this pinfold here,
Strive to keep up a frail and feverish being
Unmindful of the crown that Virtue gives,
After this mortal change, to her true servants      10
Amongst the enthron'd gods on sainted seats.
Yet some there be that by due steps aspire
To lay their just hands on that golden key
That opes the palace of Eternity :
To such my errand is, and but for such
I would not soil these pure ambrosial weeds
With the rank vapours of this sin-worn mould.
    But to my task.  Neptune, besides the sway
Of every salt flood and each ebbing stream,
Took in by lot 'twixt high and nether Jove      20
Imperial rule of all the sea-girt isles
That like to rich and various gems inlay
The unadorned bosom of the deep,
Which he, to grace his tributary gods,
By course commits to several government,
And gives them leave to wear their sapphire crowns
And wield their little tridents ; but this Isle,
The greatest and the best of all the main,
He quarters to his blue-hair'd deities.
And all this tract that fronts the falling sun      30

54

A noble Peer of mickle trust and power
Has in his charge, with temper'd awe to guide
An old and haughty nation, proud in arms :
Where his fair offspring, nursed in princely lore,
Are coming to attend their father's state
And new-entrusted sceptre.   But their way
Lies through the perplex'd paths of this drear wood,
The nodding horror of whose shady brows
Threats the forlorn and wandering passenger ;
And here their tender age might suffer peril,          40
But that by quick command from sovran Jove
I was despatch'd for their defence and guard :
And listen why, for I will tell you now
What never yet was heard in tale or song
From old or modern bard in hall or bower.
  Bacchus, that first from out the purple grape
Crush'd the sweet poison of misusèd wine,
After the Tuscan mariners transform'd,
Coasting the Tyrrhene shore, as the winds listed,
On Circe's island fell.   (Who knows not Circe,          50
The daughter of the Sun ? whose charmed cup
Whoever tasted lost his upright shape,
And downward fell into a grovelling swine.)
This Nymph, that gaz'd upon his clust'ring locks,
With ivy berries wreath'd, and his blithe youth,
Had by him, ere he parted thence, a son
Much like his father but his mother more,
Whom therefore she brought up, and Comus nam'd :
Who ripe and frolic of his full-grown age,
Roving the Celtic and Iberian fields,          60
At last betakes him to this ominous wood,
And in thick shelter of black shades imbower'd
Excels his mother at her mighty art ;
Off'ring to every weary traveller
His orient liquor in a crystal glass
To quench the drouth of Phoebus, which as they taste
(For most do taste through fond intemperate thirst),

Soon as the potion works, their human count'nance,
Th' express resemblance of the gods, is chang'd
Into some brutish form of wolf or bear          70
Or ounce or tiger, hog or bearded goat,
All other parts remaining as they were ;
And they, so perfect is their misery,
Not once perceive their foul disfigurement,
But boast themselves more comely than before,
And all their friends and native home forget
To roll with pleasure in a sensual sty.
Therefore when any favour'd of high Jove
Chances to pass through this advent'rous glade,
Swift as the sparkle of a glancing star          80
I shoot from heaven to give him safe convoy,
As now I do.  But first I must put off
These my sky-robes spun out of Iris' woof,
And take the weeds and likeness of a swain
That to the service of this house belongs,
Who with his soft pipe and smooth-dittied song
Well knows to still the wild winds when they roar
And hush the waving woods ;  nor of less faith,
And in this office of his mountain watch
Likeliest, and nearest to the present aid          90
Of this occasion.  But I hear the tread
Of hateful steps ;  I must be viewless now.

[Comus *enters, with a charming-rod in one hand, his glass
in the other ; with him a rout of monsters, headed
like sundry sorts of wild beasts, but otherwise like
men and women, their apparel glistering. They
come in making a riotous and unruly noise, with
torches in their hands.*

*Comus.*  The star that bids the shepherd fold
Now the top of heaven doth hold ;
And the gilded car of day
His glowing axle doth allay

In the steep Atlantic stream ;
And the slope sun his upward beam
Shoots against the dusky pole,
Pacing toward the other goal                    100
Of his chamber in the east.
Meanwhile welcome joy and feast,
Midnight shout and revelry,
Tipsy dance and jollity.
Braid your locks with rosy twine,
Dropping odours, dropping wine.
Rigour now is gone to bed,
And advice with scrupulous head,
Strict Age and sour Severity
With their grave saws in slumber lie.           110
We that are of purer fire
Imitate the starry quire,
Who in their nightly watchful spheres
Lead in swift round the months and years.
The sounds and seas with all their finny drove
Now to the moon in wavering morrice move,
And on the tawny sands and shelves
Trip the pert faeries and the dapper elves ;
By dimpled brook and fountain brim
The wood-nymphs, deck'd with daisies trim,      120
Their merry wakes and pastimes keep :
What hath night to do with sleep ?
Night hath better sweets to prove ;
Venus now wakes, and wakens Love.
Come let us our rites begin,
'Tis only daylight that makes sin
Which these dun shades will ne'er report.
Hail goddess of nocturnal sport,
Dark-veil'd Cotytto, t' whom the secret flame
Of midnight torches burns ; mysterious dame,    130
That ne'er art call'd but when the dragon womb
Of Stygian darkness spets her thickest gloom
And makes one blot of all the air,

Stay thy cloudy ebon chair,
Wherein thou rid'st with Hecat', and befriend
Us thy vow'd priests, till utmost end
Of all thy dues be done, and none left out,
Ere the blabbing eastern scout,
The nice Morn on the Indian steep,
From her cabin'd loop-hole peep                              140
And to the tell-tale Sun descry
Our conceal'd solemnity.
Come, knit hands, and beat the ground
In a light fantastic round.


## THE MEASURE

Break off, break off ! I feel the different pace
Of some chaste footing near about this ground.
Run to your shrouds within these brakes and trees ;
Our number may affright. Some virgin sure
(For so I can distinguish by mine art)
Benighted in these woods ! Now to my charms,      150
And to my wily trains : I shall ere long
Be well stock'd with as fair a herd as graz'd
About my mother Circe. Thus I hurl
My dazzling spells into the spongy air,
Of power to cheat the eye with blear illusion
And give it false presentments, lest the place
And my quaint habits breed astonishment
And put the damsel to suspicious flight ;
Which must not be, for that's against my course.
I, under fair pretence of friendly ends             160
And well-plac'd words of glozing courtesy
Baited with reasons not unplausible,
Wind me into the easy-hearted man
And hug him into snares. When once her eye
Hath met the virtue of this magic dust
I shall appear some harmless villager,
Whom thrift keeps up about his country gear.

But here she comes ; I fairly step aside,
And hearken, if I may, her business here.

*The* Lady *enters.*

*Lady.* This way the noise was, if mine ear be true,
My best guide now.   Methought it was the sound
Of riot and ill-manag'd merriment,                            172
Such as the jocund flute or gamesome pipe
Stirs up among the loose unletter'd hinds,
When for their teeming flocks and granges full
In wanton dance they praise the bounteous Pan
And thank the gods amiss.   I should be loth
To meet the rudeness and swill'd insolence
Of such late wassailers ; yet O where else
Shall I inform my unacquainted feet                           180
In the blind mazes of this tangled wood ?
My brothers, when they saw me wearied out
With this long way, resolving here to lodge
Under the spreading favour of these pines,
Stepp'd, as they said, to the next thicket side
To bring me berries or such cooling fruit
As the kind hospitable woods provide.
They left me then when the grey-hooded Even
Like a sad votarist in palmer's weed                          189
Rose from the hindmost wheels of Phoebus' wain.
But where they are, and why they came not back,
Is now the labour of my thoughts.   'Tis likeliest
They had engag'd their wandering steps too far,
And envious darkness, ere they could return,
Had stole them from me : else, O thievish Night,
Why shouldst thou, but for some felonious end,
In thy dark lantern thus close up the stars
That Nature hung in heaven, and fill'd their lamps
With everlasting oil, to give due light
To the misled and lonely traveller ?                          200
This is the place, as well as I may guess,
Whence even now the tumult of loud mirth

Was rife, and perfect in my listening ear ;
Yet nought but single darkness do I find.
What might this be ?   A thousand fantasies
Begin to throng into my memory,
Of calling shapes, and beckoning shadows dire,
And airy tongues that syllable men's names
On sands and shores and desert wildernesses.
These thoughts may startle well, but not astound  210
The virtuous mind, that ever walks attended
By a strong siding champion, Conscience.—
O welcome, pure-eyed Faith, white-handed Hope,
Thou hovering angel girt with golden wings,
And thou unblemish'd form of Chastity !
I see ye visibly, and now believe
That He, the Supreme Good, t' whom all things ill
Are but as slavish officers of vengeance,
Would send a glistering guardian, if need were,
To keep my life and honour unassail'd.            220
Was I deceiv'd, or did a sable cloud
Turn forth her silver lining on the night?
I did not err, there does a sable cloud
Turn forth her silver lining on the night,
And casts a gleam over this tufted grove.
I cannot hallo to my brothers, but
Such noise as I can make to be heard farthest
I'll venture, for my new-enliven'd spirits
Prompt me ; and they perhaps are not far off.

## SONG

Sweet Echo, sweetest nymph that liv'st unseen   230
    Within thy airy shell
  By slow Meander's margent green,
And in the violet-imbroider'd vale
    Where the love-lorn nightingale
Nightly to thee her sad song mourneth well:
Canst thou not tell me of a gentle pair

That likest thy Narcissus are ?
   O if thou have
Hid them in some flowery cave,
   Tell me but where,             240
Sweet Queen of Parley, Daughter of the sphere :
So may'st thou be translated to the skies,
And give resounding grace to all heaven's harmonies.

   *Comus.*   Can any mortal mixture of earth's mould
Breathe such divine enchanting ravishment ?
Sure something holy lodges in that breast,
And with these raptures moves the vocal air
To testify his hidden residence.
How sweetly did they float upon the wings
Of silence, through the empty-vaulted night,    250
At every fall smoothing the raven down
Of darkness till it smil'd.   I have oft heard
My mother Circe with the Sirens three,
Amidst the flowery-kirtled Naiades
Culling their potent herbs and baleful drugs,
Who as they sung would take the prison'd soul
And lap it in Elysium :  Scylla wept
And chid her barking waves into attention,
And fell Charybdis murmur'd soft applause.
Yet they in pleasing slumber lull'd the sense,    260
And in sweet madness robb'd it of itself ;
But such a sacred and home-felt delight,
Such sober certainty of waking bliss,
I never heard till now.   I'll speak to her,
And she shall be my queen.—Hail foreign wonder,
Whom certain these rough shades did never breed
Unless the goddess that in rural shrine
Dwell'st here with Pan or Silvan, by blest song
Forbidding every bleak unkindly fog    269
To touch the prosperous growth of this tall wood.
   *Lady.*   Nay, gentle shepherd, ill is lost that praise
That is address'd to unattending ears.

Not any boast of skill, but éxtreme shift
How to regain my sever'd company
Compell'd me to awake the courteous Echo
To give me answer from her mossy couch.

    *Comus.*   What chance, good Lady, hath bereft you
               thus ?
    *Lady.*   Dim darkness and this leavy labyrinth.
    *Comus.*   Could that divide you from near-ushering
               guides ?
    *Lady.*   They left me weary on a grassy turf.   280
    *Comus.*   By falsehood, or discourtesy, or why ?
    *Lady.*   To seek i' the valley some cool friendly
               spring.
    *Comus.*   And left your fair side all unguarded, Lady?
    *Lady.*   They were but twain, and purpos'd quick
               return.
    *Comus.*   Perhaps forestalling night prevented them.
    *Lady.*   How easy my misfortune is to hit !
    *Comus.*   Imports their loss, beside the present need ?
    *Lady.*   No less than if I should my brothers lose.
    *Comus.*   Were they of manly prime, or youthful
               bloom ?
    *Lady.*   As smooth as Hebe's their unrazor'd lips.
    *Comus.*   Two such I saw, what time the labour'd ox
In his loose traces from the furrow came    292
And the swink'd hedger at his supper sat.
I saw them under a green mantling vine
That crawls along the side of yon small hill,
Plucking ripe clusters from the tender shoots ;
Their port was more than human, as they stood :
I took it for a faëry vision
Of some gay creatures of the element
That in the colours of the rainbow live    300
And play i' the plighted clouds.   I was awe-strook,
And as I pass'd, I worshipp'd.   If those you seek,
It were a journey like the path to Heaven
To help you find them.

*Lady.*                    Gentle villager,
What readiest way would bring me to that place?
   *Comus.*   Due west it rises from this shrubby point.
   *Lady.*   To find out that, good shepherd, I suppose,
In such a scant allowance of star-light,
Would overtask the best land-pilot's art,
Without the sure guess of well-practis'd feet.   310
   *Comus.*   I know each lane and every alley green,
Dingle or bushy dell of this wild wood,
And every bosky bourn from side to side,
My daily walks and ancient neighbourhood;
And if your stray attendance be yet lodg'd
Or shroud within these limits, I shall know
Ere morrow wake or the low-roosted lark
From her thatch'd pallet rouse. If otherwise,
I can conduct you, Lady, to a low
But loyal cottage, where you may be safe   320
Till further quest.
   *Lady.*                  Shepherd, I take thy word
And trust thy honest-offer'd courtesy,
Which oft is sooner found in lowly sheds
With smoky rafters, than in tap'stry halls
And courts of princes, where it first was nam'd
And yet is most pretended. In a place
Less warranted than this or less secure
I cannot be, that I should fear to change it.   328
Eye me, blest Providence, and square my trial
To   my   proportion'd   strength.   Shepherd,   lead
   on. . . .                                  [*Exeunt.*

*Enter the* Two Brothers.

   *Eld. Bro.*   Unmuffle, ye faint stars; and thou, fair
               moon,
That wont'st to love the traveller's benison,
Stoop thy pale visage through an amber cloud
And disinherit Chaos that reigns here
In double night of darkness and of shades;

Or if your influence be quite damn'd up
With black usurping mists, some gentle taper,
Though a rush-candle from the wicker hole
Of some clay habitation, visit us
With thy long levell'd rule of streaming light,    340
And thou shalt be our star of Arcady
Or Tyrian Cynosure.

   *Sec. Bro.*           Or if our eyes
Be barr'd that happiness, might we but hear
The folded flocks, penn'd in their wattled cotes,
Or sound of pastoral reed with oaten stops,
Or whistle from the lodge, or village cock
Count the night-watches to his feathery dames,
'Twould be some solace yet, some little cheering
In this close dungeon of innumerous boughs.
But O that hapless virgin, our lost sister !    350
Where may she wander now, whither betake her
From the chill dew, amongst rude burs and thistles ?
Perhaps some cold bank is her bolster now
Or 'gainst the rugged bark of some broad elm
Leans her unpillow'd head fraught with sad fears :
What if in wild amazement and affright,
Or while we speak within the direful grasp
Of savage hunger or of savage heat !

   *Eld. Bro.*   Peace, brother, be not over-exquisite
To cast the fashion of uncertain evils ;    360
For grant they be so, while they rest unknown
What need a man forestall his date of grief
And run to meet what he would most avoid ?
Or if they be but false alarms of fear,
How bitter is such self-delusion !
I do not think my sister so to seek,
Or so unprincipled in virtue's book
And the sweet peace that goodness bosoms ever,
As that the single want of light and noise
(Not being in danger, as I trust she is not)    370
Could stir the constant mood of her calm thoughts

And put them into misbecoming plight.
Virtue could see to do what virtue would
By her own radiant light, though sun and moon
Were in the flat sea sunk.   And Wisdom's self
Oft seeks to sweet retired solitude,
Where with her best nurse, Contemplation,
She plumes her feathers and lets grow her wings,
That in the various bustle of resort
Were all-to ruffled and sometimes impair'd.               380
He that has light within his own clear breast
May sit i' the centre and enjoy bright day,
But he that hides a dark soul and foul thoughts
Benighted walks under the mid-day sun—
Himself is his own dungeon.
   *Sec. Bro.*          'Tis most true
That musing meditation most affects
The pensive secrecy of desert cell,
Far from the cheerful haunt of men and herds,
And sits as safe as in a senate-house ;
For who would rob a hermit of his weeds,               390
His few books or his beads or maple dish,
Or do his grey hairs any violence ?
But beauty, like the fair Hesperian tree
Laden with blooming gold, had need the guard
Of dragon watch, with unenchanted eye,
To save her blossoms and defend her fruit
From the rash hand of bold incontinence.
You may as well spread out the unsunn'd heaps
Of miser's treasure by an outlaw's den
And tell me it is safe, as bid me hope               400
Danger will wink on opportunity
And let a single helpless maiden pass
Uninjur'd in this wild surrounding waste.
Of night or loneliness it recks me not ;
I fear the dread events that dog them both,
Lest some ill-greeting touch attempt the person
Of our unowned sister.

*Eld. Bro.*     I do not, brother,
Infer as if I thought my sister's state
Secure without all doubt or controversy ;
Yet where an equal poise of hope and fear   410
Does arbitrate the event, my nature is
That I incline to hope rather than fear,
And gladly banish squint suspicion.
My sister is not so defenceless left
As you imagine ; she has a hidden strength
Which you remember not.
  *Sec. Bro.*    What hidden strength,
Unless the strength of Heaven, if you mean that ?
  *Eld. Bro.* I mean that too, but yet a hidden
     strength
Which, if Heaven gave it, may be term'd her own.
'Tis chastity, my brother, chastity :   420
She that has that, is clad in complete steel,
And like a quiver'd nymph with arrows keen
May trace huge forests and unharbour'd heaths,
Infamous hills and sandy perilous wilds,
Where through the sacred rays of chastity
No salvage fierce, bandite or mountaineer
Will dare to soil her virgin purity ;
Yea there where very desolation dwells,
By grots and caverns shagg'd with horrid shades,
She may pass on with unblench'd majesty,   430
Be it not done in pride or in presumption.
Some say no evil thing that walks by night,
In fog or fire, by lake or moorish fen,
Blue meagre hag or stubborn unlaid ghost
That breaks his magic chains at curfew time,
No goblin or swart faëry of the mine,
Hath hurtful power o'er true virginity.
Do ye believe me yet, or shall I call
Antiquity from the old schools of Greece
To testify the arms of chastity ?   440
Hence had the huntress Dian her dread bow,

Fair silver-shafted queen for ever chaste,
Wherewith she tam'd the brinded lioness
And spotted mountain pard, but set at nought
The frivolous bolt of Cupid ; gods and men
Fear'd her stern frown, and she was queen o' the
    woods.
What was that snaky-headed Gorgon shield
That wise Minerva wore, unconquer'd virgin,
Wherewith she freez'd her foes to congeal'd stone,
But rigid looks of chaste austerity,        450
And noble grace that dash'd brute violence
With sudden adoration and blank awe ?
So dear to Heaven is saintly chastity
That when a soul is found sincerely so
A thousand liveried angels lackey her,
Driving far off each thing of sin and guilt,
And in clear dream and solemn vision
Tell her of things that no gross ear can hear,
Till oft converse with heavenly habitants
Begin to cast a beam on the outward shape,   460
The unpolluted temple of the mind,
And turns it by degrees to the soul's essence,
Till all be made immortal.   But when lust
By unchaste looks, loose gestures and foul talk,
But most by lewd and lavish act of sin,
Lets in defilement to the inward parts,
The soul grows clotted by contagion,
Imbodies and imbrutes, till she quite lose
The divine property of her first being :
Such are those thick and gloomy shadows damp  470
Oft seen in charnel vaults and sepulchres
Lingering, and sitting by a new-made grave
As loth to leave the body that it lov'd,
And link'd itself by carnal sensualty
To a degenerate and degraded state.
   *Sec. Bro.*  How charming is divine Philosophy !
Not harsh and crabbed, as dull fools suppose,

But musical as is Apollo's lute,
And a perpetual feast of nectar'd sweets
Where no crude surfeit reigns.

    *Eld. Bro.*             List, list, I hear  480
Some far-off hallo break the silent air.

    *Sec. Bro.*   Methought so too ; what should it be ?

    *Eld. Bro.*               For certain
Either some one like us night-founder'd here,
Or else some neighbour woodman, or at worst
Some roving robber calling to his fellows.

    *Sec. Bro.*   Heaven keep my sister ! Again, again,
             and near !
Best draw, and stand upon our guard.

    *Eld. Bro.*               I'll hallo.
If he be friendly he comes well : if not,
Defence is a good cause, and Heaven be for us.

    *He hallos. The* Attendant Spirit *hallos again and
          enters habited like a shepherd.*

    *Eld. Bro.*   That hallo I should know. What are
            you ? speak.                   490
Come not too near ; you fall on iron stakes else.

    *Spir.*   What voice is that ? my young Lord ? speak
        again.

    *Sec. Bro.*   O brother, 'tis my father's shepherd, sure.

    *Eld. Bro.*   Thyrsis ! whose artful strains have oft
           delay'd
The huddling brook to hear his madrigal,
And sweeten'd every musk-rose of the dale.
How cam'st thou here, good swain ? Hath any ram
Slipp'd from the fold, or young kid lost his dam,
Or straggling wether the pent flock forsook ?   499
How couldst thou find this dark sequester'd nook ?

    *Spir.*   O my lov'd master's heir, and his next joy,
I came not here on such a trivial toy
As a stray'd ewe, or to pursue the stealth
Of pilfering wolf ; not all the fleecy wealth

That doth enrich these downs is worth a thought
To this my errand, and the care it brought.
But O my virgin Lady, where is she ?
How chance she is not in your company ?
    *Eld. Bro.* To tell thee sadly, Shepherd, without
           blame
Or our neglect, we lost her as we came.       510
    *Spir.* Ay me unhappy ! then my fears are true.
    *Eld. Bro.* What fears, good Thyrsis ? Prithee
           briefly shew.
    *Spir.* I'll tell ye. 'Tis not vain or fabulous
(Though so esteem'd by shallow ignorance)
What the sage poets, taught by th' heavenly Muse,
Storied of old in high immortal verse
Of dire Chimeras and enchanted isles,
And rifted rocks whose entrance leads to Hell,
For such there be, but unbelief is blind.
    Within the navel of this hideous wood,     520
Immur'd in cypress shades, a sorcerer dwells,
Of Bacchus and of Circe born, great Comus,
Deep skill'd in all his mother's witcheries,
And here to every thirsty wanderer
By sly enticement gives his baneful cup,
With many murmurs mix'd, whose pleasing poison
The visage quite transforms of him that drinks,
And the inglorious likeness of a beast
Fixes instead, unmoulding reason's mintage
Character'd in the face. This have I learnt     530
Tending my flocks hard by i' the hilly crofts
That brow this bottom glade, whence night by night
He and his monstrous rout are heard to howl
Like stabled wolves, or tigers at their prey,
Doing abhorred rites to Hecatè
In their obscured haunts of inmost bowers ;
Yet have they many baits and guileful spells
To inveigle and invite the unwary sense
Of them that pass unweeting by the way.

This evening late, by then the chewing flocks    540
Had ta'en their supper on the savoury herb
Of knot-grass dew-besprent, and were in fold,
I sate me down to watch upon a bank
With ivy canopied and interwove
With flaunting honeysuckle, and began
Wrapt in a pleasing fit of melancholy
To meditate my rural minstrelsy,
Till fancy had her fill ; but ere a close
The wonted roar was up amidst the woods
And fill'd the air with barbarous dissonance,    550
At which I ceas'd, and listen'd them a while,
Till an unusual stop of sudden silence
Gave respit to the drowsy-frighted steeds
That draw the litter of close-curtain'd Sleep.
At last a soft and solemn-breathing sound
Rose like a steam of rich distill'd perfumes
And stole upon the air, that even Silence
Was took ere she was ware, and wish'd she might
Deny her nature and be never more
Still to be so displac'd ; I was all ear,    560
And took in strains that might create a soul
Under the ribs of Death.   But O ere long
Too well I did perceive it was the voice
Of my most honour'd Lady, your dear sister.
Amaz'd I stood, harrow'd with grief and fear ;
And ' O poor hapless nightingale,' thought I,
' How sweet thou sing'st, how near the deadly
    snare ! '
Then down the lawns I ran with headlong haste
Through paths and turnings often trod by day,
Till guided by mine ear I found the place    570
Where that damn'd wisard, hid in sly disguise
(For so by certain signs I knew), had met
Already, ere my best speed could prevent,
The aidless innocent lady, his wish'd prey,
Who gently ask'd if he had seen such two,

Supposing him some neighbour villager.
Longer I durst not stay, but soon I guess'd
Ye were the two she meant ; with that I sprung
Into swift flight, till I had found you here ;
But further know I not.

    *Sec. Bro.*           O night and shades,    580
How are ye join'd with hell in triple knot
Against th' unarmed weakness of one virgin,
Alone and helpless ! Is this the confidence
You gave me, brother ?

    *Eld. Bro.*           Yes, and keep it still ;
Lean on it safely ; not a period
Shall be unsaid for me. Against the threats
Of malice or of sorcery, or that power
Which erring men call Chance, this I hold firm :
Virtue may be assail'd but never hurt,
Surpris'd by unjust force but not enthrall'd ;    590
Yea even that which mischief meant most harm
Shall in the happy trial prove most glory.
But evil on itself shall back recoil
And mix no more with goodness, when at last
Gather'd like scum and settled to itself
It shall be in eternal restless change
Self-fed and self-consum'd : if this fail,
The pillar'd firmament is rottenness
And earth's base built on stubble. But come, let's on!
Against the opposing will and arm of Heaven    600
May never this just sword be lifted up ;
But for that damn'd magician, let him be girt
With all the grisly legions that troop
Under the sooty flag of Acheron,
Harpies and Hydras, or all the monstrous forms
'Twixt Africa and Inde, I'll find him out
And force him to return his purchase back,
Or drag him by the curls to a foul death
Curs'd as his life.

    *Spir.*           Alas good vent'rous youth,

I love thy courage yet and bold emprise,                   610
But here thy sword can do thee little stead ;
Far other arms and other weapons must
Be those that quell the might of hellish charms :
He with his bare wand can unthread thy joints
And crumble all thy sinews.

    *Eld. Bro.*                   Why, prithee Shepherd,
How durst thou then thyself approach so near
As to make this relation ?

    *Spir.*                   Care and utmost shifts
How to secure the Lady from surprisal
Brought to my mind a certain shepherd lad,
Of small regard to see to, yet well skill'd          620
In every virtuous plant and healing herb
That spreads her verdant leaf to the morning ray.
He lov'd me well, and oft would beg me sing ;
Which when I did, he on the tender grass
Would sit, and hearken even to ecstasy,
And in requital ope his leathern scrip
And shew me simples of a thousand names,
Telling their strange and vigorous faculties.
Amongst the rest a small unsightly root,
But of divine effect, he cull'd me out ;          630
The leaf was darkish and had prickles on it
But in another country, as he said,
Bore a bright golden flower, but not in this soil ;
Unknown, and like esteem'd, and the dull swain
Treads on it daily with his clouted shoon,
And yet more med'cinal is it than that Moly
That Hermes once to wise Ulysses gave.
He called it Haemony, and gave it me,
And bade me keep it as of sovran use
'Gainst all enchantments, mildew blast or damp          640
Or gastly Furies' apparition.
I purs'd it up, but little reckoning made
Till now that this extremity compell'd,
But now I find it true ; for by this means

I knew the foul enchanter though disguis'd,
Enter'd the very lime-twigs of his spells
And yet came off.   If you have this about you
(As I will give you when we go) you may
Boldly assault the necromancer's hall ;
Where if he be, with dauntless hardihood          650
And brandish'd blade rush on him, break his glass
And shed the luscious liquor on the ground ;
But seize his wand.   Though he and his curst crew
Fierce sign of battle make and menace high,
Or like the sons of Vulcan vomit smoke,
Yet will they soon retire if he but shrink.
   *Eld. Bro.*   Thyrsis, lead on apace, I'll follow thee ;
And some good angel bear a shield before us.


*The Scene changes to a stately palace, set out with all manner
     of deliciousness ; soft music, tables spread with all
     dainties.   Comus appears with his rabble, and the
     Lady set in an enchanted chair ; to whom he offers
     his glass, which she puts by and goes about to rise.*


   *Comus.*   Nay Lady, sit ; if I but wave this wand,
Your nerves are all chain'd up in alabaster          660
And you a statue, or as Daphne was
Root-bound, that fled Apollo.
   *Lady.*                                Fool, do not boast.
Thou canst not touch the freedom of my mind
With all thy charms, although this corporal rind
Thou hast immanacled while Heaven sees good.
   *Comus.*   Why are you vex'd, Lady ? why do you
        frown ?
Here dwell no frowns nor anger, from these gates
Sorrow flies far.   See here be all the pleasures
That fancy can beget on youthful thoughts,
When the fresh blood grows lively and returns          670
Brisk as the April buds in primrose season.
And first behold this cordial julep here

73

That flames and dances in his crystal bounds,
With spirits of balm and fragrant syrups mix'd ;
Not that Nepenthes which the wife of Thone
In Egypt gave to Jove-born Helena
Is of such power to stir up joy as this,
To life so friendly or so cool to thirst.
Why should you be so cruel to yourself,
And to those dainty limbs which Nature lent     680
For gentle usage and soft delicacy ?
But you invert the cov'nants of her trust,
And harshly deal like an ill borrower
With that which you receiv'd on other terms,
Scorning the unexempt condition
By which all mortal frailty must subsist,
Refreshment after toil, ease after pain,
That have been tir'd all day without repast
And timely rest have wanted.   But fair virgin,
This will restore all soon.

    *Lady.*                'Twill not, false traitor ;   690
'Twill not restore the truth and honesty
That thou hast banish'd from thy tongue with lies.
Was this the cottage and the safe abode
Thou told'st me of ?   What grim aspects are these,
These ugly-headed monsters ?   Mercy guard me !
Hence with thy brew'd enchantments, foul deceiver :
Hast thou betray'd my credulous innocence
With vizor'd falsehood and base forgery,
And wouldst thou seek again to trap me here
With lickerish baits fit to ensnare a brute ?   700
Were it a draught for Juno when she banquets,
I would not taste thy treasonous offer ;  none
But such as are good men can give good things,
And that which is not good is not delicious
To a well-govern'd and wise appetite.

    *Comus.*   O foolishness of men !  that lend their ears
To those budge doctors of the Stoic fur
And fetch their precepts from the Cynic tub,

74

Praising the lean and sallow Abstinence.
Wherefore did Nature pour her bounties forth    710
With such a full and unwithdrawing hand,
Covering the earth with odours, fruits, and flocks,
Thronging the seas with spawn innumerable,
But all to please and sate the curious taste ?
And set to work millions of spinning worms,
That in their green shops weave the smooth-hair'd silk
To deck her sons ;  and that no corner might
Be vacant of her plenty, in her own loins
She hutch'd th' all-worshipp'd ore and precious gems
To store her children with.   If all the world    720
Should in a pet of temperance feed on pulse,
Drink the clear stream and nothing wear but frieze,
Th' All-giver would be unthank'd, would be unprais'd,
Not half his riches known, and yet despis'd ;
And we should serve him as a grudging master,
As a penurious niggard of his wealth,
And live like Nature's bastards not her sons,
Who would be quite surcharg'd with her own weight
And strangled with her waste fertility :
The earth cumber'd, and the wing'd air dark'd with
      plumes,                                           730
The herds would over-multitude their lords,
The sea o'erfraught would swell, and the unsought
      diamonds
Would so emblaze the forehead of the deep
And so bestud with stars, that they below
Would grow inur'd to light, and come at last
To gaze upon the sun with shameless brows.
List Lady, be not coy, and be not cozen'd
With that same vaunted name, Virginity ;
Beauty is Nature's coin, must not be hoarded
But must be current, and the good thereof    740
Consists in mutual and partaken bliss,
Unsavoury in the enjoyment of itself ;
If you let slip time, like a neglected rose

It withers on the stalk with languish'd head.
Beauty is Nature's brag, and must be shewn
In courts, at feasts and high solemnities,
Where most may wonder at the workmanship ;
It is for homely features to keep home,
They had their name thence ;  coarse complexions
And cheeks of sorry grain will serve to ply          750
The sampler and to tease the huswife's wool.
What need a vermeil-tinctur'd lip for that,
Love-darting eyes or tresses like the morn ?
There was another meaning in these gifts ;
Think what, and be advis'd ;  you are but young yet.
       *Lady.*   I had not thought to have unlock'd my lips
In this unhallow'd air, but that this juggler
Would think to charm my judgment as mine eyes,
Obtruding false rules prank'd in reason's garb.
I hate when vice can bolt her arguments          760
And virtue has no tongue to check her pride.
Imposter !  do not charge most innocent Nature,
As if she would her children should be riotous
With her abundance.   She, good cateress,
Means her provision only to the good,
That live according to her sober laws
And holy dictate of spare Temperance.
If every just man that now pines with want
Had but a moderate and beseeming share
Of that which lewdly-pamper'd Luxury          770
Now heaps upon some few with vast excess,
Nature's full blessings would be well dispens'd
In unsuperfluous even proportion,
And she no whit encumber'd with her store ;
And then the Giver would be better thank'd,
His praise due paid :  for swinish gluttony
Ne'er looks to Heaven amidst his gorgeous feast,
But with besotted base ingratitude
Crams, and blasphemes his Feeder.   Shall I go on ?
Or have I said enough ?   To him that dares          780

Arm his profane tongue with contemptuous words
Against the sun-clad power of Chastity
Fain would I something say, yet to what end ?
Thou hast nor ear nor soul to apprehend
The sublime notion and high mystery
That must be utter'd to unfold the sage
And serious doctrine of Virginity ;
And thou art worthy that thou shouldst not know
More happiness than this thy present lot.
Enjoy your dear wit and gay rhetoric,                    790
That hath so well been taught her dazzling fence ;
Thou art not fit to hear thyself convinc'd.
Yet should I try, the uncontrolled worth
Of this pure cause would kindle my rapt spirits
To such a flame of sacred vehemence
That dumb things would be mov'd to sympathise,
And the brute Earth would lend her nerves and shake
Till all thy magic structures, rear'd so high,
Were shatter'd into heaps o'er thy false head.
  *Comus.*   She fables not.   I feel that I do fear    800
Her words set off by some superior power ;
And though not mortal, yet a cold shuddering dew
Dips me all o'er, as when the wrath of Jove
Speaks thunder and the chains of Erebus
To some of Saturn's crew.   I must dissemble,
And try her yet more strongly.—Come, no more,
This is mere moral babble, and direct
Against the canon laws of our foundation.
I must not suffer this ; yet 'tis but the lees
And settlings of a melancholy brood.           •        810
But this will cure all straight ; one sip of this
Will bathe the drooping spirits in delight
Beyond the bliss of dreams.   Be wise, and taste . . .
  [*The* Brothers *rush in with swords drawn, wrest his glass
      out of his hand, and break it against the ground : his
      rout make sign of resistance, but are all driven in.
      The* Attendant Spirit *comes in.*

77

*Spir.* What ! have you let the false enchanter
    'scape ?
O ye mistook, ye should have snatch'd his wand
And bound him fast.  Without his rod revers'd,
And backward mutters of dissevering power,
We cannot free the Lady that sits here
In stony fetters fix'd and motionless.
Yet stay, be not disturb'd ; now I bethink me,    820
Some other means I have which may be us'd,
Which once of Melibaeus old I learnt,
The soothest shepherd that e'er pip'd on plains.

    There is a gentle Nymph not far from hence,
That with moist curb sways the smooth Severn stream:
Sabrina is her name, a virgin pure ;
Whilom she was the daughter of Locrine,
That had the sceptre from his father Brute.
She, guiltless damsel, flying the mad pursuit
Of her enraged stepdame, Guendolen,    830
Commended her fair innocence to the flood
That stay'd her flight with his cross-flowing course ;
The water-nymphs that in the bottom play'd
Held up their pearled wrists and took her in,
Bearing her straight to aged Nereus' hall,
Who piteous of her woes rear'd her lank head,
And gave her to his daughters to imbathe
In nectar'd lavers strew'd with asphodil,
And through the porch and inlet of each sense
Dropt in ambrosial oils, till she reviv'd    840
And underwent a quick immortal change,
Made Goddess of the river.  Still she retains
Her maiden gentleness, and oft at eve
Visits the herds along the twilight meadows,
Helping all urchin blasts and ill-luck signs
That the shrewd meddling elf delights to make,
Which she with precious vial'd liquors heals :
For which the shepherds at their festivals
Carol her goodness loud in rustic lays,

And throw sweet garland wreaths into her stream    850
Of pansies, pinks, and gaudy daffodils.
And, as the old swain said, she can unlock
The clasping charm and thaw the numbing spell,
If she be right invok'd in warbled song ;
For maidenhood she loves, and will be swift
To aid a virgin such as was herself,
In hard-besetting need.    This will I try,
And add the power of some adjuring verse.

### SONG

Sabrina fair,
      Listen where thou art sitting                    860
Under the glassy, cool, translucent wave,
      In twisted braids of lilies knitting
The loose train of thy amber-dropping hair ;
      Listen for dear honour's sake,
      Goddess of the silver lake,
            Listen and save !
Listen, and appear to us
In name of great Oceanus,
By the earth-shaking Neptune's mace
And Tethys' grave majestic pace,                      870
By hoary Nereus' wrinkled look
And the Carpathian wisard's hook,
By scaly Triton's winding shell
And old soothsaying Glaucus' spell,
By Leucothea's lovely hands
And her son that rules the strands,
By Thetis' tinsel-slipper'd feet
And the songs of Sirens sweet,
By dead Parthenope's dear tomb
And fair Ligea's golden comb                          880
Wherewith she sits on diamond rocks
Sleeking her soft alluring locks,
By all the nymphs that nightly dance

79

Upon thy streams with wily glance ;
Rise, rise, and heave thy rosy head
From thy coral-paven bed,
And bridle in thy headlong wave
Till thou our summons answer'd have.

Listen and save !

*Sabrina rises, attended by Water-nymphs, and sings.*

*Sabr.*   By the rushy-fringèd bank        890
Where grows the willow and the osier dank
   My sliding chariot stays,
Thick set with agate and the azurn sheen
Of turkis blue and emerald green
   That in the channel strays,
Whilst from off the waters fleet
Thus I set my printless feet
O'er the cowslip's velvet head,
   That bends not as I tread ;
Gentle swain, at thy request        900
   I am here.
   *Spir.*   Goddess dear,
We implore thy powerful hand
To undo the charmed band
Of true virgin here distress'd
Through the force and through the wile
Of unblest enchanter vile.
   *Sabr.*   Shepherd, 'tis my office best
To help ensnared chastity.
Brightest Lady, look on me :        910
Thus I sprinkle on thy breast
Drops that from my fountain pure
I have kept of precious cure,
Thrice upon thy finger's tip,
Thrice upon thy rubied lip ;
Next this marble venom'd seat,
Smear'd with gums of glutinous heat,
I touch with chaste palms moist and cold.

Now the spell hath lost his hold ;
And I must haste ere morning hour          920
To wait in Amphitrite's bower.

Sabrina *descends, and* the Lady *rises out of her seat.*

   *Spir.*   Virgin, daughter of Locrine,
Sprung of old Anchises' line,
May thy brimmed waves for this
Their full tribute never miss
From a thousand petty rills
That tumble down the snowy hills :
Summer drouth or singed air
Never scorch thy tresses fair,
Nor wet October's torrent flood          930
Thy molten crystal fill with mud ;
May thy billows roll ashore
The beryl and the golden ore ;
May thy lofty head be crown'd
With many a tower and terrace round,
And here and there thy banks upon
With groves of myrrh and cinnamon.
   Come Lady, while Heaven lends us grace
Let us fly this cursed place,
Lest the sorcerer us entice          940
With some other new device :
Not a waste or needless sound
Till we come to holier ground.
I shall be your faithful guide
Through this gloomy covert wide ;
And not many furlongs thence
Is your Father's residence,
Where this night are met in state
Many a friend to gratulate
His wish'd presence, and beside          950
All the swains that there abide
With jigs and rural dance resort.
We shall catch them at their sport,

And our sudden coming there
Will double all their mirth and cheer.
Come let us haste, the stars grow high
But Night sits monarch yet in the mid sky.

*The Scene changes, presenting Ludlow Town, and the
President's Castle : then come in Country Dancers ;
after them the* Attendant Spirit *with the two* Brothers
*and the* Lady.

### SONG

   *Spir.*  Back shepherds, back, enough your play
Till next sun-shine holiday.
Here be, without duck or nod,        960
Other trippings to be trod
Of lighter toes, and such court guise
As Mercury did first devise
With the mincing Dryades
On the lawns and on the leas.

*This second Song presents them to their Father and Mother.*

Noble Lord and Lady bright,
I have brought ye new delight.
Here behold so goodly grown
Three fair branches of your own.
Heaven hath timely tried their youth,   970
Their faith, their patience, and their truth,
And sent them here through hard assays
With a crown of deathless praise,
   To triumph in victorious dance
O'er sensual folly and intemperance.

*The dances ended, the* Spirit *epiloguizes.*

   *Spir.*  To the Ocean now I fly,
And those happy climes that lie
Where day never shuts his eye,
Up in the broad fields of the sky.

There I suck the liquid air                                980
All amidst the gardens fair
Of Hesperus, and his daughters three
That sing about the golden tree ;
Along the crisped shades and bowers
Revels the spruce and jocund Spring,
The Graces and the rosy-bosom'd Hours
Thither all their bounties bring ;
There eternal Summer dwells,
And west winds with musky wing
About the cedarn alleys fling                              990
Nard and cassia's balmy smells.
Iris there with humid bow
Waters the odorous banks that blow
Flowers of more mingled hew
Than her purfled scarf can shew,
And drenches with Elysian dew
(List, mortals, if your ears be true)
Beds of hyacinth and roses
Where young Adonis oft reposes,
Waxing well of his deep wound                             1000
In slumber soft, and on the ground
Sadly sits the Assyrian queen ;
But far above in spangled sheen
Celestial Cupid, her fam'd son advanc'd,
Holds his dear Psyche sweet entranc'd
After her wandering labours long,
Till free consent the gods among
Make her his eternal bride,
And from her fair unspotted side
Two blissful twins are to be born,                        1010
Youth and Joy—so Jove hath sworn.
    But now my task is smoothly done :
I can fly or I can run
Quickly to the green earth's end
Where the bow'd welkin slow doth bend,
And from thence can soar as soon

To the corners of the moon.
    Mortals that would follow me
Love Virtue, she alone is free.
She can teach ye how to climb          1020
Higher than the sphery chime ;
Or if Virtue feeble were
Heaven itself would stoop to her.

# LYCIDAS

*In this Monody the Author bewails a learned Friend, unfortunately
drowned in his passage from Chester on the Irish Seas, 1637.
And by occasion foretells the ruine of our corrupted Clergy then
in their height*

YET once more, O ye laurels, and once more
Ye myrtles brown, with ivy never sere,
I come to pluck your berries harsh and crude,
And with forc'd fingers rude
Shatter your leaves before the mellowing year.
Bitter constraint and sad occasion dear
Compels me to disturb your season due :
For Lycidas is dead, dead ere his prime,
Young Lycidas, and hath not left his peer.
Who would not sing for Lycidas ? he knew                    10
Himself to sing, and build the lofty rhyme.
He must not float upon his watery bier
Unwept, and welter to the parching wind
Without the meed of some melodious tear.
   Begin then, Sisters of the sacred well
That from beneath the seat of Jove doth spring,
Begin, and somewhat loudly sweep the string ;
Hence with denial vain and coy excuse.
So may some gentle Muse
With lucky words favour my destin'd urn,                    20
And as he passes turn
And bid fair peace be to my sable shroud.
For we were nurs'd upon the self-same hill,
Fed the same flock, by fountain, shade and rill.
   Together both, ere the high lawns appear'd

Under the opening eyelids of the morn,
We drove a-field, and both together heard
What time the gray-fly winds her sultry horn,
Battening our flocks with the fresh dews of night
Oft till the star that rose at evening bright                    30
Toward Heaven's descent had slop'd his westering
    wheel.
Meanwhile the rural ditties were not mute,
Temper'd to the oaten flute ;
Rough Satyrs danc'd, and Fauns with cloven heel
From the glad sound would not be absent long,
And old Damoetas lov'd to hear our song.

    But O the heavy change, now thou art gone,
Now thou art gone and never must return !
Thee Shepherd, thee the woods and desert caves,
With wild thyme and the gadding vine o'ergrown,
And all their echoes mourn.                    41
The willows and the hazel copses green
Shall now no more be seen
Fanning their joyous leaves to thy soft lays.
As killing as the canker to the rose,
Or taint-worm to the weanling herds that graze,
Or frost to flowers that their gay wardrope wear
When first the white-thorn blows :
Such, Lycidas, thy loss to shepherds' ear.

    Where were ye, Nymphs, when the remorseless
    deep                    50
Clos'd o'er the head of your lov'd Lycidas ?
For neither were ye playing on the steep
Where your old bards, the famous Druids, lie,
Nor on the shaggy top of Mona high,
Nor yet where Deva spreads her wisard stream.
Ay me, I fondly dream !
Had ye been there—for what could that have done ?
What could the Muse herself that Orpheus bore,
The Muse herself for her enchanting son
Whom universal Nature did lament,                    60

When by the rout that made the hideous roar
His gory visage down the stream was sent,
Down the swift Hebrus to the Lesbian shore ?
  Alas ! what boots it with uncessant care
To tend the homely slighted shepherd's trade,
And strictly meditate the thankless Muse ?
Were it not better done as others use,
To sport with Amaryllis in the shade
Or with the tangles of Neaera's hair ?
Fame is the spur that the clear spirit doth raise   70
(That last infirmity of noble mind)
To scorn delights and live laborious days ;
But the fair guerdon when we hope to find
And think to burst out into sudden blaze,
Comes the blind Fury with the abhorred shears
And slits the thin-spun life.   " But not the praise,"
Phoebus replied, and touch'd my trembling ears ;
" Fame is no plant that grows on mortal soil,
Nor in the glistering foil
Set off to the world nor in broad rumour lies,   80
But lives and spreads aloft by those pure eyes
And perfect witness of all-judging Jove ;
As he pronounces lastly on each deed,
Of so much fame in Heaven expect thy meed."
  O fountain Arethuse, and thou honour'd flood,
Smooth-sliding Mincius, crown'd with vocal reeds,
That strain I heard was of a higher mood :
But now my oat proceeds,
And listens to the herald of the sea
That came in Neptune's plea.   90
He ask'd the waves, and ask'd the felon winds,
What hard mishap hath doom'd this gentle swain ?
And question'd every gust of rugged wings
That blows from off each beaked promontory.
They knew not of his story ;
And sage Hippotades their answer brings,
That not a blast was from his dungeon stray'd,

The air was calm, and on the level brine
Sleek Panope with all her sisters play'd.
It was that fatal and perfidious bark,                    100
Built in the eclipse and rigg'd with curses dark,
That sunk so low that sacred head of thine.

Next Camus, reverend sire, went footing slow,
His mantle hairy and his bonnet sedge,
Inwrought with figures dim, and on the edge
Like to that sanguine flower inscrib'd with woe.
" Ah ! who hath reft " (quoth he) " my dearest
    pledge ? "
Last came, and last did go,
The Pilot of the Galilean Lake ;
Two massy keys he bore of metals twain              110
(The golden opes, the iron shuts amain) ;
He shook his mitred locks, and stern bespake :
" How well could I have spar'd for thee, young
    swain,
Anow of such as for their bellies' sake
Creep and intrude and climb into the fold !
Of other care they little reckoning make
Than how to scramble at the shearers' feast
And shove away the worthy bidden guest.
Blind mouths ! that scarce themselves know how to
    hold
A sheep-hook, or have learnt aught else the least   120
That to the faithful herdman's art belongs !
What recks it them ?  What need they ?  They are
    sped ;
And when they list, their lean and flashy songs
Grate on their scrannel pipes of wretched straw ;
The hungry sheep look up and are not fed,
But swoln with wind and the rank mist they draw
Rot inwardly, and foul contagion spread ;
Besides what the grim wolf with privy paw
Daily devours apace, and nothing said.
But that two-handed engine at the door               130

Stands ready to smite once, and smite no more."
   Return, Alpheus, the dread voice is past
That shrunk thy streams ; return, Sicilian Muse,
And call the vales and bid them hither cast
Their bells and flowrets of a thousand hues.
Ye valleys low where the mild whispers use
Of shades and wanton winds and gushing brooks,
On whose fresh lap the swart star sparely looks,
Throw hither all your quaint enamell'd eyes
That on the green turf suck the honied showers,   140
And purple all the ground with vernal flowers.
Bring the rathe primrose that forsaken dies,
The tufted crow-toe, and pale jessamine,
The white pink, and the pansy freakt with jet,
The glowing violet,
The musk-rose, and the well-attir'd woodbine,
With cowslips wan that hang the pensive head,
And every flower that sad embroidery wears ;
Bid amaranthus all his beauty shed,
And daffadillies fill their cups with tears,   150
To strew the laureate hearse where Lycid lies.
For so to interpose a little ease
Let our frail thoughts dally with false surmise.
Ay me ! whilst thee the shores and sounding seas
Wash far away, where'er thy bones are hurl'd,
Whether beyond the stormy Hebrides
Where thou perhaps under the whelming tide
Visit'st the bottom of the monstrous world ;
Or whether thou to our moist vows denied
Sleep'st by the fable of Bellerus old,   160
Where the great Vision of the guarded mount
Looks toward Namancos and Bayona's hold :
Look homeward Angel now, and melt with ruth ;
And, O ye dolphins, waft the hapless youth.
   Weep no more, woeful shepherds weep no more,
For Lycidas your sorrow is not dead,
Sunk though he be beneath the watery floor ;

So sinks the day-star in the ocean bed,
And yet anon repairs his drooping head
And tricks his beams, and with new-spangled ore
Flames in the forehead of the morning sky :   171
So Lycidas sunk low, but mounted high,
Through the dear might of Him that walk'd the waves,
Where other groves and other streams along
With nectar pure his oozy locks he laves,
And hears the unexpressive nuptial song
In the blest kingdoms meek of joy and love.
There entertain him all the saints above
In solemn troops and sweet societies,
That sing, and singing in their glory move,   180
And wipe the tears for ever from his eyes.
Now Lycidas the shepherds weep no more ;
Henceforth thou art the Genius of the shore
In thy large recompense, and shalt be good
To all that wander in that perilous flood.

Thus sang the uncouth swain to the oaks and rills,
While the still Morn went out with sandals gray ;
He touch'd the tender stops of various quills,
With eager thought warbling his Doric lay :
And now the sun had stretch'd out all the hills,   190
And now was dropt into the western bay ;
At last he rose, and twitch'd his mantle blue :
To-morrow to fresh woods and pastures new.

# SONNETS

## I

### TO THE NIGHTINGALE

O NIGHTINGALE, that on yon bloomy spray
    Warblest at eve, when all the woods are still,
    Thou with fresh hope the lover's heart dost fill
    While the jolly hours lead on propitious May ;
Thy liquid notes that close the eye of day,      5
    First heard before the shallow cuckoo's bill,
    Portend success in love.   O if Jove's will
    Have link'd that amorous power to thy soft lay,
Now timely sing, ere the rude bird of hate
    Foretell my hopeless doom in some grove nigh ;  10
    As thou from year to year hast sung too late
For my relief, yet hadst no reason why :
    Whether the Muse or Love call thee his mate,
    Both them I serve, and of their train am I.

## II

### ON HIS BEING ARRIVED TO THE AGE
### OF TWENTY-THREE

How soon hath Time, the subtle thief of youth,
    Stolen on his wing my three-and-twentieth year !
    My hasting days fly on with full career,
    But my late spring no bud or blossom shew'th.

Perhaps my semblance might deceive the truth    5
    That I to manhood am arriv'd so near,
    And inward ripeness doth much less appear
    That some more timely-happy spirits endu'th.
Yet be it less or more, or soon or slow,
    It shall be still in strictest measure even    10
    To that same lot, however mean or high,
Toward which Time leads me, and the will of
    Heaven;
    All is, if I have grace to use it so,
    As ever in my great Task-Master's eye.

# III

## WHEN THE ASSAULT WAS INTENDED
### TO THE CITY

CAPTAIN, or Colonel, or Knight in arms,
    Whose chance on these defenceless doors may
      seize,
    If deed of honour did thee ever please,
    Guard them, and him within protect from
      harms.
He can requite thee ; for he knows the charms    5
    That call fame on such gentle acts as these,
    And he can spread thy name o'er lands and
      seas,
    Whatever clime the sun's bright circle warms.
Lift not thy spear against the Muses' bower :
    The great Emathian conqueror bid spare    10
    The house of Pindarus, when temple and
      tower
Went to the ground ; and the repeated air
    Of sad Electra's poet had the power
    To save the Athenian walls from ruin bare.

## IV

### To a Virtuous Young Lady

LADY that in the prime of earliest youth
    Wisely hast shunn'd the broad way and the green,
    And with those few art eminently seen
    That labour up the hill of heavenly Truth,
The better part with Mary and with Ruth       5
    Chosen thou hast ; and they that overween,
    And at thy growing virtues fret their spleen,
    No anger find in thee, but pity and ruth.
Thy care is fix'd and zealously attends
    To fill thy odorous lamp with deeds of light,   10
    And hope that reaps not shame. Therefore be
        sure
Thou, when the Bridegroom with his feastful friends
    Passes to bliss at the mid-hour of night,
    Hast gain'd thy entrance, Virgin wise and pure.

## V

### To the Lady Margaret Ley

DAUGHTER to that good Earl, once President
    Of England's Council and her Treasury,
    Who liv'd in both unstain'd with gold or fee,
    And left them both more in himself content,
Till the sad breaking of that Parlament       5
    Broke him, as that dishonest victory
    At Chaeronea, fatal to liberty,
    Kill'd with report that old man eloquent ;
Though later born than to have known the days
    Wherein your father flourish'd, yet by you,   10
    Madam, methinks I see him living yet :

So well your words his noble virtues praise
    That all both judge you to relate them true
    And to possess them, honour'd Margaret.


## VI

### ON THE DETRACTION WHICH FOLLOWED UPON MY WRITING CERTAIN TREATISES

A book was writ of late call'd *Tetrachordon*,
    And woven close, both matter, form and style ;
    The subject new : it walk'd the town a while,
    Numbering good intellects ; now seldom por'd
    on.
Cries the stall-reader, " Bless us ! what a word on  5
    A title-page is this ! " ;  and some in file
    Stand spelling false, while one might walk to Mile-
End Green.   Why, is it harder, sirs, than *Gordon*,
*Colkitto*, or *Macdonnel*, or *Galasp* ?
    Those rugged names to our like mouths grow
    sleek        10
    That would have made Quintilian stare and gasp.
Thy age, like ours, O soul of Sir John Cheek,
    Hated not learning worse than toad or asp,
    When thou taught'st Cambridge and King
    Edward Greek.


## VII

### ON THE SAME

I did but prompt the age to quit their clogs
    By the known rules of ancient liberty,
    When straight a barbarous noise environs me
    Of owls and cuckoos, asses, apes and dogs ;

As when those hinds that were transform'd to
    frogs      5
    Rail'd at Latona's twin-born progeny,
    Which after held the Sun and Moon in fee.
But this is got by casting pearl to hogs,
That bawl for freedom in their senseless mood
    And still revolt when truth would set them
    free.      10
    Licence they mean when they cry Liberty ;
For who loves that must first be wise and good :
    But from that mark how far they rove we see,
    For all this waste of wealth and loss of blood.

# VIII

## To Mr. H. Lawes, on His Airs

Harry, whose tuneful and well-measur'd song
    First taught our English music how to span
    Words with just note and accent, not to scan
    With Midas' ears, committing short and long,
Thy worth and skill exempts thee from the throng, 5
    With praise enough for Envy to look wan ;
    To after age thou shalt be writ the man
    That with smooth air couldst humour best our
    tongue.
Thou honour'st verse, and verse must lend her
    wing
    To honour thee, the priest of Phoebus' quire    10
    That tun'st their happiest lines in hymn or
    story.
Dante shall give Fame leave to set thee higher
    Than his Casella, whom he woo'd to sing,
    Met in the milder shades of Purgatory.

## IX

### ON THE RELIGIOUS MEMORY OF MRS. CATHERINE THOMASON, MY CHRISTIAN FRIEND, DECEASED DEC. 16, 1646

WHEN Faith and Love, which parted from thee never,
　　Had ripen'd thy just soul to dwell with God,
　　Meekly thou didst resign this earthy load
Of death, call'd life, which us from life doth sever.
Thy works and alms and all thy good endeavour　5
　　Stay'd not behind, nor in the grave were trod,
　　But as Faith pointed with her golden rod
Follow'd thee up to joy and bliss for ever.
Love led them on and Faith, who knew them best
　　Thy handmaids, clad them o'er with purple
　　　　beams　10
　　And azure wings, that up they flew so drest
And spake the truth of thee on glorious themes
　　Before the Judge, who thenceforth bid thee rest
　　And drink thy fill of pure immortal streams.

## X

### ON THE NEW FORCERS OF CONSCIENCE UNDER THE LONG PARLIAMENT

BECAUSE you have thrown off your Prelate Lord,
　　And with stiff vows renounc'd his Liturgy,
　　To seize the widow'd whore Plurality
From them whose sin ye envied, not abhorr'd;
Dare ye for this adjure the civil sword　5
　　To force our consciences that Christ set free,
　　And ride us with a classic hierarchy
Taught ye by mere A. S. and Rotherford?

Men whose life, learning, faith and pure intent
    Would have been held in high esteem with
      Paul             10
    Must now be nam'd and printed heretics
By shallow Edwards and Scotch What-d'ye-call.
    But we do hope to find out all your tricks,
    Your plots and packings, worse than those of
      Trent,
              That so the Parliament   15
May with their wholesome and preventive shears
Clip your phylacteries, though baulk your ears,
          And succour our just fears,
When they shall read this clearly in your charge :
New Presbyter is but old Priest writ large.   20

## XI

### To the Lord General Fairfax, at the Siege of Colchester

Fairfax, whose name in arms through Europe
    rings
    Filling each mouth with envy or with praise
    And all her jealous monarchs with amaze
    And rumours loud, that daunt remotest kings,
Thy firm unshaken virtue ever brings     5
    Victory home, though new rebellions raise
    Their Hydra heads, and the false North displays
    Her broken league to imp their serpent wings.
O yet a nobler task awaits thy hand;
    For what can war but endless war still breed,  10
    Till truth and right from violence be freed,
And public faith clear'd from the shameful brand
    Of public fraud.  In vain doth Valour bleed
    While Avarice and Rapine share the land.

## XII

### To the Lord General Cromwell,
on the Proposals of certain Ministers at the
Committee for Propagation of the Gospel

CROMWELL, our chief of men, who through a cloud
    Not of war only, but detractions rude,
    Guided by faith and matchless fortitude,
    To peace and truth thy glorious way hast
      plough'd,
And on the neck of crowned Fortune proud    5
    Hast rear'd God's trophies and his work pur-
      sued,
    While Darwen stream with blood of Scots imbrued
    And Dunbar field resounds thy praises loud,
And Worcester's laureate wreath : yet much remains
    To conquer still ; peace hath her victories    10
    No less renown'd than war : new foes arise,
Threat'ning to bind our souls with secular chains.
    Help us to save free conscience from the paw
    Of hireling wolves whose Gospel is their maw.

## XIII

### To Sir Henry Vane the Younger

VANE, young in years but in sage counsel old,
    Than whom a better senator ne'er held
    The helm of Rome, when gowns not arms repell'd
    The fierce Epirot and the African bold,
Whether to settle peace or to unfold    5
    The drift of hollow states hard to be spell'd,
    Then to advise how war may best, upheld,
    Move by her two main nerves, iron and gold,

In all her equipage ; besides to know          9
   Both spiritual power and civil, what each means,
   What severs each thou hast learn'd, which few
      have done.
The bounds of either sword to thee we owe.
   Therefore on thy firm hand Religion leans
   In peace, and reckons thee her eldest son.


## XIV

### ON THE LATE MASSACRE IN PIEMONT

AVENGE O Lord thy slaughter'd saints, whose bones
   Lie scatter'd on the Alpine mountains cold,
   Even them who kept thy truth so pure of old
   When all our fathers worshipp'd stocks and stones,
Forget not : in thy book record their groans          5
   Who were thy sheep and in their ancient fold
   Slain by the bloody Piemontese that roll'd
   Mother with infant down the rocks.   Their moans
The vales redoubled to the hills, and they
   To heaven.   Their martyr'd blood and ashes
      sow          10
   O'er all the Italian fields where still doth sway
The triple Tyrant ; that from these may grow
   A hundredfold, who having learnt thy way
   Early may fly the Babylonian woe.


## XV

### ON HIS BLINDNESS

WHEN I consider how my light is spent,
   Ere half my days, in this dark world and wide,
   And that one talent which is death to hide
   Lodg'd with me useless, though my soul more bent

To serve therewith my Maker, and present          5
    My true account, lest He returning chide ;
    " Doth God exact day-labour, light denied ? "
    I fondly ask.   But Patience, to prevent
That murmur, soon replies, " God doth not need
    Either man's work or his own gifts.   Who best
    Bear his mild yoke, they serve him best.   His state
Is kingly :   thousands at his bidding speed        12
    And post o'er land and ocean without rest ;
    They also serve who only stand and wait."


## XVI

### To Mr. Lawrence

Lawrence, of virtuous father virtuous son,
    Now that the fields are dank and ways are mire,
    Where shall we sometimes meet, and by the fire
    Help waste a sullen day, what may be won
From the hard season gaining ?   Time will run     5
    On smoother, till Favonius reinspire
    The frozen earth and clothe in fresh attire
    The lily and rose, that neither sow'd nor spun.
What neat repast shall feast us, light and choice,  9
    Of Attic taste, with wine, whence we may rise
    To hear the lute well touch'd, or artful voice
Warble immortal notes and Tuscan air ?
    He who of those delights can judge, and spare
    To interpose them oft, is not unwise.


## XVII

### To Cyriack Skinner

Cyriack, whose grandsire on the royal bench
    Of British Themis with no mean applause

Pronounc'd, and in his volumes taught, our laws,
  Which others at their bar so often wrench ;
To-day deep thoughts resolve with me to drench   5
  In mirth that after no repenting draws ;
  Let Euclid rest, and Archimedes pause,
  And what the Swede intends, and what the
    French.
To measure life learn thou betimes, and know
  Toward solid good what leads the nearest way ; 10
  For other things mild Heaven a time ordains,
And disapproves that care, though wise in show,
  That with superfluous burden loads the day,
  And when God sends a cheerful hour, refrains.


## XVIII

### To the Same

CYRIACK, this three years' day these eyes, though
    clear
  To outward view of blemish or of spot,
  Bereft of light their seeing have forgot,
  Nor to their idle orbs doth sight appear
Of sun or moon or star throughout the year,   5
  Or man or woman.   Yet I argue not
  Against Heaven's hand or will, nor bate a
    jot
Of heart or hope, but still bear up and steer
Right onward.   What supports me, dost thou ask ?
  The conscience, friend, to have lost them over-
    plied   10
  In liberty's defence, my noble task,
Of which all Europe talks from side to side.
  This thought might lead me through the world's
    vain mask
  Content though blind, had I no better guide.

## XIX

### ON HIS DECEASED WIFE

METHOUGHT I saw my late espousèd saint
    Brought to me like Alcestis from the grave,
    Whom Jove's great son to her glad husband gave,
    Rescued from Death by force though pale and
      faint.
Mine as whom wash'd from spot of child-bed taint  5
    Purification in the Old Law did save,
    And such as yet once more I trust to have
    Full sight of her in Heaven without restraint,
Came vested all in white, pure as her mind.
    Her face was veil'd, yet to my fancied sight   10
    Love, sweetness, goodness, in her person shin'd
So clear, as in no face with more delight.
    But O as to embrace me she inclin'd
    I wak'd, she fled, and day brought back my night.

# NOTES

*Paraphrase on Psalm 114* (1624).
This and the following paraphrase, written during his schooldays, are Milton's earliest extant verse.
P. 1, l. 1.   *Terah's faithful son :*  Abraham.
   l. 3.   *Pharian :*  Egyptian.
   l. 10.   *Foil :*  repulse.

*Paraphrase on Psalm 136* (1624).
P. 3, l. 32.   *Fell :*  fierce, ruthless.
   l. 36.   *Erythraean main :*  Red Sea.
   l. 52.   " For only Og, king of Bashan, remained of the remnant of giants " (Deut. iii. 2).

*Death of a Fair Infant* (1625–1626).
The subject of this poem was the first-born child of Milton's sister Anne, the mother of Edward and John Phillips ;  the child probably died in the winter of 1625–1626.   No doubt the elegy sprang from a genuine feeling of sympathy and grief ;  it is the immaturity of manner rather than the immaturity of experience that produces an effect of artificiality.   Milton is obviously, too obviously, writing in imitation of the Spenserian school of poets ;  the flow of the verse, the mere sensuous delight in words, the Spenserian archaisms, all reveal him as the self-conscious poetic apprentice.   The conceits in the poem—the elaborate conceit, for instance, with which it opens and which affects the modern reader as an insincerity—are also in accord with a prevalent poetic fashion.   Nevertheless there are frequent phrasings and some whole passages to remind us that it is Milton writing ;  and there are themes and motives introduced that he was later to use to better purpose.
P. 5, l. 2.   *Timelessly :*  before due time.
   l. 8.   *Aquilo :*  or Boreas, the North Wind, carried off

Oreithyia, the daughter of the Athenian king Erechtheus.

l. 16. *Middle empire of the freezing air :* " Middle air " is a technical term in Milton (cp. " Nativity Ode," l. 164). Mediaeval science, still current, divided the air into three regions : the middle region was the region of clouds and winds and other meteorological phenomena, and was represented as intensely cold ; the upper region, extending from the tops of the highest mountains to the moon, was serene and mild, corresponding to the Olympian heaven of Greek mythology. The middle air was the abode of demons, the upper air the abode of angels and happy spirits.

P. 6, ll. 23–27. Hyacinthus, a beautiful youth of Sparta, was loved by Apollo but was killed one day by a quoit thrown by the god ; Apollo changed the blood of Hyacinthus into the purple flower that bears his name. Eurotas is the river of Sparta.

*Unweeting :* unwitting.

ll. 39–40. For the verbal form cp. *Lyc.* ll. 155 seq. *That high first-moving sphere :* the *primum mobile*, or outermost sphere (see Appendix, " Milton's Cosmology "). The *Elysian fields* are the region in Greek mythology where the souls of heroes go after death to enjoy the pleasures of life in perfection. Christians placed heaven beyond the highest sphere, as distinct from the older classical view of an elysium within the human universe (see note on cancelled lines in " Comus ").

P. 7, l. 43. The belief that stars are divinities, coming originally from the astrological religions of the East, constantly appears in classical literature.

l. 44. See " Comus," I., note. *Shak'd* is probably an allusion to the war waged by the Titans against the Olympian gods.

l. 45. *Behoof :* interest.

ll. 47–49. *Earth's sons :* the Giants, sons of Gaea (Earth), who in later legend became confused with the Titans and the story of their war on heaven (cp. " Paradise Lost," I. ll. 197–200). By way of accounting for the later identification of Greek with Egyptian gods, legend also said that the Olympian gods and goddesses fled from the Giants into Egypt, where they concealed themselves in the forms of various animals.

*Nectar'd head :* divine head. Nectar was the drink,

as ambrosia was the food, of the gods; both are
attributes of the immortal.

l. 50.  *That just maid :* Astraea, goddess of justice, who
dwelt on earth during the golden age but later fled from
the crimes of men ; she was identified with the constellation Virgo.

l. 53.  *[Mercy] :* In the original this line is short of the
just length by two syllables ; the emendation is based
on the similar conjunction of Mercy with Truth and
Justice in the " Nativity Ode," ll. 141–144.

l. 57.  *Golden-winged host :* angels.

l. 58.  *Human weed :* fleshly garment, body (cp. " Comus,"
l. 16).

l. 59.  *Prefixed :* preordained.
        *Post :* haste on a mission.

Pp. 7–8, ll. 66–69.  The plague, traditionally regarded as a
divine punishment for sin, was raging in London and
in England generally at this time.

## At a Vacation Exercise (1628).

The Latin speeches to which these verses belong, form the
sixth of the Prolusions or Academic Exercises which
Milton permitted to be published at the end of his life.
The speeches were delivered by Milton as the elected
" Father " or president of some annual college revel ;
at the conclusion of the second speech, full of the
scurrilities and college jokes expected of him, he
announces that he will now overleap the university
statutes (which ordained all academic discourses to be
in the learned tongues) and run off from Latin into
English.  He then recited the present verses, in which
he pays homage to his native tongue and declares his
intention of one day using it worthily on some lofty
theme.  Part of the significance of the lines lies in the
fact that it was still a debatable point whether anything
written in a modern tongue would endure and whether
a writer, therefore, who aimed at lasting fame should
not compose in Latin.  His prophetic account of the
themes he was later to handle so magnificently show
that he was already conscious of the bent of his
genius.

P. 9, l. 8.  *Latter : i.e.* at the tail-end of the Latin harangue.

l. 18.  *Wardrope :* wardrobe (Milton's habitual spelling).

l. 20.  *Late fantastics :* recent literary eccentrics.  This
couplet may be aimed at the fashionable metaphysical

school of poetry, headed by John Donne. Metaphysical poetry, like much contemporary poetry, was a revolt against the conventional in poetic thought and style ; it was individual and up-to-date ; it explored the queer ways of the individual mind and heart, and sought to surprise by its unexpected thoughts and sentiments, its incongruous and far-fetched images, its startling colloquialisms and irregular rhythms, its ingenious and often contorted language. Being fashionable at court this new poetry attracted those " wits " of the day who delighted in enlivening poetry with novelties : in their hands it became a game of hunting the paradox, the unlikely image, and above all the metaphysical " conceit " or fancy. The opening stanzas of Milton's " Death of a Fair Infant " provide a mild example of the metaphysical conceit.

l. 22.   *Wits :* minds. " Wit " still retained its original wider sense of the whole mind ; and so " wits," used personally, were men of intellect, learning, talent, the term being applied especially to authors.

P. 10, l. 27.   *Suspect :* suspicion, misgiving.

l. 34.   *Poles :* the celestial poles, skies.

l. 36.   *Thunderous throne :* Zeus, as lord of heaven, was the god of thunder.

l. 37.   *Unshorn :* the classical epithet for Apollo, god of prophecy, music and poetry.

l. 38.   *Hebe :* daughter of Zeus, cupbearer to the gods and goddess of youth.

ll. 40–44.   The poet's imagination descends again through the spheres of the stars and planets to this earth.

   *Loft :* (cp. Germ. *Luft*) originally meant sky, air, upper region, and so came to be applied to the upper part of a house ; in Milton's day it was also used of the various layers or stages either of the air or of any superstructure. Milton's use of the word is illustrated by this sentence from a seventeenth-century author : " We often see clouds as in several stories, lofts or scenes, one over another " (Goad, " Celestial Bodies," II. II. 162).

   *Neptune :* see note on " Comus," l. 18.

ll. 45–46.   The creation of the world and its earliest history.

   *Beldam :* grandmother.

ll. 48–52.   " Odyssey," viii. 601 *seq.:* Demodocus, the blind bard of King Alcinous, sings of the Trojan war and its heroes ; Ulysses covers his face to hide his emotion. In the remainder of the verses, omitted from the present text, Milton resumes his proper business of burlesquing the Aristotelian philosophy.

### Song on May Morning (?1629).

The only evidence for the date of this lyric is that Milton placed it among the university poems in the 1645 edition, before the epigram " On Shakespear " ; and that, as Professor Hanford observes, it is a lyric comment on the theme of the fifth Latin elegy written in the spring of 1629. May 1, 1629, may therefore be taken as the likely date.

### The Fifth Ode of Horace.

This poem (written perhaps during the Cambridge days) comes near perfection in the art of poetic translation. That it is both an exact translation and a characteristic poem illustrates how much the Miltonic style owes to his study and practice of Latin verse.

P. 12, ll. 13–16. *Vota :* (which Milton always renders by *vows* in English) were prayers to the gods to avert some danger, accompanied by the promise of thank-offerings if the prayers were answered ; the vow was generally accompanied by a votive tablet, which was placed on the wall of the temple and contained an inscription or picture relating to the vow (cp. " Lycidas," l. 159).

### On the Morning of Christ's Nativity (Dec. 1629).

This is the first of the poems that in design and treatment may be called Miltonic ; here for the first time Milton fully displays his power of handling universal themes and presenting the show of time and space. Another poet might have retold the simple and picturesque story of the birth at Bethlehem ; Milton unfolds a vision of the created world and of the nations of the earth acknowledging the advent of their Lord. His treatment of the subject provides the opportunity for a masterly survey of the ancient world. The first half of the Hymn celebrates Christ's fulfilment of its dreams and aspirations, enabling Milton to paint a gracious picture of what was endearing and best in classical life and literature : Christ is the mighty Pan, Lord of Nature, the true author of the Roman peace, the restorer of the Age of Gold. The second half of the Hymn presents the darker side of paganism, celebrating Christ's triumph over its superstitious errors and cruelties. If we attend to both sides of the picture we shall understand Milton's attitude to the classical world, and how in true renaissance manner he combined allegiance to Greece and Rome with his Christian faith.

In a poem so nobly conceived we look for a corresponding grandeur in style. The style, however, has been criticised as too artificial and fanciful. Certainly it is in places peculiarly romantic, and the manner is not yet assured and certain. The Spenserian influence still shows in occasional diffuseness, excessive alliteration and the flow of the verse, more especially in the alexandrine that closes the stanza ; such a line as

" Swindges the scaly horror of his folded tail " might well be thought to come from the " Faerie Queene " itself. But criticism has been chiefly directed against the ingenious and sometimes tasteless conceits, and the frequent use of what Ruskin dubbed the pathetic fallacy—the trick of investing nature with human sentiments. These " metaphysical " traits reveal the influence not merely of contemporary English but of Italian poetry, particularly Italian pastoral poetry. Yet the fact is that these faults are discernible as alien elements in a style already Miltonic in its majesty of diction and metre, a style that rises to the height of the theme.

P. 14, l. 5. *Holy sages :* the prophets of the Old Testament.

l. 6. *Deadly forfeit :* penalty of death incurred by the Fall.

l. 10. *Wont :* was wont ; past tense of *won*, " to dwell," " to be used to."

l. 15. *Vein :* peculiar talent or genius ; here equivalent to " inspiration."

P. 15, l. 23. *Star-led Wisards :* " the wise men from the East " (St. Matthew ii.).

l. 24. *Prevent :* anticipate.

l. 27. *Angel quire :* " the multitude of the heavenly host " who appeared to the shepherds in the fields of Bethlehem (St. Luke ii.).

*Quire :* the older spelling of " choir " always used by Milton.

l. 28. Alluding to the live coal from the altar with which the seraph touched the lips of Isaiah (Isaiah vi.). In the " Reason of Church Government " (1642) Milton

speaks of the great poem he hopes one day to write as
" a work not to be raised from the heat of youth, or
the vapours of wine . . . but by devout prayer to that
eternal Spirit who can enrich with all utterance and
knowledge, and sends out his Seraphim with the
hallowed fire of his Altar to touch and purify the lips
of whom he pleases." The poet, in Milton's view, was
a divinely inspired prophet.

l. 30. *While :* at the time that, when. "While " was
originally a noun meaning " time," as in certain surviving phrases—" the while," " meanwhile."

ll. 32–36. Here as elsewhere in the poem (see st. x)
Milton has in mind the pagan worship of Nature, as
the source and controlling power of life, which under
the Roman Empire took the final and universal form
of sun-worship ; this was the religion with which
Christianity had to struggle for supremacy. Actually
the date selected by the church for the commemoration
of the Nativity was the date of the pagan festival
celebrating the birth of the New Sun, when the days
first begin to lengthen after the winter solstice (cp.
st. vii).

*Trim :* fine dress.

St. II. To the worship of Nature Christians opposed the
doctrine of the " corruption " of Nature, consequent
upon the Fall of man ; Nature shared in the consciousness of sin and suffered under the divine malediction ;
as St. Paul expressed it, " the whole creation groaneth
and travaileth in pain together."

P. 16, l. 48. *The turning sphere :* the whole system of spheres,
the globe of the universe turning daily about the earth
(see Appendix; and cp. " the visible diurnal sphere,"
" Paradise Lost," vii. 22).

l. 52. There was a seven-years peace throughout the
Roman Empire at the beginning of the Christian era,
which the Church later interpreted as a divine sign.

l. 56. *Hooked :* armed with hooks.

l. 59. *Awful :* full of awe.

l. 60. *Sovran :* Milton preferred this spelling of
" sovereign."

l. 64. *Whist :* hushed. " Whist " and " hist " (cp. " Il
Penseroso," l. 55) are the same word, being onomato-
poeic words enjoining silence. " Whist " has survived
in Ireland.

l. 68. *Birds of calm :* halcyons. The classical legend was

that during seven days before and after the winter solstice there is always calm at sea while the halcyons build their nest on the waters and hatch their young.

*Charmed* : laid under a charm, spell-bound.

St. VI.  Astrology, or the worship and study of the stars as divinities controlling the world, was a religion which, like the worship of the Sun, had come to Rome from the East ; it was prevalent throughout the Roman Empire, and maintained its hold over the human mind down to the end of the seventeenth century (cp. " Il Penseroso," l. 43, note).

l. 71.  *Precious influence :* Astrology taught that an ethereal liquid flowed from the stars, which affected the character and destiny of man ; this line illustrates the origin of our word " influence."

P. 17, l. 74.  *Lucifer :*  the morning star.

St. VII.  Milton plays on the idea that the sun rises late and as it were reluctantly at this time of year.  Christ is the " Sun of righteousness " (Malachi iv. 2), the " light of men " (St. John i. 4), as opposed to the " Invincible and Eternal Sun " of pagan religion (cp. note, ll. 32–36).

l. 84.  *Axletree*, of the sun's chariot ;  " tree " has here the sense of " shaped wood " (cp. " roof-tree ").  Note that " bear " rhymes with " appear " (cp. " Il Penseroso," l. 87 and " Upon the Circumcision," l. 6).

l. 85.  *Lawn :*  grassland.  Strictly " lawn " is " a cleared space in a wood " (cp. " L'Allegro," l. 71 ;  " Il Penseroso," l. 35 ;  " Lycidas," l. 25).

l. 86.  *Or ere :*  before.

l. 88.  *Than :*  then.  These words were still used interchangeably.

l. 89.  *Pan :*  as the god of woods and pastures, of shepherds and their flocks, was the god of pastoral poetry ; in pastoral allegory he was identified with Christ, the Good Shepherd.  This mingling of pagan and Christian story is common in Renaissance poetry, and is habitual with Milton.

l. 91.  Milton thinks of them as the shepherds of pastoral poetry.

l. 92.  *Silly :*  simple, homely, innocent.

l. 97.  *Noise :*  was still used of music and all agreeable sounds.

P. 18, l. 100.  *Close :*  conclusion or cadence to a musical movement or phrase.

# NOTES

St. X. See note, ll. 32–36.

ll. 102–103. *Round of Cynthia's seat :* the sphere of the moon. The " region of the air " extended from the earth to the moon, where the region of fire began (cp. " Death of Fair Infant," l. 16, note).

l. 106. At the Day of Judgement this corrupted world shall be dissolved, and a new heaven and earth shall appear.

ll. 107–108. Alluding to the doctrine that the music of the spheres keeps " unsteady Nature to her law " (see " Arcades," ll. 63–73).

l. 116. *Unexpressive :* inexpressible, ineffable (cp. " Lycidas," l. 176).

St. XII. See Job xxxviii. 4–11.

l. 122. *Hinges :* poles. The word is a literal translation of the Latin *cardines,* the primary meaning of which is " hinge," and a secondary meaning " poles " or " axis " of the world.

Sts. XIII–XIV. See note on Music of the Spheres in Appendix.

P. 19, l. 126. *Humane :* was not differentiated from " human " until after 1700.

l. 128. *Chime :* concord (cf. " At a Solemn Music," l. 20, note).

l. 132. *Consort :* meaning " fellowship," " agreement," was confused with " concert " and so used of both " a band of musicians " and, as here, of " harmony."

l. 135. *Age of Gold :* the fabled " first " age of Cronus or Saturn, when mankind enjoyed perpetual youth, joy and peace, taking the fruits of the earth without labour.

l. 136. *Speckled :* spotted, defiled (Latin, *maculosus*).
*Vanity :* in the biblical sense of all human sins.

l. 138. *Mould :* cp. " Comus," l. 17, note.

ll. 139–140. Milton places hell in the centre of the earth (cp. " Comus," l. 382).

ll. 143–144. This is the reading of the second edition of 1673 ; the first edition of 1645 reads,
" Thy enameld Arras of the Rainbow wearing,
And Mercy set between."

l. 145. *Sheen :* brightness.

l. 146. *Tissued :* finely and richly woven, especially with gold and silver thread. Cp. " plighted clouds," " Comus," l. 301.

P. 20, l. 155. *Ychained :* the prefix *y* is a survival of the

Anglo-Saxon prefix *ge* ; by the middle of the fifteenth century it had disappeared, but the past participle formed with *y* was a feature of the archaistic language of Spenser and his school, in imitation of Chaucer.

*Sleep : i.e.* of death ; see 1 Corinthians xv. 51–52, and 1 Thessalonians iv. 13–18.

l. 156.   The comma at the end of this line, which is the punctuation of Ed. 1, is obviously right, the sentence being prolonged into the next stanza ; in Ed. 2 the comma was changed to a period.

ll. 157–159.   When Moses received the Ten Commandments (Exodus xix.).

l. 162.   *Centre :* cp. ll. 139–140, note.

l. 163.   *Session :* *-ion* is invariably disyllabic at the end of a line.

l. 164.   " They shall see the Son of man coming in the clouds of heaven with power and great glory " (Matthew xxiv. 30).   *Middle air :* see note, " Death of a Fair Infant," l. 16.

l. 166.   *Is :* vivid present for future tense.

ll. 168–172.   Revelation xii. and xx.

*Swindges :* a form of " swing " that retained the senses of " flog " and " brandish," and so was used of a beast " lashing " its tail.

*Horror :* this use of an abstract for a concrete noun, in order to obtain an effect of grandeur, is characteristic of Milton's style.

Sts. XIX–XX provide a masterly survey of the religious life of the classical world, of the various pagan cults which were brought together under the Roman Empire and with which Christianity had to contend for supremacy ; the struggle lasted several centuries, but Milton naturally uses the dramatic Christian tradition that the pagan gods were routed at the birth of Christ.   Here is the first supreme example in Milton's poetry of his imaginative control of his learning and of his art in picturing great tracts of history ; compare the more elaborate account of the pagan deities in " Paradise Lost," i. 381–521, and the vision of the kingdoms of the world in " Paradise Regained," iii. 251–440.

St. XIX.   The characteristic feature of Greek religion was the practice of divination and the authority of certain centres of divination called oracles.   Oracles were shrines where a god was believed to give responses to the inquiries of his votaries, making known his will, solving problems, and revealing the future. The two chief forms of divination were the interpretation of the frenzied cries uttered by the prophetess of the oracle when in a state of ecstasy and supposed to be possessed by the god, and the communion with gods or departed spirits in dreams specially induced. The most famous of the oracles was at the temple of Apollo at Delphi, situated on the precipitous lower slopes of Mt. Parnassus.

l. 173. It was an ancient Christian tradition that the oracles suddenly " ceased and grew mute at the coming of Christ."

l. 174. *Voice :* was the technical term for the utterance of the oracle, supposed to be the voice of the god speaking through his medium.

*Hideous hum :* describes the frenzied inarticulate utterance of the prophetesses, which is thought to account for their generic name of Bees ; *hideous* has here its original sense of " causing horror or dread."

l. 175. *Deceiving :* the responses of the oracles were usually either enigmatical or ambiguous, an immemorial precaution of prophets ; there are many stories of consultants being thus deluded, as Macbeth was by the witches.

l. 178. *Delphos :* was a common form for Delphi in the seventeenth century.

l. 179. *Nightly :* nocturnal.

*Breathed spell :* whispered incantation, to invoke the deity or spirit.

l. 180. *Pale-eyed :* it was essential to divination that the soul should be freed from the body, whether in ecstasy or sleep or by bodily weakness : thus fasting, sickness, and the approach of death were thought to produce a favourable condition.

P. 21, St. XX. Besides the Olympian gods, with their temples and oracles, Greek religion recognised the inferior spirits of Nature, the local divinities of water and earth and vegetation ; every place, as every person, had its *loci genius* or presiding spirit (cp. the " Genius of the Wood " in " Arcades " and the " Attendant Spirit " in " Comus ").

l. 185. *Poplar pale :* the white poplar.

l. 188. *Nymphs :* semi-divine maidens in Greek mythology, expressing the multiform life of Nature.

St. XXI presents the native religion of the Romans, a religion of family and tribal gods which persisted even after they had adopted the gods of Greece and other nations.

l. 189. *Consecrated earth :* the Romans *consecrated* certain spots for the sole use and habitation of their deities. Most commentators take the words in the less appropriate Christian sense of " burial ground."

l. 190. *Holy hearth :* The Roman religion was that of an agricultural people, a religion of the family and the farmstead ; the house was a kind of temple, the dwelling of divine as well as human beings, and the hearth was the centre or altar of this family worship.

l. 191. *Lars and Lemures :* Lares were the " powers " ruling over the house and its inmates, their activities, lands, and possessions ; Lemures were the spirits of departed ancestors that had to be propitiated, progenitors of the ghosts and hobgoblins of Christian Europe. Note that Milton treats the words as English words and that *Lemures* is therefore a disyllable.

l. 192. *Urns :* vessels in which the ashes of the dead were preserved.

l. 194. *Flamens :* priests of any particular deity, whose chief duty was to perform daily sacrifices.
    *Service quaint :* elaborate ritual. The original sense of " quaint " was " skilful, ingenious," then " elaborate, fine, handsome," then " curious, odd, fantastic " (cp. " Arcades," l. 47, " Comus," l. 157, " Lycidas," l. 139).

l. 195. Many ancient writers mention the bleeding and sweating of statues in the temples of the gods on the occasion of some disaster.

l. 196. *Peculiar power :* particular god (Latin, *numen*).
    *Seat :* (Latin, *sedes*) abode, temple.

Sts. XXII–XXV describe the gods of Syria and Africa, including the pagan deities mentioned in the Old Testament.

l. 197. Baal-Peor was one of the titles under which the Phoenician and Canaanitish peoples worshipped Baal, their chief male deity (Numbers xxv and xxxi.)

l. 199. Dagon, god of the Philistines ; for the story alluded to, see 1 Samuel v. 2–4.

ll. 200–201. Ashtaroth was the female Baal, represented by the crescent moon. Selden (" De Diis Syriis ") calls her " queen of heaven and mother of the gods."

# NOTES

*Shine :* a noun.

l. 203. *Libyc Hammon :* Libyan Ammon. Ammon was an Egyptian god, later identified with Zeus and Jupiter ; there was a famous oracle of Ammon at the oasis of Siwa in Lybia. He was represented by a ram with curved horns.

*Shrinks :* transitive, as in " Lycidas," l. 133.

l. 204. Ezekiel viii. 14 : " There sat women weeping for Tammuz." Thammuz, beloved of Ashtaroth, was killed by a boar while hunting in Lebanon ; his death was mourned by the Phoenician (Tyrian) women of Byblos in an annual festival, when the river Adonis ran red with soil washed down from Lebanon by the autumn rains. The story, adopted by the Greeks as that of Aphrodite (Venus) and Adonis, is a common kind of vegetation myth, representing the death of the year.

ll. 205–210. Moloch was a god of the Ammonites, often referred to in the Old Testament. Selden (" De Diis Syris ") says that his brazen image, of human form with the head of an ox, was hollow and heated from beneath, and its arms extended so that a child could be laid in them as a sacrifice ; the cries of the victim were drowned by the sound of percussion instruments, while friends and relations danced around.

P. 22, l. 211. *Brutish gods of Nile :* Egypt is often symbolised by the Nile, on which the fertility and whole life of the country depends ; Egyptian gods were worshipped under the forms of animals.

l. 212. *Isis :* sister and wife of Osiris.

*Orus :* son of Osiris.

*Anubis :* son of Osiris, worshipped under the form of a dog or jackal ; messenger of the gods, and the god of embalming. These gods and goddesses formed a sort of holy family.

l. 213. Osiris became the chief of Egyptian gods. The legend was that Osiris was a king of Egypt who set forth to subdue the world by the arts of peace ; on his return his brother Set (whom the Greeks called Typhon) killed him by shutting him in a chest, which was then thrown into the Nile. Isis wandered in search of her husband and at last found the chest ; but Set stole the body, cut it up and scattered the pieces about the earth. Isis recovered the pieces of the body, which with the aid of Anubis were put together and embalmed ; then Isis restored life to the body, and Osiris thereafter

reigned as king and judge over the dead. As Osiris
became the supreme god of the Egyptians, so the
attributes and powers of other gods were ascribed to
him ; we may say in brief that he was the god of light
(identified with the sun), of fertility and life (identified
with the Nile), and of resurrection, the pledge of personal immortality.

l. 214. The chief shrine of Osiris was at Memphis,
where the sacred bull Apis was worshipped as the god
incarnate ; there was an enclosure in which the sacred
bull could exercise himself and be seen by those who
came to worship or to consult him as an oracle.

l. 215. *Unshower'd grass :* Egypt is almost rainless and
owes its immense fertility to the annual inundation of
the Nile. One of the prayers to Osiris reads : " The
Nile appeareth at thy utterance . . . making all cultivated things green " (Budge, " Osiris and the Egyptian
Resurrection ").

l. 217. *Sacred chest :* the chest (worshipped as the chief
shrine) in which the sacred bull was buried, representing
the chest in which the recovered body of Osiris had
been laid.

ll. 219–220. The mystery of the death and resurrection
of Osiris was enacted daily and at the annual festival.
At the annual festival, after days of mourning for the
dead god, the people made a procession to the river,
attended by hymns chanted to the sound of flutes and
timbrels ; the priests in their holy robes bore the sacred
chest, having within it a little gold ark into which they
poured fresh water, and thereupon all the people gave
a great shout that Osiris was found (Plutarch, " Isis
and Osiris ").

*Timbrel'd anthems dark :* mysterious hymns chanted
to the accompaniment of timbrels.

*Sable-stoled :* black-robed.

ll. 221–222. Isaiah xix. : " Behold, the Lord rideth
upon a swift cloud, and shall come into Egypt ; and
the idols of Egypt shall be moved at his presence . . .
and it shall be afraid and fear because of the shaking
of the hand of the Lord of hosts. . . . And the land
of Judah shall be a terror unto Egypt." There was
an early Christian tradition that this prophecy was
fulfilled when Joseph and Mary fled with the infant
Jesus into Egypt : the child was taken into the temple

at Hermopolis and the idols fell down like Dagon before the ark.

l. 223. An allusion to Osiris as a god of light ; one of the symbols of Osiris was a sceptre with an eye in the head, indicating that the god surveys and rules the universe as does the sun. *Dusky eyn* may mean " darkened eyes," *dusky* being a proleptic adjective anticipating the effect of the verb " blinded " ; or it may be taken more picturesquely to mean " dark eyes " in the sense of " dark complexion." " Egyptian " and " Gipsy " (Gipsies were so called because this dark-skinned race were supposed to have come from Egypt) were synonyms for " dark colouring," then a matter of reproach as " black blood " is to-day. Plutarch says that Osiris was black-skinned, that the sacred bull was black in colour, and that Egypt is called by the same name as the black part of the eye. Milton uses " dusk ' for " dark-skinned " in " Paradise Regained," iv. 76, " Dusk faces with white silken turbants wreath'd," a quotation that brings out the picturesque effect he might intend in our present line.

l. 226. Typhon (Set) was worshipped under the form of the crocodile.

ll. 227–228. As Hercules in his cradle strangled the serpents.

St. XXVI. This simile neatly concludes the story of the triumph of Christ (although the description of the rising sun in the manner of the " metaphysical conceit " consorts ill with the Miltonic style) ; for the evil spirits, ghosts, and fairies of Christendom were the descendants of the gods and demons and nymphs of the pagan world. The simile depends on the belief that evil spirits vanish at dawn.

ll. 232–236. Cp. " A Midsummer-Night's Dream," III. ii. 379–382.

*Fetter'd ghost :* ghosts were souls of the dead whom earthly interests kept " fettered " to the scenes of their human existence (cp. " Comus," ll. 470–475).

P. 23, l. 236. *Moon-lov'd maze :* labyrinths of the woods loved by the huntress Diana, who in association with Hecate was goddess of the fairies. See note to " Comus," l. 135.

l. 240. *Youngest-teemed star :* latest born star, " teem " being used in sense of " give birth to " (cp. " Comus," l. 175).

l. 242. St. Matt. ii. 9 : " The Star which they saw in the East went before them, till it came and stood over where the young child was."

l. 244. *Bright-harness'd* : clad in bright armour.
*Serviceable* : ready to serve.

*The Passion* (1630).

The opening lines indicate that this poem was designed as a sequel to the " Nativity Ode," and was no doubt begun at the following Easter.

P. 24, l. 1. *Ethereal mirth* : heavenly rejoicing.

l. 4. Referring to " Nativity Ode," l. 27 : " And join thy voice unto the angel quire." *Divide* : share ; perhaps the word was suggested by its musical sense of playing or singing a variation on or accompaniment to a theme or plainsong.

l. 6. *I.e.* " like the shortened light of the winter solstice."

l. 7. *Out-living* : lasting inordinately (cp. *livelong*, " On Shakespear," l. 8).

l. 10. *Seize* : used of a bird of prey fastening its claws on its victim.

ll. 13–14. An allusion to the labours of the Greek hero Hercules. Cp. Hebrews ii. 10 : " For it became him . . . to make the captain of their salvation perfect through suffering." *Plight* : undertaking, of a risk or responsibility.

ll. 15–17. Milton thinks of Christ as described by St. Paul in Hebrews : " the high priest of our profession," " who is set on the right hand of the throne of Majesty in heaven," but who laid aside his divinity " to be made like unto his brethren, that he might be a merciful and faithful high priest." Anointing with oil is a ceremony of consecration, especially of a king or high priest.

l. 18. *Front* : forehead.

l. 19. *Mask* and *disguise* were both terms for masquerades and dramatic entertainments at which such masks and disguises were worn (see Introduction to " Arcades and Comus ").

l. 20. *Abide* : undergo.

P. 25, l. 22. *Latest* : Ed. 1, " latter."

l. 23. *Phoebus* : Apollo, god of poetry, and hence " muse or poetic impulse."

l. 26. *Cremona's trump* : the " Christiad," an epic on the

life of Christ by Vida of Cremona. *Trump* : trumpet, a symbol of heroic poetry.

l. 28. *Still* : gentle, quiet. See " Il Penseroso," l. 127.

l. 30. *Pole* : sky. See " At a Vacation Exercise," l. 34.

ll. 34–35. Elegies were sometimes printed in white letters on black paper : in other words the " conceit " in these lines was so common as to have found practical form.

St. VI. Ezekiel's vision of God by the river Chebar was in the form of a fiery whirlwind composed of winged creatures, " and their appearance and their work was as it were a wheel in the middle of a wheel " (Ezekiel i. 16) ; " and the spirit lifted me up between the earth and the heaven, and brought me in the visions of God to Jerusalem " (vii. 3).

l. 39. *Salem* : Jerusalem, home of sacred poetry.

l. 43. The Holy Sepulchre.

l. 44. *Store* : treasure (obsolete sense).

l. 46. *Quarry* : rock.

l. 47. *Plaining* : complaining.

*As before, i.e.* in the " Nativity Ode."

P. 26, ll. 48–49. The conceit is that the poet's tears will score his verses in the stone.

l. 51. Jeremiah ix. 10 : " For the mountains will I take up a weeping."

l. 56. The conceit is from the story of Ixion, who embraced a cloud, formed by Jupiter to the shape of Juno, and engendered the centaurs.

The poem has degenerated into conceits more and more unsuited to the subject ; the inspiration that sustained the poet in his previous ode has only too evidently failed him now, and one wonders not that he was unable to finish but that he was willing to print.

*Upon the Circumcision* (?1632–1633).

This poem follows " At a Solemn Music " and " On Time " in the Trinity MS., and the three pieces are grouped together after " The Passion " in Milton's editions ; all three are short odes with irregular rhyme and length of line, a metrical form Milton was to handle once again with such mastery in " Lycidas." They were probably written about the beginning of the Horton period.

P. 27, l. 1. As in " The Passion," Milton refers back to the " Nativity Ode." Angels are called *flaming* because of their " ethereal mould," ether being according to ancient and mediaeval physics a purer or " essential " form of fire, the material of which the heavens and stars and all heavenly beings are composed.

l. 2. *Erst :* formerly.

l. 6. *Sad share with us to bear :* *i.e.* in order to join in our sorrow. " Bear," as always in Milton, is pronounced to rhyme with " ear " and " tear " ; otherwise there would be an ugly internal rhyme with " share."

l. 7. *Fiery essence :* ethereal nature (see note, l. 1), excluding water as a contrary.

ll. 8–9. *I.e.* use our tears as the sun draws vapour from the sea : a typical metaphysical conceit.

l. 10. *Heraldry :* ceremonial proclamation.

    *Whilere :* a while ago.

ll. 12 *seq.* Circumcision was regarded as a token of the Old Covenant between God and Israel under the Mosaic Law, and by Christians as a token of man's state of sin under that law. " The Mosaic Law was a written code consisting of many precepts . . . with a promise of life to such as should keep them and a curse on such as should be disobedient " (Milton's " Christian Doctrine," ch. 26). According to Christian doctrine this Law of the Covenant was a consequence of the Fall, whereby all men continued to be subject to the just wrath of God ; obedience to the law therefore could not " justify " man or reconcile him to God. But Christ " fulfilled the law " by taking human form and suffering all the consequences of man's sin ; he satisfied the irrevocable decrees or justice of God by paying the full penalty in perfect love and obedience. Under the New Covenant of the Gospel, therefore, man was freed from the bondage of the Law and admitted to grace : " Christian liberty is enfranchisement through Christ from the bondage of sin and from the rule of man and law . . . that we may serve God in love " (" Christian Doctrine ").

l. 14. *Seize :* attack.

l. 15. *Exceeding love :* " For God so loved the world, that he gave his only begotten Son, that whosoever believeth in him should not perish, but have everlasting life " (St. John iii. 16).

l. 17. *Doom :* judgment.

    *Remediless :* without remedy (qualifying *we*).

l. 18. *Death :* " Wherefore, as by one man sin entered

into the world, and death by sin . . . so by the righteousness of one the free gift came upon all men unto justification of life " (Romans v.). In the " Christian Doctrine," ch. 12, Milton explains that all evils whatever under which this sinful world suffers are summed up in Scripture under the name of death.

l. 21. *Cov'nant :* the Old Law. Christians are still bound by the law as a code of moral and religious duties ; in the " Christian Doctrine " Milton explains that the difference under the Gospel is that its injunctions are now written by the Spirit in the hearts of believers and we obey as free sons of God instead of as slaves under a penal code.

*Still :* continually.

l. 24. *Excess :* transgression.

*On Time* (? 1632–1633).

The opening lines are explained by the sub-title in the Trinity manuscript : " to be set on a Clock-case." The poem leads up through the idea of Time, which both produces and destroys all mortal things, to the Christian hope of eternity and immortality, " when this corruption must put on incorruption, and this mortal must put on immortality."

P. 28, l. 3. *Plummet :* leaden weight of the pendulum.

l. 4. " Womb " is the grammatical object of " devours " : Time devours the Hours which themselves devour the offspring of Time, *i.e.* temporal things.

l. 12. *Individual :* inseparable.

l. 18. *Happy-making sight :* is the plain English of *beatific vision*, the vision of God granted to the saints after death.

l. 20. *Quit :* discarded.

l. 21. *Attir'd :* crowned. " Attire " was especially used of head-dress.

l. 22. *Chance :* or Fortune, was worshipped in the ancient world as the goddess of Nature and Fate, the ruler of this world of change.

*At a Solemn Music* (*circ.* 1632).

For this poem read the quotation from Milton's Second Prolusion in the note on the music of the spheres in the Appendix.

P. 29, l. 1. *Sirens :* cp. " Arcades," l. 63.           144

*Pledges :* offspring (Latin, *pignora*).

l. 4. An allusion to the legend of Orpheus (see " L'Allegro," ll. 145–150, note).

l. 5. *Phantasy :* imagination.

l. 6. *Concent :* harmony.

l. 7. *Sapphire-colour'd throne :* " And above the firmament that was over their heads was the likeness of a throne, as the appearance of a sapphire stone " (Ezekiel i. 26).

l. 9. *Jubilee :* loud rejoicing.

l. 10. Angels were classified into three hierarchies, each subdivided into three orders or choirs ; the first hierarchy consisted of Seraphim, Cherubim, and Thrones, who live in the immediate presence of God. Seraphim was said to mean in Hebrew " burning," and to express the nature of these angels (cp. " Il Penseroso," ll. 52–54, note).

ll. 14–16. Revelation vii. and xiv. : " And, lo, a great multitude . . . stood before the throne, and before the Lamb, clothed with white robes, and palms in their hands. . . . And they sung as it were a new song before the throne . . . and no man could learn that song but the hundred and forty and four thousand, which were redeemed from the earth. These are they which were not defiled with women. . . . And in their mouth was found no guile : for they are without fault before the throne of God." This was a favourite passage with Milton : " Nor did I slumber over that place expressing such high rewards of ever accompanying the Lamb, with those celestial songs to others inapprehensible but not to those who were not defiled with women " (" Apology for Smectymnuus," following the passage on the Platonic conception of chastity and true love).

l. 18. *Noise :* music (cp. " Nativity Ode," l. 96).

l. 20. *Jar* and *chime* were musical terms for " discord " and " concord."

l. 23. *Diapason :* the concord of the octave made by the eight notes of the spheres (see " Arcades," ll. 63–73, note).

l. 27. *Consort :* choir (" Nativity Ode," l. 132, note).

*On Shakespear* (1630).

These lines first appeared in the Second Folio of Shakespeare (1632) and so were the first of Milton's verses to be published. It has been plausibly argued that in 1630, the date of composition given by Milton, the editors of the Second Folio may have intended to reproduce as frontispiece the monument in Stratford church instead of the Droeshout portrait ; and that Milton's lines were written to be set over against this frontispiece.

P. 30, l. 4.    *Star-ypointing*.    For the prefix *y* see " Nativity Ode," l. 155, note ; the use of this poetical archaism with the present participle is unusual but effective.

l. 5.    *Son of memory :*  therefore brother of the nine muses, who were daughters of Mnemosyne (Memory) and Zeus.

l. 8.    *Livelong :*  lasting (which is actually the 1632 reading) ; the word was originally two words, "lief" (dear) and "long" (cp. German "die liebe lange Nacht ").

ll. 9–10.    The ease and fluency of Shakespeare's composition was well known and was attested by his fellow players, Heminge and Condell, in their preface to the First Folio : "His mind and hand went together : And what he thought he uttered with that easiness that we have scarce received from him a blot in his papers." On which Ben Jonson, one of "slow-endeavouring art," retorted, "Would he had blotted out a thousand ! . . . he flowed with that facility that sometimes it was necessary he should be stopped." There can be little doubt that Milton has Jonson in mind as Shakespeare's antitype, for in "L'Allegro," ll. 131–134, he draws a similar distinction between Jonson's "learned" plays and the "native wood notes wild" of Shakespeare.  *Whilst :*  when (see "Nativity Ode," l. 30, note).  *Numbers :*  measured or metrical writing, verses.  *Heart :*  1632 ed. reads "part," *i.e.* each *faculty*.

l. 11.    *Unvalued :*  invaluable.

ll. 12–14.    *Delphic :*  inspired by Apollo, as were the oracles of Delphi (see "Nativity Ode," St. XIX, notes) ; Apollo was the god of both prophecy and poetry. Milton associates the effect of Shakespeare on our imaginations with the ecstasy of the Delphic prophetess under the influence of the god.  The lines are further illustrated by the phrase "forget thyself to marble " in "Il Penseroso," l. 42, where he is referring to the ecstasy so often described by Socrates in Plato's dialogues, those moments of pure contemplation in which the mind escapes from and forgets the body.

*Fancy :*  imagination.  Our modern distinction be-

tween " fancy," as the faculty for inventing illustrative
or decorative imagery, and " imagination," as the
faculty for creating an ideal and self-consistent world,
is due to Coleridge.

## On the University Carrier (1631).

Thomas Hobson was a " character " in Cambridge, and
his death was the occasion of many commemorative
verses. He had been a carrier between Cambridge
and the Bull Inn, Bishopsgate Street, London, for more
than sixty years. Steele (" Spectator," 509) says that
he kept the first livery stable in England, hiring horses
to the undergraduates ; when a client came for a
horse he was obliged to take the one nearest the door,
whence arose the phrase " Hobson's choice." In the
spring of 1630 his weekly journeys to London were
suspended on account of the plague ; he escaped the
plague but died on New Year's Day, 1631, in his eighty-
seventh year. He left a fortune sufficient to provide
not only for a large family but also for public works in
Cambridge. Milton's two poems admirably convey
the laughing admiration and familiar respect with
which such a character would be universally regarded
and treated in Cambridge.

P. 31, l. 1. *Girt :* girth.
l. 5. *Shifter :* artful dodger.
l. 14. *Chamberlin :* attendant in charge of the bed-
chambers.

## Another on the Same (1631).

P. 32, l. 5. *Sphere-metal :* the ethereal substance of the
heavenly spheres, ever-moving and indestructible.
l. 7. Alluding to the Aristotelian doctrine that time is
the measure of motion.
l. 9. As in the mechanism of a pendulum clock :
Hobson's wheel and weight were his van and its
load.
l. 10. *Principles :* motive forces, whether of a machine or
person.
*Straight :* straightway.
l. 12. *Breathing :* rest (as in " breathing-time ").
l. 14. The pun is on the University " vacations " and
" terms," " vacation " also meaning " any period of
cessation from work " and " term " also meaning
" end."

l. 18. There is obviously a pun on the phrase " fetch and carry," and it looks as if *fetch'd* were used in a secondary sense of " outwitted, bettered " ; " fetches " was used for " tricks, stratagems," and " fetch in or off " for " take in or get the better of."

l. 19. *Cross Doctors :* there is probably a local or contemporary allusion here which has never been explained.

l. 20. *Put down :* suppressed. Throughout the seventeenth century there was considerable opposition, on conservative or self-interested grounds, to the increase in hackney coaches and stage waggons, and measures were periodically taken to limit or reduce their numbers.

*Bearers :* pun on the general sense " carriers " and the special sense " coffin-bearers."

l. 22. *Heaviness :* melancholy.

ll. 29–31. Every month Hobson made a regular number of journeys at regular times between Cambridge and London, so that the course of his life, like the tides, was ruled by the moon.

*Date :* term or period of life.

*Reciprocal :* (literally) back and forth.

*Mutual :* correspondent.

P. 33, l. 32. *Wain :* waggon, with pun on " wane."

l. 33. The carrier of these days was also " postman."

l. 34. *Superscription :* both an " inscription on a tomb " and an " address on a letter."

*An Epitaph on the Marchioness of Winchester* (1631).

The subject of this poem was Jane Savage, daughter of Viscount Savage and wife of the Marquis of Winchester, and through her mother heir of the Earl of Rivers. She died in childbirth on April 15, 1631, at the age of twenty-three. Her death was the occasion of poems by Ben Jonson, Davenant, and others.

P. 34, l. 13. *Nature* governs the events of this world, but *Fate* is a superior overruling power.

l. 17. *Virgin quire :* bride's maids.

*Request :* invoke.

l. 18. Hymen, with his lighted torch.

l. 22. *Cypress bud :* emblematic of a funeral.

l. 23. *Early :* timely.

*Matrons :* was a term used specifically of women who helped in childbirth.

l. 24. *Greet her of :* congratulate her on.

P. 35, l. 26. *Lucina :* Roman goddess of childbirth.

l. 28.   The three Fates were Clotho, who spun the thread of life, Lachesis, who determined its length, and Atropos, who cut it.

ll. 31–32.   The child was stillborn.

l. 35.   *Slip :* sprig.

l. 50.   *Seize :* possess (see " The Passion," l. 10, note).

l. 55.   *Tears :* was the name given to mourning verses pinned to the coffin or bier (cp. " Lycidas," l. 103).

l. 56.   *Helicon :* mountain in Boeotia, the home of the Muses.

l. 59.   *Came :* river Cam at Cambridge.

l. 62.   Rachel, Jacob's wife (Genesis xxix. *seq.*).

## *L'Allegro* and *Il Penseroso* (? 1631–1632).

The exact date of these poems is uncertain ; but critics are agreed that they were written at Horton, whether during a University vacation or after Milton had finally settled there. In either case we may accept them as a psychological picture of his life at Horton, presented under two alternating moods which he calls Melancholy and Mirth. Dr. Johnson observes : " I know not whether the characters are kept sufficiently apart. No mirth can, indeed, be found in his melancholy ; but I am afraid that I always meet some melancholy in his mirth." But L'Allegro and Il Penseroso are not two different characters ; nor are they, as others have supposed, two different and incompatible attitudes towards life. Both are recognisably Milton himself ; and certainly Milton was no Dr. Jekyll and Mr. Hyde, that we should expect either division or contradiction in his personality. The key to the poems is in the meaning of the term " melancholy." Milton uses it in the sense, now obsolete, of the serious, pensive mood ; Il Penseroso is the solitary, meditative man. Such a mood, indulged to excess, gives rise of course to melancholy in the special sense that survives today, the sense which Johnson gives it and in which he himself was a melancholy man ; Milton only presents melancholy under this aspect at the beginning of " L'Allegro," when bidding it depart. But the mood invoked and portrayed in " Il Penseroso " is the contemplative mood in which the poet abstracts himself into the world of thought and imagination ; it is the mood consequently not only of study and meditation but of poetic composition. The

# NOTES

word is used exactly in this sense by the Attendant Spirit in " Comus," when he appears in the guise of the shepherd Thyrsis and tells, in conventional, pastoral manner, how that evening

> " I . . . began,
>    Wrapt in a pleasing fit of melancholy,
>    To meditate my rural minstrelsy."

It may be noted how the descriptions of Nature in " Il Penseroso " suggest this mood of poetic reverie and at certain points reveal the poet's imagination, as it were, in the very act of creation. " L'Allegro " depicts the corresponding mood, when the mind wearies of its own world of brooding thought and looks for entertainment from without, in the scenes and social activities of country and town. But L'Allegro too is the scholar and poet ; he too finds much of his entertainment in the imaginative world of art, and the world he sees about him is full of literary romance and fiction. That is why the moods of the two poems, although subtly distinguished throughout, present no sharp contrast to each other.

## L'Allegro

P. 37.  *L'Allegro :*  the Cheerful Man.
 l. 2.  *Cerberus :*  was the three-headed dog who guarded the entrance to the lower world.
 l. 3.  *Stygian :*  adjectival form of Styx, one of the four rivers of Hades and so a synonym for the world of the dead.
 l. 5.  *Uncouth :*  out-of-the-way, desolate.
 l. 8.  *Low-brow'd :*  frowning.
 l. 10.  *Cimmerian.*  The Cimmerians were a mythical people dwelling " beyond the Ocean Stream " in a land of perpetual darkness.
 l. 11.  *Free :*  of gentle birth and breeding. " Fair and free " was a stock phrase of compliment for women.
 l. 12.  *Yclep'd :*  named. The three Graces were Euphrosyne (Mirth), Aglaia (Festive Beauty), and Thalia (Youthful Bloom and Vigour).
 l. 18.  *Breathes :*  exhales (Latin, *spirat*).
 l. 20.  *A-maying :*  celebrating May-day.
 l. 24.  *Buxom* originally meant " pliant," and so " gracious, lively, jolly."
    *Debonair :*  gracious, affable.
 l. 27.  *Quips :*  " We great girders call it [quip] a short

127

SHORTER POEMS OF JOHN MILTON

saying of a sharp wit, with a bitter sense in a sweet
word " (Lyly, " Alexander and Campaspe," III. II).
*Cranks :* fanciful and humorous turns of speech.
*Wanton Wiles :* sportive tricks.

l. 28. *Becks :* bows.

l. 29. *Hebe :* cupbearer of the gods, personifying youth.

P. 38, l. 30. *Sleek :* smooth and soft, used especially of
well-conditioned fur or skin.

l. 33. *Trip it :* dance.

l. 36. The hills have always been associated with liberty.

l. 39. *Her :* i.e. Liberty.

l. 40. *Unreproved :* unreprovable, innocent.

ll. 45–48. The syntax and punctuation of the original
editions indicate that it is the poet who comes to the
window. There are three distinct statements dependent
on " Mirth admit me of thy crew," which are separated
by semicolons and are each introduced by an infinitive :
" To live with her . . .," " To hear the lark . . .,"
" Then to come. . . ." At l. 41 the poet begins to
enumerate the successive pleasures of his day, which
provide the subject matter of the rest of the poem :
first he is awakened by the lark, then he comes to his
window, listens to the sounds of the rousing world,
walks abroad, and so on. It would have been un-
necessary to labour this point had not many commentators supposed Mirth or the lark to be the subject
of " Then to come" : what should have decided the
point long ago is that only one reading makes good
poetic sense.

*In spite of :* in scorn or defiance of.

*Bid good-morrow :* The phrase seems to be used
absolutely, either as a salutation to the day or simply
to express the cheerful holiday mood of general good-
will.

*Eglantine :* is the same as sweet-briar, but " twisted "
suggests that Milton perhaps meant the honeysuckle.

ll. 49–52. The punctuation of the original editions,
which I have retained, indicates that these lines are
adverbial clauses subordinate to " Oft list'ning,"
etc.

l. 55. *Hoar :* grey with age (a traditional epithet ; cp.
" Arcades," l. 98).

l. 57. *Not unseen :* Contrast " Il Penseroso," l. 65, " I
walk unseen " ; L'Allegro is sociable, Il Penseroso
solitary.

128

l. 60. *State :* The sense of the word as used here is retained in the phrase " to ride or lie in state," *i.e.* with all the pomp and ceremony belonging to high rank.

l. 62. *Liveries :* uniforms of servants and retainers.

*Dight :* being arrayed. Milton has a similar description of the sunrise in his First Prolusion : " And the clouds, in robes of various colours, seem to attend the god in ceremonial train and long procession."

P. 39, ll. 67–68. This is the ideal shepherd of pastoral poetry.

l. 70. *Lantskip :* landscape (Milton's invariable spelling).

l. 71. *Russet :* was a homespun of grey or neutral colour, and the word came to be used for these shades.

*Lawns :* grasslands (see " Nativity Ode," l. 85, note).

*Fallows :* ploughlands left uncropped.

l. 75. *Pied :* parti-coloured (a stock epithet for daisies).

l. 79. *Lies :* lodges, dwells (cp. " the court lay at Windsor ").

l. 83. *Corydon and Thyrsis :* together with *Phyllis* (l. 86) and *Thestylis* (l. 88), are stock names in pastoral poetry.

*Met :* having met.

l. 85. *Messes :* dishes.

l. 87. *Bower :* has here its earlier meaning " cottage," rather than " chamber " as in " Comus," l. 45.

l. 89. *Lead :* direct.

l. 91. *Secure :* free from care (Latin, *securus*).

l. 94. *Rebeck :* early fiddle.

l. 99. *Livelong :* see " On Shakespear," l. 8, note.

l. 102. *Mab :* see " Romeo and Juliet," I. iv. 54–95.

*Junkets :* any delicacies made from milk (left for the fairy to eat).

l. 103. *She :* *i.e.* one of the company who tells the tale.

*Pinch'd and pulled :* as punishment for laziness and sluttishness. Falstaff had reason to know that fairies show their displeasure in this way (" Merry Wives of Windsor," V. v.).

P. 40, l. 104. This is the 1673 reading ; the 1645 ed. gives " And he by Friar's Lanthorn led," thus introducing a second speaker. The correction was evidently made in the interest of the syntax, to smooth the transition to the next line.

The *Friar's Lanthorn* was the will-o'-the-wisp, supposed to be a deluding spirit who, like Shakespeare's Puck, misleads " night wanderers, laughing at their harms."

l. 105. *Tells* : *i.e.* " she tells."

*Drudging goblin* : Robin Goodfellow or Hobgoblin, Shakespeare's Puck ; he was as malicious as the other fairies but would perform prodigies of work during the night for those who treated him well. " A bigger kind there is of them (fairies) called with us hobgoblins, or Robin Goodfellows, that would in those superstitious times grind corn for a mess of milk, cut wood, or do any manner of drudging work " (Burton, " Anatomy of Melancholy," I. II. 1, 2).

l. 108. *Shadowy* : insubstantial, unreal.

l. 110. *Lubber* : big, clumsy lout, stupid drudge ; an exact rendering of Shakespeare's title for Puck, " thou lob of spirits."

l. 111. *Chimney's* : ingle-nook's.

l. 114. *Matin* : prayer recited at daybreak. The services of the Church, as other set times, were announced by bell-ringing. The first cock-crow was the signal for the departure of spirits and ghosts.

ll. 118–128. See Bacon's " Of Masques and Triumphs."

l. 120. *Weeds* : garments.

*Triumphs* : public festivities, in the form especially of tournaments and jousts.

l. 121. *Store* : plenty, crowd (perhaps with the suggestion of " precious " : cp. " The Passion," l. 44, note).

l. 122. *Rain influence* : a metaphor from astrology (cp. " Nativity Ode," l. 71).

l. 123. *Of wit or arms* : Tournaments, a survival of chivalry, might still to some extent be a display of skill in arms and horsemanship but they had become more and more mimetic, an affair of pageantry, of dramatic shows of the same character as the Court masques, and an occasion for courtly compliments in speech and poem.

ll. 125–126. This couplet suggests one of the many masques for a wedding, in which Hymen always appeared in a saffron robe and holding his torch.

l. 127. *Pomp* : festival procession or pageantry.

*Revelry* : theatrical entertainments such as it was the business of the Master of the Revels to arrange at Court.

l. 128. *Antique pageantry* : " Pageants " were the separate scenes or tableaux presented on movable stages in the religious and allegorical plays of mediaeval times ; they were still used in public entertainments for royalty and

# NOTES

distinguished persons, and they survive to-day in the
Lord Mayor's Show.

l. 130. *Haunted:* cp. "Nativity Ode," l. 184.

l. 131. *Well-trod:* implies the skill of the actor.

l. 132. *Sock:* light shoe (*soccus*) worn by comic actors in
the ancient theatre, which came to stand for comedy
itself. *Learned* is the most appropriate single epithet
for Ben Jonson's deliberate, laborious, and often
pedantic work.

l. 133. *Fancy's:* Imagination's (see "On Shakespear,"
ll. 12–14, note).

l. 134. *Native:* natural, untutored. In his epitaph
"On Shakespear" Milton insists on this same contrast
between laboured and spontaneous verse.

l. 136. *Lydian airs:* sweet, plaintive music, characterised
by the Greeks as soft and effeminate ; the other two
modes of Greek music were the Phrygian (warlike) and
Dorian (simple and solemn).

l. 139. *Bout:* bend, involution. The word comes from
"bow" and is used of the coils of ropes and chains.
Spenser uses it of the folds of a serpent.

P. 41, l. 141. *Cunning:* skill.

ll. 145–150. Orpheus was the mythical poet whose song
had power even over wild beasts and inanimate things.
When his wife Eurydice died he followed her into the
underworld and his music prevailed on Persephone,
Pluto's queen, to allow his wife to return with him,
only provided that he should forbear to look back as
he led her up to the world of light ; when Orpheus
turned to see if she was following, Eurydice was caught
back to Hades.

l. 152. In the original editions "*thee*" is followed by a
comma, which was the usual method of emphasising a
word as we do by italics.

### Il Penseroso

P. 42. *Il Penseroso:* the Thoughtful Man.

l. 3. *Bested:* help, avail (cp. "stand in good stead").

l. 4. *Fixed:* settled, steady.
*Toys:* trifles.

l. 6. *Fond:* foolish, doting.

l. 10. *Pensioners:* attendants, retainers.
*Morpheus:* god of sleep.

l. 14. *Hit:* suit, agree with.

l. 17. At this time dark colouring in a woman was
disparaged.

l. 18. The Ethiopian prince Memnon, son of Tithonus
and Eos (Dawn), was called by Ulysses the handsomest
of men ; mediaeval writers gave him a sister Hemera
(Day), who was equally beautiful.

ll. 19–21. Cassiopeia, wife of the Ethiopian king Cepheus,
boasted that she was fairer than the Nereids (sea
nymphs), who then prevailed on Neptune to punish
her profanity by sending a flood and a sea monster
against the country ; her daughter Andromeda was
about to be sacrificed to the monster in expiation when
she was rescued by Perseus.

*Starr'd :* Cassiopeia was transformed into the constellation of that name.

l. 23. *Vesta :* was the Roman goddess of the hearth (see
" Nativity Ode," l. 190, note), worshipped under the
symbol of the eternal fire which it was the duty of the
vestal virgins to keep alight ; she corresponded to the
Greek Hestia, daughter of Cronus (Roman Saturn).
Vesta was the type of chastity.

l. 24. *Solitary Saturn :* The epithet indicates the astrological view of Saturn as representing " melancholy."
Being farthest from the earth, the planet Saturn is
" solitary and appears to move most deliberately " ;
those born under its influence were therefore of a
corresponding " melancholic " temperament—sluggish,
unsociable, meditative, cold, and gloomy. (This was
the original meaning of " saturnine.")

ll. 25–30. Saturn ruled from Mt. Ida in Crete until he
was overthrown by his son Jupiter ; his reign was the
Golden Age (" Nativity Ode," l. 135, note).

P. 43, l. 33. *Grain :* dye, colour.

l. 35. *Stole :* either a long robe or an ecclesiastical vest-
ment consisting of a strip of linen or silk hanging from
the back of the neck over the shoulders and down to the
knees ; here it may be used in the latter sense to mean
" shawl."

*Cypress lawn :* a black transparent material used for
mourning.

l. 41. *Still :* is here an adjective.

l. 42. Cp. " On Shakespear," l. 13.

l. 43. *Sad :* serious.

*Leaden :* the saturnian or melancholy colour. The
theory of astrology was that, the universe being one,

the heavenly bodies must exercise a constant influence on earthly conditions ; astrology was accordingly enlarged until it was brought into relation with practically all the known sciences. Colours, metals, stones, plants, and animal and human life in all its aspects were assigned to their respective planets and stars. Thus Saturn was associated with the colour grey, the metal lead, and so on, as well as with the melancholy temperament.

l. 44. *Fast :* fixedly.

ll. 46–48. In his Latin " Elegy VI " Milton observes that he who would write on high and serious themes must " live sparingly and let herbs furnish his innocent diet " (cp. " Lycidas," ll. 15–16, note).

ll. 52–54. The imagery of these lines is from Ezekiel (see particularly ch. x. cp. " The Passion," st. vi.). But the main idea is taken from mediaeval angelology (" At a Solemn Music," l. 10, note) ; Cherubim, signifying " fulness of knowledge," were those angels who lived in the contemplation of God, of the divine beauty and wisdom.

l. 55. *Hist :* is a verb in the imperative mood, answering to " bring " (l. 51) (cp. " Nativity Ode," l. 64, note).

l. 56. *Philomel :* the nightingale.

*Deign :* vouchsafe.

l. 59. *Cynthia :* Diana, the moon.

*Yoke :* a pair of draught animals. In classical mythology it is Ceres, goddess of Earth, whose chariot is drawn by dragons ; but Ceres became associated in worship with her daughter Proserpina, goddess of the Underworld, and Proserpina was in turn joined with Diana and Hecate as the triple goddess of the Moon. Although ancient writers never speak of the Moon's car being drawn by dragons, Ovid so describes the magical aerial car of Medea, devotee of Hecate (" Metamorphoses," vii.) ; and it was probably in connection with Hecate, goddess of witchcraft and enchantments, that dragons became associated in post-classical authors with night and the moon. In his Latin elegy on the Bishop of Ely, Milton writes, " I saw the triform goddess controlling her dragons with reins of gold " (cp. " Comus," l. 135, note).

l. 60. *Accustom'd oak :* In " Epitaphium Damonis " Milton says that he did not feel the loss of his friend until he returned home and sat beneath " the accustomed elm " (*assueta seditque sub ulmo*).

l. 63. *Chauntress* : songstress.

P. 44, l. 68. *Highest noon* : the moon's meridian.

l. 73. *Plat* : plot.

l. 74. *Curfew* : The curfew bell was rung in the Middle Ages to announce the time for extinguishing all fires ; the custom continued in many places (and still continues in a few) after the regulation was no longer enforced.

l. 75. *Shore* : land bordering on water, whether sea or lake or river ; or the shallow water of such an area (cp. " Lycidas," l. 154, note).

l. 77. *Air* : weather.

l. 83. *Bellman* : night-watchman, who on his rounds cried the hours and the state of the weather, commonly prefacing his call with a benediction.

*Charm* : verse or formula having magic or exorcising power.

ll. 87–96. This passage reflects Renaissance platonism, a dominating influence in the thought and literature of the age. There had been a great revival of platonism in the sixteenth century, in reaction to mediaeval aristotelianism ; but it was an uncritical platonism, drawn from many sources and assuming many forms. It derived partly from the renewed study of Plato's own works ; partly from the mystical development of Plato's teaching by the neoplatonists during the first centuries of our era, which had considerably influenced Christian theology and Western thought ; and partly from a debased form of this neoplatonism which had survived in the practice of astrology, alchemy, and magic, and which received the general name of the hermetic philosophy. The fundamental doctrine of this Renaissance platonism is that the universe is a single organism animated by a world soul or divine intelligence. The world soul has manifested itself in the unchanging heavens ; and the stars, moving ever in accordance with eternal law, are the gods who govern and direct the created universe. That is why science consists in a knowledge of the stars. But ranked in orders under the stars are subordinate divinities or daemons, both beneficent and malignant, who inhabit and have immediate control of all things beneath the sphere of the moon. Daemons live and work in the four elements of our sublunary world (in fire, air, water, and earth), and are classified accordingly ; they correspond to what to-day we should call natural as distinct from super-natural forces, producing all the phenomena of mortal life, all the varied activity of growth and change in the world of Nature. It is the aim of magic to learn to control these spirits in order to control the materials and forces they represent, just as it is the aim of astrology to learn to interpret the stars. Each person has his individual daemon or genius who controls the mortal part of his nature and his earthly destiny ; but the soul is immortal and akin to the stars. In the " Timaeus " Plato represents in a myth how God, having created the universe, made human souls of the same divine substance as the soul of the universe ; he made " as many souls as there are stars, assigning to each soul a star ; and causing each soul to go up into her star as into a chariot, he showed her the true nature and laws of the universe. . . . And those souls that lived well for the time appointed them on earth should return to their natal stars and dwell there, and have a life hence-forth blessed and proper to their nature." This passage explains Milton's phrase " unsphere the spirit of Plato."

l. 87. The constellation of the Great Bear never sets. Note that " Bear " rhymes with " sphere."

l. 88. *Thrice great Hermes :* The neoplatonists of Alex-andria identified the Egyptian god Thoth, inventor of all arts and sciences, with the Greek Hermes, giving him the title of Hermes Trismegistus or Thrice Great ; he was regarded as the author and patron deity of alchemy, magic, and all occult doctrines. The forty-two Hermetic books, attributed to him but actually written by the neoplatonists, had a great influence on thought and belief during the sixteenth and seventeenth centuries.

l. 93. *And of :* i.e. " and tell of," the verb being included in " unfold " (l. 89) by a zeugma.

l. 95. *Consent :* agreement, concord.

l. 97. *Gorgeous :* magnificently dressed.

l. 98. *Sceptred :* regal. Alluding to the fact that royal persons are the protagonists in Greek tragedy ; similarly in the " Tractate of Education " he speaks of " Attic tragedies of stateliest and most regal argu-ment."

135

SHORTER POEMS OF JOHN MILTON

*Pall :* mantle worn by tragic actors in ancient drama (Latin, *palla*).

ll. 99–100. An epitome of some of the themes of Greek tragedy. Thebes is the scene of Aeschylus' " Seven Against Thebes " and Sophocles' " Oedipus Rex " ; Pelops' descendants included Agamemnon, Orestes, Iphigenia, and Electra, all of them subjects of Greek tragedy ; and the tale of Troy is represented by Euripides' " Trojan Women," " Andromache " and " Hecuba."

ll. 101–102. In the preface to " Samson Agonistes " Milton speaks of " Aeschylus, Sophocles and Euripides, the three tragic poets unequalled yet by any, and the best rule to all who endeavour to write tragedy," and observes that modern plays have brought the form into " the small esteem, or rather infamy, which in the account of many it undergoes at this day with their common Interludes ; happening through the poet's error of intermixing comic stuff with tragic sadness and gravity or introducing trivial and vulgar persons." This is clearly a condemnation of Shakespeare and of Elizabethan drama in general.

*Buskin'd stage :* Greek tragic actors wore a high boot or buskin, which thus became the emblem of tragic drama (cp. note on " sock," " L'Allegro," l. 132).

l. 103. *Sad Virgin, i.e.* Melancholy.

P. 45, l. 104. *Musaeus :* mythical Greek poet and seer, in some legends said to be the son of Orpheus.

*Bower :* abode.

ll. 105–108. See " L'Allegro," ll. 145–150, note. It is in keeping with the theme and mood of " Il Penseroso " that the poet should dwell on what is dark and mysterious in poetic literature—the lost poems and songs of a legendary age, an unfinished poem of Chaucer's, and the allegorical romance.

ll. 109–115. " The Squire's Tale " was left unfinished by Chaucer. It is a story of the Tartar king, Cambuscan, and his three children, Algarsyf, Cambalo, and Canace ; and of the unknown lover of Canace, who gave her a magic ring, enabling its wearer to understand the language of birds and the medicinal properties of herbs, and a magic mirror that revealed the future, and who also offered her father the Horse of Brass that could carry its rider any distance within twenty-four hours.

136

*Virtuous* : endued with peculiar power (cp. " Comus," l. 621).

ll. 116–120. The reference is to the whole literature of chivalric romance down to Spenser's " Faerie Queene."

*Trophies hung* : in antiquity the spoils of victory were hung up as an offering to the gods, and this rite was followed in mediaeval tournaments.

*Drear* : the original sense of this word is " bloody," and so " cruel, dire."

l. 121. *Career* : was especially used of the courses of the sun, moon, and planets.

l. 122. *Civil-suited* : soberly dressed (as distinct from the brilliance of military uniform). Cp. " Romeo and Juliet," " Come, civil night, thou sober-suited matron."

l. 123. *Trick'd* : decked, adorned (cp. " Lycidas," l. 170).

*Frounc'd* : with hair frizzled and curled or with clothes elaborately puffed and pleated.

l. 124. *The Attic boy* : Cephalus, whom Eos (the Dawn) fell in love with as she saw him hunting one morning.

l. 125. *Kerchieft* : A kerchief was a scarf worn as a head-dress by women.

l. 130. *Minute-drops* : drops falling at minute intervals (cp. " minute gun," " minute bell ").

l. 134. *Brown* : dark (original meaning of the word).

*Silvan* : Sylvanus was a Roman god of woods and trees, later identified with Pan.

l. 135. *Monumental* : massive and enduring.

P. 46, l. 145. *Consort* : harmony (cp. " Nativity Ode," l. 132, note).

ll. 147–150. The sense seems to be, " Let some dream come fluttering on the wings of sleep, displaying itself in a stream of images that are laid lightly on the eyelids."

l. 154. *Genius of the wood* : cp. " Arcades."

l. 156. *Pale* : enclosure.

l. 158. *Antic* : quaintly carved.

*Massy proof* : The words are not hyphened in Milton's editions, but it seems best to treat them as a compound adjective meaning " secure in their massiveness."

l. 159. *Dight* : adorned.

l. 163. *High* : shrill, loud.

ll. 170–173. *i.e.* make all knowledge his province ; cp. note to ll. 87–96. Burton writes, " the heaven is God's instrument, by mediation of which he governs and disposes these elementary bodies ; or a great book, whose letters are the stars . . . wherein are written many strange things for such as can read " (" Anatomy of Melancholy," I. 2, i., iv).

*Rightly spell :* read, interpret aright (cp. Sonnet VI, l. 7).

## *Arcades* and *Comus.*

These two poems may be considered together since the same personal connections occasioned them, and they are both examples, however different in scale and character, of the seventeenth-century masque. " Arcades " may have been written in 1633, though some put it as early as 1630. It was, as Milton informs us, " part of an entertainment to the Countess Dowager of Derby at Harefield by some noble members of her family." The Countess, now some seventy or more years of age and the head of a large and distinguished family, derived her title from her first husband, who had died in 1594. In 1600 she married Thomas Egerton, himself a widower, who became Baron Ellesmere and Viscount Brackley ; they settled at Harefield, about twelve miles from Horton, where the Countess lived for the remainder of her life. Among the " noble persons " who honoured the Countess on this occasion would be the family of her stepson, John Egerton Earl of Bridgewater, for whom Milton wrote " Comus " ; the Earl's children, who took the principal parts in " Comus," no doubt acted also in " Arcades." The entertainment was probably devised by Henry Lawes, who was musical tutor in the Egerton family and who later superintended the production of " Comus." Lawes was one of the musicians attached to the Court of Charles I and a well-known composer ; both as a composer and a singer he took a prominent part in the masques produced at Court. That Lawes was one of Milton's closest friends is proved by the sonnet addressed to him in 1645 ; and, since there were probably few musicians in London with whom Milton's father was not acquainted, the friendship may well go back to Milton's boyhood. There can be little doubt that it was Lawes who asked Milton to write the verses both for the family affair at Harefield and for the more public occasion at Ludlow in 1634.

In 1631 the Earl of Bridgewater had been appointed Lord President of the Council of Wales and its Marches, but it was not until the autumn of 1634 that he was inaugurated into his office at Ludlow Castle, the official residence of the Lord President. " Comus " was written for the celebrations attending this event, being performed in the great hall of Ludlow Castle on September 29th. The parts of the Lady and her two brothers were taken by the Earl's three children, Lady Alice Egerton, Lord Brackley, and Mr. Thomas Egerton, whose ages ranged from about fifteen to twelve. That Lawes was the producer and himself took the part of the Attendant Spirit is practically certain ; his musical settings of several of the " Comus " lyrics have been preserved, and it was he who first published the text in 1637, because, as he says in the dedication, it was " so much desired that the often copying it hath tired my pen to give my several friends satisfaction."

These were the circumstances in which the poems were produced ; it remains to consider them as examples of a dramatic form that flourished during the first forty years of the seventeenth century. Originally, as introduced from Italy early in the sixteenth century, the masque was simply a visit in masquerade to the house of a friend or person of honour, usually at a time of festival ; the masquers, having done obeisance and paid ceremonious compliment to the master of the house, would entertain the company with dances performed either by themselves alone or with partners selected from the onlookers. This gives the essential characteristics of the masque ; even when it had developed under James I into the distinct species of theatrical art known as the Court masque, it remained a social entertainment with the pageantry and the dances of the masquers as its central feature. The Court masques of the reigns of James and Charles were most elaborate and costly productions, requiring the services of the stage architect, the dramatist, the musician, the ballet-master, and the professional actor. Like the modern revue, they were theatrical spectacles, presenting a general idea chiefly by means of pageantry, music, and dance. The mere staging of these shows, as recorded in the texts of Ben Jonson's masques and in the drawings of Inigo Jones, reveals their character ; they were mag-

nificently mounted, dresses and scenes being designed
as a unit, and not only were there complete changes of
scenes but transformation scenes were effected in full
view of the audience.  Being designed as compliments
to those in whose honour they were given, the common
themes were Virtue, Beauty, Honour, Fame, Learning,
and so on.  Some episode from classical mythology or
some allegorical legend would provide the plot ;  the
characters were classical gods and goddesses and
heroes, figures from pastoral literature, and personi-
fications of virtue and vice.  In construction the fully
developed masque consists of two main parts, the antimasque and the masque proper.  First the action and
purport of the piece, including its complimentary
significance, was explained in a prologue ;  the prologue soon developed into a dramatic scene between
two or more characters, and out of this in turn developed
the antimasque.  The antimasque was a preliminary
masque serving as a contrast or foil to the main masque ;
and since the latter was an expression of heroic virtue
and beauty, the antimasque was realistic, ribald, and
grotesque.  For instance, Jonson's "Masque of Queens,"
in which the Queen and some of her ladies took part,
celebrates "honourable and true Fame, bred out of
Virtue " ;  the antimasque accordingly presents twelve
witches "sustaining the persons of Ignorance, Suspicion, Credulity, etc., the opposites of good fame,"
who appear in an opening scene similar to that in the
Fourth Act of "Macbeth," and perform grotesque
dances "full of preposterous change and gesticulation."
During this preliminary part of the entertainment,
whatever form it took, the masquers proper were concealed within the scene, and it was the dramatist's and
producer's principal care to render their first appearance
as effective as possible ;  for this was the dramatic
climax of the show.  At the appropriate moment they
were revealed either by a transformation scene or by a
part of the scene opening in the form of a shell or a
cave, or some such device.  They were then welcomed
in speech or song by the other characters ; after which
they moved in procession down from the stage to the
dancing floor in the middle of the hall and performed
their three or four sets of formal courtly dances.  The
dances were interspersed with songs which served both
to interpret their dramatic significance and to give the

dancers a breathing space ; and between the second and third set usually came the ordinary social dances in which the masquers chose partners from the audience. After their final dance the masquers withdrew to the stage and the play concluded with a final song.

What does Milton make of this form of entertainment? " Arcades," to begin with, is a good example of the poetic text of a masque on a small scale, the simpler sort of masque that would be given on such a private occasion. It may have been performed either indoors or out ; in either case Milton's verses would be delivered in dramatic manner with the usual pageantry, dancing and musical accompaniment. " Comus," on the other hand, was composed to fulfil all the purposes of a Court masque. There is the usual mythological story expressing a moral theme, which is made appropriate to the occasion and yields all the necessary compliments and topical allusions—the allusions to Welsh history and legend, the graceful compliments to the Lord President and his office, to his daughter and sons, and to Henry Lawes. All the typical features of the form are reproduced : " Comus " opens with a prologue in which the story and moral are explained, followed by the antimasque of Comus's crew ; there are three changes of scene, five songs, and three separate dances. And yet, despite these correspondences in form and purpose, " Comus " differs fundamentally in plan from the ordinary masque. In the Court masque the principal figures were the ladies and gentlemen of the Court who appeared as the masquers ; all that was required of the masquers was to make a brave show and to dance, but they and their dances were the principal part of the entertainment ; the speaking and singing parts were subordinate, and were taken by professionals. In " Comus " there are, strictly speaking, no masquers at all, only the antimasquers of Comus's crew ; the principal figures are anything but dumb and they do not dance. The one dance in the body of the piece is a burlesque performance of the Measures in the antimasque of Comus's crew ; the country dances (which are also proper only to an antimasque) and the dances of the courtiers come as a graceful epilogue, long after the dramatic climax has passed. Milton in fact has made the structural elements of the masque subsidiary features and has substituted

dramatic speech for pageantry and dance as his basis
of construction, so converting a theatrical spectacle into
a literary form ; he has written a dramatic poem in the
guise of a masque.  That is why the text of " Comus,"
unlike other masques, is complete in itself and can be
read as an independent work.

Yet in reading " Comus " as a dramatic poem it is
still necessary to remember that it was composed and
successfully produced as a masque, in order that we
may not misjudge its dramatic methods.  Read as
normal drama, it will appear full of faults : the action
is lacking in incident and variety, and is often improb-
able ;  the conflict consists in the simple opposition of
virtue to vice ;  the characters are too inflexible and
without subtlety, the speeches too long and argu-
mentative.  These methods would never do in a drama
of character, but they are the methods proper to the
kind of drama Milton is writing.  " Comus " should
be read as a dramatised debate on a moral or philosophical theme, a sort of Platonic dialogue in verse ;
and although there are moments of ordinary drama,
the main dramatic interest, as in a Platonic dialogue,
consists in following the developments and turns in a
skilfully conducted debate.  No one knew better than
Milton how to turn such matters into the right kind of
dramatic poetry.

## *Arcades* (? 1633)

**P. 47.** *Arcades :* Arcadians.  Arcadia was a state of ancient
Greece on the central plateau of the Peloponnesus ;
shut off by mountain barriers, the Arcadians were a
nation of shepherds and huntsmen, leading simple lives
and retaining their ancient customs.  In Renaissance
literature Arcadia became the imaginary land of the
pastoral convention, where shepherds and shepherdesses
lived innocently and happily as in the Golden Age.

*Seat of state :* raised throne placed centrally for the person
in whose honour the entertainment was being given.

l. 6.  *Vows :* prayers.  The Countess is addressed as a
deity.

ll. 8–13.  Spenser and other poets had honoured the
Countess in verse.

*Erst :* formerly.

l. 14.  *State :* cp. " L'Allegro," l. 60, note.

l. 20.  *Latona :* mother of Apollo and Diana.

**l. 21.** *Cybele :* Rhea, mother of the Olympian gods, was identified by the Greeks with the Asiatic Cybele, " Mother of gods and men," goddess of the productive powers of Nature and also of the arts of civilisation ; in the latter character Cybele was regarded as the founder of cities and so represented with a diadem of towers. These mythological compliments to the Countess and her family are in the customary vein of the masque writer.

**P. 48, l. 23.** *Odds :* allowance to an inferior competitor. The line recalls the famous contest between Juno, Minerva, and Venus for the golden apple inscribed " For the Fairest," which Paris was called on to decide.

**l. 24.** *Clime :* The earth's surface between the equator and each of the poles was divided into twenty-four climes or climates ; Milton also uses the word, as here, when contrasting the ethereal atmosphere of heaven with that of earth (cp. " Comus," l. 977).

*Genius of the Wood :* The Romans assigned a protective spirit or genius to every place as to every person (cp. note on daemons, " Il Penseroso," ll. 87–96). This part was probably taken by Henry Lawes.

**l. 26.** *Gentle :* well-born.

*Swains :* rustic servants. The form of address is therefore an oxymoron, the explanation of which is introduced by *for.*

**l. 27.** *Honour :* quality of a man of birth and breeding.

**ll. 29–31.** Alpheus, the main river of the Peloponnesus, was worshipped as the chief river-god in Arcadia ; like many streams in that country it passes underground for a part of its course. The legend was that Arethusa, a fountain nymph, was bathing in the Alpheus when the river-god fell in love with her ; she fled to Ortygia in Sicily, where Diana changed her to a fountain, but Alpheus flowed on under the sea to unite with her there (cp. " Lycidas," l. 85).

*So often sung :* Homer is the first of many poets to write of the sacred river.

**l. 33.** *Silver-buskin'd :* The lady masquers would be so clad as nymphs of Diana. The buskin was a boot reaching to the calf or knee.

*As great and good :* equal to the swains in birth.

**l. 34.** *Quest :* hunt.

*Free intent :* courteous object.

**l. 39.** *Solemnity :* festival (Latin, *solemnitas*).

l. 44. *Lot :* allotment (cp. " Comus," l. 20).
 *Pow'r :* local divinity (Latin, *numen*).

l. 47. *Quaint :* cunningly made, elaborate, fantastic (cp. " Nativity Ode," l. 198, note).
 *Wanton :* unrestrained.
 *Wove :* woven.

ll. 47–53. Cp. " Comus," ll. 843–847.

l. 51. *Thwarting :* going athwart, zigzag. *Thunder* was used of both thunder and lightning.

l. 52. A malign influence was attributed to Saturn (cp. " Epitaphium Damonis," ll. 78–80) : " Some star is casting an evil spell over you ; Saturn's star has often been baleful to shepherds, and strikes with his slant [*obliquo*] leaden shaft your inmost breast."
 *Cross :* looking askance, hostile (Latin, *obliquus*).
 *Dire-looking :* of evil aspect, in the astrological sense. The evils due to Saturn are described by Chaucer in " The Knight's Tale," ll. 2453–2469.

l. 53. *Canker'd :* infected with canker, a disease of plants.

P. 49, l. 60. *Murmurs :* incantations (cp. " Comus," l. 526).

l. 61. *Else :* at other times (obsolete).

ll. 63–73. See Appendix, " Milton's Cosmology." The present lines summarise the " Vision of Er " at the close of Plato's " Republic," in which Socrates describes in a myth the judgment of souls in the other world. The souls come to a place where they see the Spindle of Necessity (*i.e.* the law of the universe), made of adamant, which holds the universe together and by which its revolutions are produced and maintained ; it is driven as an axis through the centre of the earth and the eight spheres, and rests in the lap of Necessity. On each of the spheres sits a siren who utters one note at one pitch, the eight notes making together the harmony of the octave. Seated at equal distances about Necessity are the Fates, Lachesis and Clotho and Atropos, the daughters of Necessity ; Lachesis sings of the past, Clotho of the present and Atropos of the future, and it is they who turn the Spindle of Necessity.

l. 65. Strictly speaking only Atropos held the shears, cutting the thread of life her sisters spun and drew out.

l. 71. *Measured :* musically regular, rhythmical.

l. 73. *Mould :* cp. " Comus," l. 17, note.

l. 74. *Blaze :* proclaim (cp. " Lycidas," l. 74, note).

l. 76. *Lustre :* splendour of beauty or renown.

*Leads :* is foremost (may be used here in the specific sense of " lead the dance ").

l. 78. *Go :* i.e. in the procession of the masquers towards the seat of state, which may have been in the form of a " measure " or grave stately dance.

l. 79. *Lesser gods :* a genius was one of the *indigetes* or lesser Roman divinities.

l. 80. *Assay :* attempt.

l. 81. *Attend :* accompany.

*State :* chair of state.

l. 82. *Stem :* stock.

l. 84. *Enamell'd :* i.e. smooth and bright as enamel ; Dante describes a lawn as " green enamel " (" Inferno," iv. 118).

P. 50, ll. 97–102. *Ladon :* tributary of the Alpheus ; *sandy* was the stock epithet for the stream. *Lycaeus, Cyllene, Maenalus :* mountains of Arcadia. *Erymanthus :* name of both a mountain and a river in Arcadia.

l. 104. *Grace :* either " honour and credit " or " good fortune " (obsolete).

ll. 106–107. *Pan* was originally an Arcadian god of hills and woods, the protecting deity of flocks, herdsmen, and hunters. *Syrinx* was a daughter of the river-god Ladon ; fleeing one day from the enamoured Pan, she was changed by her sister nymphs into a reed on the banks of the Ladon. Pan was said to have made from the reed the musical instrument called a syrinx or Pan's pipe.

### Comus (1634)

P. 52. *The Copy of a Letter written by Sir Henry Wotton :* Wotton, who had been James the First's ambassador at Venice and was now Provost of Eton, has been described as " the most cultivated Englishman of his time."

*Mr. H. :* almost certainly John Hales, whose learning won for him the epithet " ever memorable."

*Banded :* bandied, discussed.

*Tragical :* dramatic.

*Doric :* theocritean or pastoral (cp. " Lycidas," l. 189).

*Mr. R. :* probably John Rouse, Bodley's Librarian, to whom Milton wrote a Latin ode in 1647. Milton had been incorporated M.A. at Oxford in 1635 and probably made the acquaintance of Rouse then.

*The late R.'s Poems :* possibly the poems of Thomas Randolph, which were printed at Oxford in 1638 ;

but no copies of Randolph's poems bound up with " Comus " (*i.e.* Lawes' edition of 1637) have been discovered.

*Con la bocca dolce :* with a pleasant taste in the mouth.

*Blanch :* miss, omit.

*Mr. M. B. :* Michael Branthwaite, diplomatic agent at Paris.

*Young Lord S. :* the son of Lord Scudamore, English ambassador at Paris. Milton says in the " Defensio Secunda " that Lord Scudamore received him courteously and gave him an introduction to the famous Hugo Grotius.

P. 53. *I pensieri stretti ed il viso sciolto :* your thoughts close and your countenance open.

P. 54. *Attendant Spirit :* in both the Trinity MS. and the Bridgewater MS. (which is the acting copy) the description is " A Guardian Spirit, or Daemon " ; the daemon or genius, who in ancient belief protected and governed the life of a person, corresponds to the guardian angel of Christian belief.

*Descends :* suggests stage machinery. In the performance, as we know from the Bridgewater MS., the Attendant Spirit enters with a song beginning " From the Heavens now I fly," which is transferred with appropriate alterations from the epilogue, l. 975 *seq.* ; then followed the speech with which our text opens.

ll. 1–17. This first paragraph of the prologue, stating the theme from which the whole argument of the poem proceeds, is based on Plato's " Phaedo " (see " Life "). In that dialogue Socrates is represented on the day of his death discussing the immortality of the soul. He starts from the Orphic doctrine that the soul undergoes a succession of incarnations in the forms of men and animals, before it is finally purified and released from the Cycle of Birth ; this implies that the soul existed before entering the body and will continue to exist after the body's death. Indeed the true life of the soul is altogether apart from the body in which it is temporarily imprisoned : the body belongs to this illusory world of change and decay, but the soul belongs to the divine and real world of Ideas. Even in this life the soul can withdraw from and forget the body in contemplation of the abstract truth which alone is real. Those who have pursued this path of knowledge, not deceived by sensual desires and earthly interests, are

the virtuous souls ; and they at death are released
from the claims of the body, going as free spirits to
dwell for ever with the gods. In conclusion these views
are embodied in a typical Platonic myth. I believe,
says Socrates, that the earth is a globe in the centre of
the universe, and within its surface are many hollows
where we and other races of men dwell. But the true
surface of the earth is above in the pure air of heaven,
which we call the ether and of which the air and mist
and water collecting in our hollows are the sediment.
We who dwell in these hollows ignorantly suppose that
we are living on the true surface of the earth ; but if a
man could arrive at the surface he would see the true
earth, and the true heaven beyond. On the true earth
all things are fairer than here ; and men are living
there, some inland, some on the coasts of the air as we
on the coasts of the sea, and some on islands in the air :
for air is to them what the sea is to us, and the ether
what air is to us. Also they have temples where the
gods really dwell, and they see and talk with them face
to face. Now those who are judged to have been holy
in their lives on earth come to those pure mansions
above and dwell on the true earth ; whilst those who
have purified themselves by philosophy go to the
heaven beyond and live for ever without bodies in
mansions fairer still. Wherefore, concludes Socrates,
having regard to these things, it behoves us to leave
nothing undone to obtain virtue and wisdom in this
life : fair is the prize, and the hope great.

From this abstract of the " Phaedo " it will be seen
that Milton was writing the opening lines of " Comus "
with Plato's dialogue fresh in his mind. Other
classical sources naturally enter into the composition ;
and Milton in the usual renaissance manner is con-
sciously using pagan forms to express what are also
Christian ideas and sentiments. But the immediate
inspiration, not only in these lines but throughout the
poem, is platonic.

In the Trinity MS. fourteen rejected verses follow l. 4,
some of the phrases being worked into the text later
(cp. ll. 393–395) :—

" Amidst th' Hesperian gardens, on whose banks
  Bedew'd with nectar and celestial songs
  Eternal roses grow and hyacinth
  And fruits of golden rind, on whose fair tree

The scaly-harnest dragon ever keeps
His uninchanted eye ; and round the verge
And sacred limits of this blissful Isle
The jealous Ocean, that old river, winds
His far-extended arms, till with steep fall
Half his waste flood the wide Atlantic fills
And half the slow unfadom'd Stygian pool.
But soft I was not sent to court your wonder
With distant worlds and strange removed climes :
Yet thence I come and oft from thence behold
The smoke and stir of this dim narrow spot."

This is a description of the Isles of the Blest in the
western Ocean, the Elysium or Earthly Paradise
imagined by Greek poets, of which Plato's True Earth
is a celestial version. Although the lines were cancelled,
it is necessary to have a clear picture of the mythical
world they present in order to understand many
allusions in the course of the poem ; for that world
was constantly present to Milton's imagination in
writing " Comus."
Among the early Greeks, when the known world was
confined to the lands surrounding the Mediterranean,
the earth was conceived as a flat disc dividing the upper
from the lower world, Heaven from Tartarus. The
Ocean was a stream flowing round the earth and
meeting the confines of Heaven and Tartarus ; it was
personified as the " great Oceanus " (cp. l. 868), god
of primeval water and parent of all seas, rivers, fountains and lakes both on earth and in the lower world.
The setting sun was supposed to enter the Ocean Stream
in the west and be carried round the northern limits
of the earth to rise again in the east (cp. ll. 95–101) ;
and on the borders of Ocean, where the sun set, were
the Gardens of the Hesperides (cp. ll. 393–397 and
ll. 981–983). As Mediterranean seamen pushed west-
wards to the Atlantic board the idea of a river surrounding the earth was exchanged for that of a great
outer sea ; henceforth Ocean and Atlantic were inter-
changeable terms (cp. ll. 95–97), although " Ocean
River " and " Ocean Stream," being Homeric terms,
continued to be used in poetry. Now the Greek poets
imagined their fabulous lands and their elysiums to lie
in the far and unknown west. It is on the western edge
of the earth, beside the Ocean Stream, that Homer
places the Elysian Fields. an earthly paradise where

certain select heroes are translated in the flesh to enjoy for ever perfect happiness. Hesiod and Pindar transfer this elysium to islands out in the western Ocean, known as the Isles of the Blest; and it became associated or identified with the Gardens of the Hesperides. The conception of this earthly paradise corresponds to the Olympian Heaven (cp. l. 1, note). It is, like the summit of Olympus, simply an inaccessible part of the earth's surface, where perpetual summer reigns and elected mortals, endowed with the physical immortality of the gods, enjoy as gods all the pleasures of life. When in time, however, the conception of the gods became more spiritual and their abode was removed to the vault of the sky, it was natural that the oceanic elysium should be transferred there too, as it is by Plato. The True Earth of the " Phaedo " is a celestial, a more spiritual version of the older view of an earthly paradise; and Plato's aerial islands are an attempt to fit the Isles of the Blest into his mythical landscape.

Milton's cancelled lines show that he appreciated the relation of the Platonic to the older poetic conception. In the epilogue, which in performance was the opening song, he brings the older and later conceptions together into one picture :—

> " To the Ocean now I fly,
> And those happy climes that lie
> Where day never shuts his eye,
> Up in the broad fields of the sky."

On which the best comment is the later lines :—

> " I can fly and I can run
> Quickly to the green earth's end,
> Where the bow'd welkin slow doth bend,
> And from thence can soar as soon
> To the corners of the moon."

l. 1. *The starry threshold of Jove's court :* Olympus was the abode of the higher gods; its summit, rising above the clouds, was imagined to touch the sky, and here Jove held his court.

l. 2. *Mansion :* Milton is referring to the mansions on Plato's Earthly Paradise or True Earth; but there is of course the allusion also to St. John xiv. 2 : " In my Father's house are many mansions. . . . I go to prepare a place for you."

l. 3. *Inspher'd :* see " Il Penseroso," l. 88, note.

l. 6. *Which men call Earth :* as distinct *i.e.* from the

" True Earth " of the " Phaedo." " Men " serves as the subject of both its own subordinate clause and the succeeding main clause.

l. 7. *Pester'd :* shackled, tethered (also " encumbered, overcrowded ").

*Pinfold :* pound or enclosure for stray or distrained cattle (cp. the " hollows " of the " Phaedo " myth). This line represents the platonic view that the soul is a lost wanderer in this world until it shall be redeemed from the body.

ll. 8–9. See Plato's " Republic," Bk. X, where Socrates is speaking on the same theme as in the " Phaedo " and is contrasting those who strive for the short-lived success of this world with those who pursue virtue and lay up for themselves " treasure in heaven " : " The successful unjust men of this world are like runners who run well at the beginning of the race but not at the finish ; they get off quickly from the mark but in the end look ridiculous as they slink away uncrowned. But the true runners come to the finishing post and receive the prizes and are crowned."

l. 10. *Mortal change :* change to mortality (cp. l. 841), the change that befalls the soul when in the Cycle of Birth it is committed to this mortal body (cp. Wordsworth's " Ode on Intimations of Immortality "). The phrase is well illustrated by another passage in the section of the " Republic " quoted from above : " But to see the soul as she really is in her original purity, not as we see her now marred by conjunction with the body and other evils, you must contemplate her with the eye of reason ; then her full beauty will be revealed. . . . Hitherto we have spoken of her only as she appears at present, in a condition like to that of the sea-god Glaucus whose original image can hardly be discerned because his members are broken and crushed and damaged by the waves and encrusted with sea-weed and shells, so that he is more like some monster than his natural self."

l. 16. *Ambrosial :* The root meaning of this word is " immortal " ; it was the epithet applied to the food, raiment, etc., of the gods.

*Weeds :* garments (now confined to the phrase " widow's weeds ").

l. 17. *Rank :* corrupt (cp. " Lycidas," l. 126).

*Mould :* the earth of which man is fashioned (cp.

l. 244). Milton uses " mould " for both (1) the stuff or substance, and (2) the shape and character of things and persons, human or celestial.

l. 18. *Sway :* rule.

l. 20. *Nether Jove :* Pluto, ruler of the underworld. In the " Iliad," xv. 190 *seq.,* Neptune describes how he and his two brothers, after Saturn had been overthrown, divided the universe between them by casting lots.

l. 24. *Grace :* honour with title or dignity.

l. 25. *By course :* duly.

*Several :* i.e. each island to the government of a particular deity.

l. 27. *Tridents :* the trident was the sceptre of Neptune.

l. 28. *Main :* sea.

l. 29. *Quarters :* apportions.

l. 30. *This tract :* Wales and the Welsh Marches.

P. 55, l. 31. *Noble Peer :* the Earl of Bridgewater.

*Mickle trust :* great authority.

l. 33. *Nation :* the Welsh.

*Proud in arms :* a translation of the phrase Vergil applies to the Romans (" Aeneid," i. 21), intended for a complimentary allusion to the tradition, embodied in British legend, of the Roman origin of the Welsh people.

l. 35. *Attend :* wait on, pay homage to.

*State :* throne (cp. note on " seat of state," " Arcades ").

l. 37. *Perplex'd :* entangled, intricate, perplexing (Latin, *perplexus*).

l. 38. *Horror :* terror (Latin, *horror ;* cp. *horrid,* l. 429).

l. 39. *Forlorn :* lost.

l. 41. *Sovran :* Milton's customary spelling of " sovereign."

l. 45. *Hall or bower :* a frequent phrase in mediaeval romance and in Spenser ; the hall was the large common room and the bower the more private chamber.

l. 48. *After the Tuscan mariners transform'd :* i.e. after they had been transformed (a Latin construction). The story is that Bacchus, being seized by Italian (Tuscan) pirates, transformed them into dolphins.

l. 50. Circe was the daughter of Helios (the Sun) and an ocean nymph ; the visit of Ulysses to her island of Aeaea is described in the " Odyssey," Bk. X.

l. 55. *Ivy berries :* as the god of wine Bacchus is usually represented with a crown of vine and ivy leaves.

l. 57. Comus was like his father as a god of riot and intemperance, but more like his mother in his sorceries.

l. 60. *Celtic :* French.

*Iberian :* Spanish.

l. 65. *Orient :* bright (the meaning arose from the association of the East with pearls and gems and brilliant colouring).

l. 67. *Fond :* foolish.

P. 56, ll. 68–77. In the " Odyssey " Circe transforms her victims into swine by mixing drugs with their food. In the previous book Homer has described the Lotophagi, who, eating the fruit of the lotus, forget their homes and friends ; and Plato in the " Republic," Bk. X, likens profligate youths to the lotus-eaters, who not only refuse to listen to the voice of their friends but in their intoxication think themselves more comely.

l. 71. *Ounce :* a kind of lynx.

l. 73. *Perfect :* complete.

*Misery :* misfortune (Latin, *miseria*).

l. 79. *Advent'rous :* full of hazards, perilous.

l. 83. *Iris :* one of the Oceanides, a messenger of the gods and identified with the rainbow.

ll. 84–91. A compliment to Henry Lawes, put into his own mouth.

l. 87. *Knows to :* knows how to, a Latinism not uncommon in Elizabethan verse.

l. 88. *Faith :* fidelity in service.

l. 89. *Office :* duty (Latin, *officium*).

l. 90. *Likeliest :* most promising, fittest (cp. " a likely lad ").

ll. 90–91. *Nearest . . . occasion :* the nearest help for the present occasion (a Latin construction).

(Stage Direction) With the entry of Comus's crew begins what corresponds in " Comus " to the usual anti-masque. *Rout :* rabble (used of a pack of animals as well as of a tumultuous crowd of persons).

l. 93. *I.e.* the evening star, as being the first to appear.

l. 94. *I.e.* has climbed to the meridian.

ll. 95–97. See note on cancelled lines, ll. 1–17 above.

*The steep Atlantic stream* is the Ocean Stream into which the sun sinks and which " with steep fall . . . the wide Atlantic fills " (see cancelled lines). The fancy is frequently met with in classical literature that the waves hissed as the sun's chariot touched them.

*Allay :* cool.

P. 57, ll. 98–101.　*Slope :*　aslant, on an inclined course.

　*Dusky pole :*　the Bridgewater MS. reads " Northren pole," which is also a cancelled reading in the Trinity MS.　During the summer the sun's course is inclined towards the northern pole and its light is visible there throughout the twenty-four hours : Milton characteristically adapts the scientific fact to the fabulous conception of the sun carried round by the Ocean Stream.

l. 105.　*Rosy twine :*　twined roses.

l. 110.　*Saws :*　maxims.

l. 111.　*Purer fire :*　the celestial fire of which the stars and the soul are composed, but which in ordinary mortals is mixed with baser elements (see notes to " Upon the Circumcision," l. 1, and " Il Penseroso," ll. 87–96). It is a characteristic claim on Comus's part.

l. 115.　*Sounds and seas :*　straits and open seas.

l. 116.　*Morrice :*　a folk dance, associated with May-day and danced round the maypole to a lively step.

l. 118.　*Pert :*　brisk, sprightly.

l. 121.　*Wakes :*　nocturnal revels.

l. 123.　*Prove :*　try.

l. 129.　*Cotytto :*　a goddess whose licentious rites were performed in secret at night ; she was associated with Hecate as a goddess of night and the underworld.

l. 131.　*Dragon womb :*　an allusion to Night's dragons (see " Il Penseroso," l. 59, note).

l. 132.　*Stygian darkness :*　darkness of the underworld (the Styx, one of the four rivers of Hades, being a synonym for the underworld).

　*Spets :*　spits (a common Elizabethan form).

P. 58, l. 135.　*Hecat' :*　here a disyllable, but at l. 534 given its full trisyllabic form.　As a goddess of the underworld Hecate was closely associated with Proserpina, and as a goddess of night with Diana ; together these three formed the triple goddess of the moon (see " Il Penseroso," l. 59, note).　Hecate became in particular the goddess of ghosts and spirits of the night, of magic and witchcraft (cp. " Macbeth ").

l. 137.　*Dues :*　rites in honour of the goddess.

l. 138.　*Blabbing :*　cp. " 2 Henry VI," IV. 1.: " The gaudy, *blabbing* and remorseful day."

l. 139.　*Nice :*　fastidious, critical, precise.

　*Indian steep :*　cp. " A Midsummer-Night's Dream," II. 1. 69 : " the farthest steep of India."　India represented the far east.

l. 140. *Cabin'd :* narrow (cp. " Macbeth," III. IV. 24 : " cabin'd, cribb'd, confin'd "). Such verbal and stylistic evidence of the influence of Shakespeare can be produced from many other passages of " Comus."

l. 142. *Solemnity :* see " Arcades," l. 39, note.

l. 144. *Round :* a country dance.

*The Measure* was a slow and stately Court dance ; Comus's crew perform it in a burlesque manner, for the stage direction in the Trinity and Bridgewater MSS. is " The measure in a wild, rude and wanton Antick." It was, in short, the dance of the antimasque.

l. 147. *Shrouds :* coverts. " Shroud " originally meant " garment," and so " covering," " shelter," " hiding-place." Warton states that it was still used in the eighteenth century for " the branches of a tree (cp. " Nativity Ode," l. 218).

*Brakes :* thickets, brushwood.

The Trinity and Bridgewater MSS. supply the Stage Direction, " They all scatter."

l. 151. *Trains :* allurements, baits.

l. 154. *Dazzling :* Trinity MS. has cancelled reading " powder'd " (cp. " magic dust," l. 165).

l. 156. *False presentments :* unreal shows, illusions.

l. 157. *Habits :* dress (cp. " riding habit ").

l. 159. *Course :* purpose.

l. 161. *Glozing :* fawning, cajoling, specious (the same word as " gloss "). Cp. " Paradise Lost," ix. 549-550 :—

" So glozed the Tempter, and his proem tuned ;
Into the heart of Eve his words made way."

l. 165. *Virtue :* inherent power, efficacy (commonly used of the magical and medicinal properties of plants).

ll. 166–168. The 1673 ed. reads :—

" I shall appear some harmless villager
And hearken, if I may her business hear."

l. 167. *Gear :* affairs (in its more specific sense of " apparatus, tackle " the word is still in use).

P. 59, l. 168. *Fairly :* softly, quietly.

l. 172. *Ill-managed :* disorderly.

l. 174. *Hinds :* farm servants, rustics.

ll. 175–177. A harvest-home.

*Teeming :* bearing young, multiplying (cp. " Nativity Ode," l. 240, note).

*Granges :* granaries.

154

NOTES

*Pan :* see notes, " Arcades," l. 106, and " Nativity Ode," l. 89.

l. 178. *Swill'd insolence :* drunken insolence (cp. " Paradise Lost," i. 501–502 : " Sons of Belial, flown with insolence and wine ").

l. 179. *Wassailers :* carousers. " Wassail " (*Good health !*) was originally a salutation used in drinking ; it came to mean both the custom of drinking healths and the spiced ale in which the healths were drunk at Twelfth-night and Christmas-eve celebrations ; and so to the general meaning of " carousal."

l. 184. *Favour :* friendly protection.

l. 189. *Sad :* serious, grave.

*Votarist :* one consecrated by vow to a religious life.

*Palmer :* a pilgrim returned from the Holy Land (in token of which he carried a palm leaf) ; also an itinerant monk under vow of poverty.

l. 195. *Stole :* this incorrect form is evidently an alteration in the interest of euphony, for the Trinity and Bridgewater MSS. give *stolne.*

l. 198. *And fill'd :* a Latin construction.

P. 60, l. 203. *Rife :* plentiful, strong.

*Perfect :* complete, distinct (cp. l. 73). Perhaps Milton had in mind the musical use of the term. " *Perfect,* in music, denotes something that fills, and satisfies the mind, and the ear " (" Chambers's Cyclopaedia," 1727–1741).

ll. 207–209. Burton describes the belief in such spirits who haunt waste places : " Ambulones, that walk about midnight on great heaths and desert places, which (saith Lavater) ' draw men out of their way ' . . . these have several names in several places ; we commonly call them Pucks." Then he refers to Marco Polo's account of such spirits in the desert of Lop in Asia : " Various apparitions of spirits are seen and heard there by day, and more often by night. So that travellers must take care not to lose touch with their companions or to lag too far behind . . . for voices are heard there which call solitary travellers by their own names and which counterfeit the voices of their companions, in order to lead these stragglers to destruction " (" Anatomy of Melancholy," I. ii. 1, 2).

l. 212. *Conscience :* a trisyllable.

ll. 213–215. Milton substitutes Chastity for Love in the Christian trinity of virtues : Chastity *is* Love, in the

155

Platonic sense of love of the " Supreme Good " which subdues the lower passions and produces " those happy twins of her divine generation, knowledge and virtue."

l. 216.  *I see ye visibly :*  Plato maintains that if we could *see* the Good we should be entranced by its beauty and pursue it with the devotion of lovers.

ll. 221–225.  This artifice of question and answer with its return of the words is a frequent device in classical literature ; the verbal repetition, which is its essential feature, Milton learned to use with consummate art. (For an elaborate example see " Paradise Lost," iv. 641–656.)

l. 226.  *Hallo :*  spelt *hallow* in the original editions, which indicates the right pronunciation.

l. 230.  *Echo :*  a mountain nymph, daughter of Air and Earth ; she loved the beautiful Narcissus and, being scorned by him, pined away till nothing remained of her but her voice.

l. 231.  *Airy shell :*  This is usually taken to mean the " vault of heaven " (cp. " hollow round of Cynthia's seat," " Nativity Ode," l. 102), but the interpretation does not agree with the next line ; it is better to take the words in their plain sense. The Trinity MS. gives the alternative reading "cell," which shows that Milton was thinking simply of the cave or cavern in which the poets usually place Echo.

l. 232.  *Meander :*  a river of Asia Minor, proverbially famous for its winding course ; Strabo tells of the rich soil with which it fertilises its plains.

*Margent :*  marginal.

l. 236.  *Gentle :*  of gentle birth (cp. " Arcades," l. 26).

P. 61, l. 241.  *Parley :*  talk.

*Daughter of the sphere :*  cp. " At a Solemn Music," l. 2.

l. 243.  *Give resounding grace :*  the Bridgewater MS. and the MS. of the songs in the British Museum give the reading " hold a counterpoint," which is also a cancelled reading in the Trinity MS. ; this is a stronger line than that of the printed text, though perhaps it describes an echo less accurately. *Resounding* literally means " echoing." Note the fine metrical effect of the alexandrine.

ll. 246–248.  See Appendix for the Music of the Spheres, and cp. " Nativity Ode," ll. 125–132, " At a Solemn Music," and " Arcades," ll. 63–73.

l. 251.  *Fall :*  cadence.

**l. 253.** *The Sirens :* who lured mariners to destruction by their singing, dwelt on an island between Circe's isle and Scylla.

l. 254. *Naiades :* nymphs of rivers and springs.

    *Kirtle :* gown or tunic.

ll. 257–259. Scylla was a monster on a rock that confronted the whirlpool of Charybdis in the Sicilian straits ; a ship that tried to avoid the one was said to be in danger of falling a prey to the other.

l. 268. *Silvan :* see " Il Penseroso," l. 134, note.

P. 62, l. 273. *Boast of :* vain-glorious belief in.

    *Extreme :* last.

    *Shift :* an expedient under stress of circumstances.

ll. 277–290. These lines are an imitation of the device in Greek tragedy known as stichomythia, in which the dialogue proceeds in alternate verses of question and answer.

l. 285. *Prevented :* anticipated.

l. 290. *Hebe :* see " L'Allegro," l. 29, note.

l. 293. *Swink'd :* work-tired.

l 294. *Mantling :* enveloping as a mantle.

l. 297. *Port :* deportment.

l. 299. *Element :* sky.

l. 301. *Plighted :* either folded or interwoven (cp. " tissued clouds," " Nativity Ode," l. 146).

P. 63, l. 313. *Bosky bourn :* wooded stream (" bourn " is the southern form of " burn," and " bosky " a variant of " bushy ").

l. 315. *Attendance :* attendants. Such use of an abstract for a concrete noun is a marked feature of Milton's later style.

l. 316. *Shroud :* shelter (see l. 147, note).

    *Limits :* bounds.

ll. 317–318. The lark's nest is made of plaited dry grass and placed in a hollow on the ground.

    *Pallet :* straw mattress.

l. 321. *Quest :* search.

l. 324. *Tap'stry :* The walls of wealthy houses were hung with tapestry.

l. 327. *Warranted :* protected, secure (" warrant " is a doublet of " guarantee ").

l. 331. *Unmuffle :* to remove hood or veil from the face.

l. 332. *Benison :* benediction, blessing ; Milton seems to use it here in the sense of " welfare." An uncharacteristically weak line.

l. 333.   *Stoop :* cp. " Il Penseroso," ll. 71–72.

l. 334.   *Disinherit :* dispossess.—In Greek mythology Night was the daughter of Chaos.

P. 64, l. 336.   *Influence :* cp. " Nativity Ode," l. 71, note.

ll. 338–339.   *Wicker . . . habitation :* a wattle hut daubed with clay, of which the only window would be a hole in the wall.

ll. 341–342.   *Star of Arcady or Tyrian Cynosure :* guiding star.   The mythical Arcadian princess Callisto and her son Arcas, from whom the Arcadians traced their descent, were translated to the sky, Callisto as the constellation of the Greater Bear and Arcas as Arcturus (Watcher of the Bear).   The Greeks navigated by a star in the Greater Bear ; whereas the Phoenicians or Tyrians navigated by our pole star in the tail of the Lesser Bear, which the Greeks called Cynosura (literally Dog's Tail).   " Star of Arcady " therefore means the Greek pole star, and " Tyrian Cynosure " the Phoenician (or our) pole star.

l. 344.   *Wattled cotes :* sheepfolds of hurdles.

l. 345.   *Pastoral reed :* the conventional shepherd's pipe of pastoral poetry (cp. " Arcades," l. 106, note).

*Oaten :* " Oat " was a traditional word for the pastoral pipe, being a literal translation of Vergil's " avena " (cp. " Lycidas," ll. 33, 88).

l. 346.   *Lodge :* hut in a forest or other uninhabited part (cp. " shooting lodge ").

l. 349.   *Innumerous :* innumerable (Latin, *innumerus*).

l. 359.   *Over-exquisite :* too curious (Milton has in mind the root sense of the Latin *exquisitus*—" carefully sought out ").

l. 360.   *Cast :* calculate, forecast (metaphor from " casting a horoscope ").

*Fashion :* form.

l. 365.   *Delusion :* four syllables.

l. 366.   *To seek :* at a loss.

l. 367.   *Unprincipled :* ungrounded (in the principles).

P. 65, ll. 375–380.   This central passage once more reveals the influence of Plato.   Note first the transition from virtue to wisdom : " Wisdom's self " (which we might translate by the platonic " Philosopher ") is introduced as the ideal of virtue.   Secondly, the imagery derives from Plato's " Phaedrus," in which Socrates discusses the subject of love in terms of the platonic ideas we have previously illustrated : love is desire for that heavenly beauty the soul once knew and of which earthly beauty arouses the remembrance. In a typical Platonic myth Socrates likens the soul to a winged chariot, the wings representing the desire and power of the soul to mount to the heaven from which it is an exile ; the wings of the virtuous soul are quickened and nourished by the desire and search for the truth, but the wings of the soul intent on worldly affairs and carnal desires are maimed and drooping.

l. 376. *Seeks to :* resorts to.

l. 377. *Contemplation :* five syllables.

l. 378. *Plume :* preen (cp. " plume oneself on ").

l. 380. *All-to :* thoroughly (intensive adverb). Cp. Judges ix. 53 : " And a certain woman cast a piece of a millstone upon Abimelech's head, and all to brake his skull."

l. 382. *Centre : i.e.* of the earth, the underworld ; in mediaeval theology hell was placed at the centre of the earth.

l. 391. *Beads :* rosary.

*Maple :* made of maple wood.

ll. 393-395. The golden apples that grew in the Garden of the Hesperides were guarded by the sleepless dragon Ladon ; it was one of the labours of Hercules to overcome the dragon and obtain three of the apples.

l. 401. *Danger :* power over a person, especially power to hurt or harm ; cp. " Merchant of Venice," IV. i., " You stand within his danger, do you not ? "

*Wink on :* shut the eye to.

l. 404. *It recks me not :* does not trouble me (cp. " Lycidas," l. 122).

P. 66, l. 410. *Poise :* weight.

l. 411. *Arbitrate :* judge, determine.

*Event :* outcome.

l. 422. *Quiver'd nymphs :* nymphs of Diana's train, bound to chastity.

l. 423. *Trace :* traverse.

*Unharbour'd :* without shelter.

l. 424. *Infamous :* of evil repute.

l. 426. *Mountaineer :* people living in mountainous and therefore inaccessible districts were taken as a type of the savage and uncouth.

l. 429. *Shagg'd :* was used of long unkempt hair.

*Horrid :* bristling, savage, terrifying (Latin, *horridus*).

l. 430. *Unblench'd :* undismayed, unflinching.

l. 433. *I.e.* the Will-o'-the-wisp or Jack-o'-Lantern (cp. " L'Allegro," l. 104), which is actually a phosphorescent light seen hovering or flitting over marshy land. See " Paradise Lost," ix. 634–644.

l. 434. *Blue :* livid.
   *Meagre :* emaciated.
   *Hag :* evil spirit in female form (also used of a witch).

l. 436. It was a widespread belief that mines were inhabited by evil spirits (cp. " Il Penseroso," ll. 93–94).
   *Swart :* swarthy.

l. 439. *Schools of Greece :* Greek philosophy.

P. 67, l. 442. *Silver-shafted :* armed with silver arrows, as *queen* (*i.e.* goddess) of the moon.

l. 443. *Brinded :* brindled.

l. 444. *Pard :* panther or leopard.

l. 445. *Bolt :* arrow.

ll. 447–449. Minerva, virgin goddess of wisdom, was represented holding a shield with the Gorgon's head of Medusa in the centre ; the Gorgon's head, with its locks of serpents, turned the observer to stone.
   *Unconquered virgin :* refers particularly to Minerva's resisting the violence of Vulcan.

ll. 460–463. It is a fundamental idea of Milton's that all life is one, as proceeding from God, and that the material forms may pass into the spiritual or the spiritual into the material ; that body and spirit are not different kinds but only different degrees in the scale of existence. See " Paradise Lost," v. 469–503.

ll. 467–475. These lines are practically a translation from Plato's " Phaedo " : " If the soul departs from the body [at death] polluted and impure, as having constantly held communion with the body, and having served and loved it, bewitched by sensual desires and pleasures, thinking that there is nothing real except the corporeal, which one can touch and see, eat and drink, and employ for sensual purposes . . . such a soul after death is weighed down and drawn again into the visible world . . . wandering, as it is said, amongst monuments and tombs, about which indeed certain shadowy phantoms of souls have been seen."

l. 473. *It :* *i.e.* each particular shadow.

l. 474. *link'd itself :* linked itself to.

P. 68, l. 478. *Apollo's lute :* as god of the muses Apollo was represented with a lute or lyre ; there are the famous stories of his musical contests with Marsyas and Pan, who presumed to compete with him. He was also the god of philosophy. In the "Phaedo" Socrates is represented as the servant of Apollo, and in the "Republic" Plato remarks that philosophy tempered by music is the best friend and guardian of man's virtue.

The Stage Direction after l. 489 is based on the manuscript versions.

l. 494. *Thyrsis :* traditional name for a shepherd in pastoral poetry. A second compliment is paid to Lawes similar to that in ll. 86–88.

l. 495. *Madrigal :* part-song for unaccompanied voices. Note that ll. 495–512 are rhymed heroic couplets, which, as Masson points out, is the form largely used in the English pastoral.

P. 69, l. 506. *To :* compared to.

l. 512. *Shew :* spelling and rhyme indicate what is an obsolete pronunciation.

l. 516. *Storied :* narrated.

    *High :* cp. "lofty rhyme," "Lycidas," l. 11.

l. 517. *Chimeras :* the Chimaera was a fire-breathing monster, part lion, part goat and part serpent, which was slain by Bellerophon.

    *Enchanted isles :* such as the isle of Circe.

l. 518. Caves leading into the earth were imagined by the ancients to be entrances to the lower world.

l. 520. *Navel :* centre.

l. 526. *Murmurs :* incantations (cp. "Arcades," l. 60).

l. 529. *Reason's :* "reason" is always used by Milton in the Platonic sense of the chief faculty of the soul.

    *Mintage :* form stamped on a coin.

l. 530. *Character'd :* stamped or engraved.

l. 531. *Crofts :* enclosed fields.

l. 532. *Brow :* overlook, overhang.

l. 533. *Monstrous rout :* rabble of monsters.

l. 534. Cp. description of Circe's island in "Aeneid," vii. *Stabled wolves :* wolves inside the sheepfolds (a translation from Vergil, "Eclogues," iii. 80).

l. 539. *Unweeting :* unwitting.

P. 70, l. 540. *By then :* by the time that.

l. 542. *Besprent :* besprinkled.

l. 546. *Melancholy :* the contemplative, poetic mood celebrated in "Il Penseroso."

l. 547. A translation from Vergil, "Eclogues," i. 2. Vergil was one of the two main sources of the pastoralism represented by Thyrsis. *Meditate :* study, practise (Latin, *meditor*) (cp. " Lycidas," l. 66).

l. 548. *Fancy :* poetic or creative imagination (cp. " On Shakespear," ll. 12–14, note).

l. 553. *Drowsy-frighted :* drowsy but frighted. Many editors adopt the reading of the Trinity MS., " drowsy flighted " ; but all three printed versions and the Bridgewater MS. give our present reading.

l. 558. *Took :* charmed, laid under a spell (cp. " Hamlet," I. i. 163, " No fairy takes ").

l. 561. *Strains :* passages of song or poetry.

l. 568. *Lawns :* glades between the trees. (See " Nativity Ode," l. 85, note).

P. 71, l. 583. *Confidence :* assurance.

l. 585. *Period :* in the grammatical sense.

l. 591. *Meant most harm :* meant to do most harm.

l. 592. *Happy trial :* trial happy in the outcome (a proleptic epithet).

l. 594. *At last :* i.e. at the Day of Judgment.

l. 598. *Pillar'd firmament :* Homer represents heaven as resting on pillars supported by Atlas.

l. 603. *Legions :* trisyllabic.

l. 604. *Acheron :* one of the rivers of Hades, and so Hades itself (cp. l. 132).

l. 605. *Harpies :* rapacious monsters with a woman's face and the wings and claws of a bird of prey.

*Hydras :* the Hydra was a water-serpent whose many heads grew again as fast as they were cut off.

l. 606. *'Twixt Africa and Inde :* between Africa and India, the region of black enchantments.

l. 607. *Purchase :* booty (cancelled reading in Trinity MS., " release his new got prey ").

l. 608. *Curls :* Knightley observes : " Comus, as a voluptuary, is properly represented with curls, such being worn by men of fashion at that time, under the name of *lovelocks.*"

P. 72, l. 610. *Yet :* still.

*Emprise :* chivalric or other adventurous enterprise.

l. 611. *Stead :* service.

l. 617. *Relation :* report.

*Utmost shifts :* cp. l. 273, note.

ll. 619–641. The *shepherd lad*, as Professor Hanford has pointed out, is Milton himself, who here commemorates his friendship with Henry Lawes. The phrase " of small regard to see to " is characteristic in its proud

modesty, corresponding to the " uncouth swain " of
" Lycidas." The virtuous plants and healing herbs are
the knowledge and skill already acquired which one
day he will put to their intended poetic use. *Haemony*
is the platonic philosophy expressed in " Comus," a
symbol of that " sage and serious doctrine " which will
protect its owner against sensual enchantments and
deceits.

l. 620. *Regard :* account.

   *See to :* look at.

l. 621. *Virtuous :* cp. l. 165, note.

l. 626. *Scrip :* wallet, pouch.

l. 627. *Simples :* medicinal herbs (originally a single or
" simple " ingredient in a compounded medicine).

ll. 629–633. These lines describe the dark and difficult
nature of philosophy, which can yet flower into poetry.
In his Latin poem " De Idea Platonica " Milton calls
on Plato, if he desires that his doctrines should be made
current and effective, to recall the poets he had banished
from his Republic. The statement that the plant does
not flower in " this soil " refers to the Renaissance
belief that the northern climates were not as congenial
to poetic genius as those of Greece and Italy. Milton
frequently alludes to this belief : in the " Areopagitica," he speaks of his " natural endowments haply
not the worse for two and fifty degrees of northern
latitude " ; in the " History of Britain " he says, " the
sun, which we want, ripens wits as well as fruits " ;
in the " Reason of Church Government " he writes
of his ambition to write a great poem if " there be
nothing adverse in our climate, or the fate of this
age " ; and finally there are the well-known lines in
" Paradise Lost," ix. 44–46.

l. 634. *Like esteem'd :* accordingly unvalued.

l. 635. *Clouted shoon :* patched shoes, or shoes studded
with nails.

l. 636. *Moly :* the plant that made Ulysses proof against
the enchantments of Circe, " black at the root but the
flower like to milk " (" Odyssey," x. 281 *seq.*). Milton
concludes his first Latin elegy (1626) with a passage
that is interesting in the present connection : " But I
am preparing, while Cupid permits, to leave as soon
as possible this city of delights [London] and, with the
aid of the divine Moly, to flee far from the infamous
halls of the faithless Circe."

l. 638.  *Haemony* :  the name Milton gives his plant may be a reference to Haemonia, an old name for Thessaly, the land of magic and enchantments.

l. 639.  *Sovran* :  commonly used of remedies in the sense of " supremely efficacious."

l. 640.  *Mildew blast* :  blight, an infection attributed to the breath of a malignant fairy.

*Damp* :  noxious gas or vapour.  Still in use among coal miners.

These are conventional evils in pastoral poetry.

l. 642.  *Little reckoning made* :  took small heed.

P. 73, l. 646.  *Lime-twigs* :  twigs smeared with lime to catch birds.

l. 655.  *Vulcan* :  the god of fire, whose son Cacus was a fire-spitting giant ;  Vulcan was also the father of all " spirits of fire."

l. 660.  *Nerves* :  sinews.

*Alabaster* :  was much used for statues and monuments.

ll. 661–662.  The nymph Daphne, fleeing the amorous Apollo, was changed at her own entreaty into a laurel tree.

l. 672.  *Cordial julep* :  sweet stimulating drink.

P. 74, ll. 675–676.  *Nepenthes* :  (literally " pain-dispelling ") was the drug Helen gave to her husband Menelaus : " She presently cast into the wine a drug that frees men from pain and anger and brings forgetfulness of all ills. . . . Drugs of such virtue had the daughter of Jove, which were given her by Polydamna, an Egyptian, wife of Thone " (" Odyssey," iv. 220 *seq.*).

l. 685.  *Unexempt* :  from which there is no exemption.

l. 688.  *That* :  the antecedent is *you*, l. 682.

l. 698.  *Vizor'd* :  masked.

*Forgery* :  deceit.

l. 700.  *Lickerish* :  lecherous (of which it is a variant).

ll. 707–708.  The Stoics and Cynics were the philosophical sects of the classical world who most despised the pleasures of the senses.

*Budge* :  a kind of fur used on university gowns, which thus acquired the meaning " academic " and, by an easy transition, " formal, pompous, surly."

*Stoic fur* :  similarly means Stoic gown or sect.

*Cynic tub* :  the famous tub that the Cynic philosopher Diogenes, to show his contempt for luxury, used as a dwelling.

P. 75, l. 733. *Deep :* Taking this to mean " sea," commentators have remarked that diamonds do not belong to the sea ; but it is obvious that " deep " means here the depths of the earth in which the gold and precious stones, of which Comus has previously spoken, are stored. This interpretation is proved by the original, cancelled version in the Trinity MS., " Would so bestud the centre with their starlight," where " centre " means, as at l. 381, " the centre of the earth, the underworld."

l. 734. *They below :* ghosts and spirits of the underworld, who would no longer flee from the light of day.

ll. 737–755. These lines are not in the Bridgewater MS. and were therefore not spoken when " Comus " was first performed.

l. 737. *Cozen'd :* duped.

P. 76, l. 745. *Brag :* had various related meanings : bray of a trumpet, challenging boast, display and pomp.

l. 746. *Solemnities :* festivals.

l. 748. *Homely :* plain.

l. 750. *Grain :* colour.

l. 752. *Vermeil-tinctur'd :* vermilion-tinted.

l. 757. *Juggler :* mountebank magician.

l. 759. *Prank'd :* decked out.

l. 760. *Bolt :* sift, pick (from the milling process of bolting or sifting the meal from the bran). The use of the word is well illustrated from Milton's attack on his adversary in the " Animadversions upon the Remonstrant's Defence " : " To sift Mass into no Mass, and popish into no popish : yet saving this passing fine sophistical boulting-hatch. . . ."

P. 77, l. 791. *Fence :* art of fencing.

l. 793. *Uncontrolled :* undeniable (obsolete sense).

l. 797. *Lend :* assist with (cp. " lend a hand ").

*Nerves :* sinews, strength.

ll. 803–805. Jove overthrew Saturn and the Titans by his thunderbolts, and imprisoned the Titans in Erebus (the underworld).

*Speaks :* Used, by the figure known as zeugma, in the double sense of *utters* (thunder) and *pronounces sentence of* (the chains).

l. 808. *Canon laws :* ecclesiastical laws.

*Foundation :* endowed institution, such as a monastery.

ll. 809–810. An expression taken from the old physiological system, which accounted for the state of body

and mind by the action of various "humours." Todd
quotes from Nash's "Terrors of the Night" (1594) :
"The grossest part of our blood is the melancholy
humour . . . (Melancholy) sinketh down to the
bottom like the lees of the wine."

P. 78, ll. 816–817. It was a principle of magic that dis-
enchantment was effected by reversing the spells.

l. 822. *Melibaeus :* is Spenser, who relates the tale of
Sabrina in the "Faerie Queene," ii. 10. The original
source is Geoffrey of Monmouth's "British History,"
in accordance with which Milton tells the story again
in his "History of Britain," Bk. I.

l. 823. *Soothest shepherd :* most truthful poet. Milton,
unlike the modern poetaster, was not afraid to commend a poet for his teaching (see "Life," p. xxv).

l. 824 *seq.* The story as told by Geoffrey of Monmouth
is that Brutus, a descendant of Aeneas, conquered
Albion and renamed it Britain. On his death he left
the country divided between his three sons, except that
Cornwall was held by Corineus, an old companion-in-
arms. Locrine, the eldest son, married Gwendolen,
daughter of Corineus ; but when Corineus died he
divorced his wife and made Estrildis queen, whom he
had taken in battle with the Huns and by whom he
had a daughter named Sabra. Gwendolen, having
raised an army in Cornwall, defeated and killed
Locrine. "But not so ends the fury of Gwendolen :
for Estrildis and her daughter Sabra she throws into a
river : and, to leave a monument of revenge, proclaims
that the stream be henceforth called after the daughter's
name, which by length of time is now changed to
Sabrina or Severn."

l. 834. *Pearled wrists :* Pearls were conventionally associated with water deities. "White wrists" is the cancelled reading in the Trinity MS.

l. 835. *Nereus :* was a sea god, father of the fifty Nereids.
He was represented as an old man (cp. l. 871) and,
like all sea gods, had the gift of prophecy ; he and his
daughters were benevolent beings, well disposed towards
mortals.

l. 838. *Lavers :* meant (i) water weeds, (ii) washing
vessels, specifically such religious vessels as the baptismal
font.

*Asphodil :* a flower of the lily kind in Southern
Europe, which Homer describes as covering the fields

in which Ulysses met the spirits of the dead at the entrance to the underworld ; it became in poetry a symbol of immortality.

l. 840. *Ambrosial :* immortal-making (cp. l. 16, note).

l. 841. *Quick :* means " living " as well as " prompt."

*Immortal change :* change to immortality (cp. l. 10, note).

l. 845. *Helping :* relieving, curing.

*Urchin :* mischievous fairy, who often took the form of an urchin or hedgehog.

*Blasts :* cp. l. 640.

*Ill-luck signs :* omens of misfortune. Many everyday incidents (stumbling, nose-bleeding, salt-spilling, etc.) were superstitiously regarded as ominous and believed to be contrived by the fairies. The health of the shepherd's flock was the symbol of virtue and prosperity in pastoral poetry.

l. 846. *I.e.* Puck. *Shrewd :* malicious.

P. 79, l. 852. *The old swain :* Meliboeus.

l. 862. *Braids :* ribbons entwined in the hair.

l. 863. *Amber-dropping :* amber or ambergris was used in perfumery. " Their hair they ware loose . . . whose dangling amber trammels . . . seem to drop balm on their delicious bodies " (Nash, " Terrors of the Night ").

l. 864. *Honour :* chastity.

ll. 868–882. Milton follows the classical poets closely in this description of the water deities.

*Oceanus :* see note on cancelled lines, ll. 1–17.

*Earth-shaking :* the classical epithet for Neptune.

*Mace :* trident.

*Tethys :* wife of Oceanus (in Homer the original Mother of all Things, as Oceanus was the Father of all Things ; they live in dignity and peace together in the far West, aloof from both the contentions of the Olympian gods and the affairs of the human world).

*Carpathian wizard's hook :* Proteus, a deity who dwelt in the Carpathian (East Mediterranean) sea, is called " wisard " by Homer because he could change his shape at will ; he carried a hook or crook as shepherd of the seals or " herds of Neptune."

*Triton :* son of Neptune, usually represented riding the sea-horses and blowing his shell trumpet ; his lower part was in the form of a fish ; *winding* may here mean either " sounding " or " twisting," or both.

*Glaucus :* the Boeotian fisherman who, having eaten

a certain herb, was changed into a water deity ; like other water deities he possessed the gift of sooth-saying or divination.

*Leucothea . . . and her son :* Ino, when she threw herself into the sea with her son Melicertes, became Leucothea, the " White Goddess " ; her son became Palaemon, whom the Romans identified with Portumnus, god of harbours and ports ; *strand* had the meaning " quay " or " landing-place," as well as the more general meaning " shore."

*Thetis :* daughter of Nereus and mother of Achilles ; Homer's epithet for her is " silver-footed."

*Parthenope* and *Ligea :* two of the Sirens ; Parthenope's tomb was at Naples, a town sacred to her ; in his description of Ligea Milton obviously has in mind the mermaids of northern mythology.

P. 80, l. 894. *Turkis :* turquoise.

l. 913. *Cure :* power to cure.

P. 81, l. 921. *Amphitrite :* wife of Neptune.

l. 922. *Anchises :* father of Aeneas and therefore ancestor of Locrine. See note to l. 824 *seq.*

ll. 924–937. This invocation is again in the manner of pastoral poetry.

l. 924. *Brimmed :* brimming.

ll. 934–935. Milton here reverts to the idea of the river personified as a maiden : Sabrina, like Cybele (cp. " Arcades," l. 21), is crowned with towers ; the literal allusion is of course to the towers and terraces overlooking the Severn.

ll. 936–937. These lines are awkwardly turned : the sense would seem to be, " May thy banks be crowned here and there with groves of myrrh and cinnamon."

(Stage Direction) Trinity MS. gives " country dances and such like gambols," which in a Court masque would only have occurred in the antimasque.

P. 82, l. 960. *Duck :* bobbing curtsy. The rustic dancers now make way for the gentry and their more courtly dances, which are the only dances in " Comus " that could have been performed in the main part of a true Court masque.

l. 963. *Mercury :* the Greek Hermes, winged messenger of the gods, inventor of music and god of gymnastic skill, was thought happiest when leading the dances of the nymphs.

l. 964. *Mincing :* daintily moving.

NOTES

    *Dryades :* wood nymphs.
l. 965.  *Leas :* open ground.
l. 972.  *Assays :* trials.
ll. 976–979.  See end of note on cancelled lines, 1–17.
l. 977.  *Climes :* see " Arcades," l. 24, note.
P. 83, l. 984.  *Crisped :* curled (referring to the foliage ; cp. " Arcades," ll. 46–47).
l. 985.  *Spruce :* gay, both in manner and appearance.
l. 986.  *Graces :* the three goddesses who personify the charm and beauty of Nature and human life.
    *Hours :* goddesses, closely associated with the Muses and Graces, who personified the times and seasons, and were thought of as presiding especially over the happy seasons of spring and summer ; according to Homer they guard the clouds that are the gateway to the Olympian heaven, and at dawn they lead forth and harness the steeds of the sun's chariot (cp. Sonnet I, l. 4).
l. 990.  *Cedarn :* adjective from " cedar."
l. 991.  *Nard :* spikenard, a herb used to make an aromatic ointment.
    *Cassia :* a fragrant plant.
l. 993.  *Blow :* bloom with (an uncommon use).
l. 995.  *Purfled :* embroidered.
l. 997.  This line admonishes the reader of the allegorical nature of what follows.
ll. 998–1002.  See " Nativity Ode," l. 204, note ; by referring to Venus as the Assyrian Queen, Milton reminds us that the story of Venus and Adonis was originally the eastern story of Ashtaroth and Thammuz.
ll. 1004–1011.  The story of the marriage of Cupid and Psyche is told by Apuleius in " The Golden Ass." Psyche (the Soul) is separated from Cupid by the envious Venus and put to many trials and sufferings ; at length the gods decree that the lovers shall be reunited in heaven, and Psyche " is delivered of a child whom we call Pleasure." *Advanc'd* means " raised " (viz. to heaven), as in " advancing " a standard or banner ; the word is really a comment on " Celestial Cupid," *i.e.* heavenly as opposed to earthly Love (see Spenser's " Hymns in Honour of Love and Beauty " as the best commentary on this whole passage).
P. 84, ll. 1020–1021.  The meaning is that the virtuous soul will escape from this mortal world and pass beyond the music of the spheres to the heaven of heavens. The idea

is probably inspired by the myth of the " Phaedrus "
(cp. ll. 375–380, note), where Plato describes how the
souls who have been lovers of the beauty of truth and
goodness follow Zeus and the gods in their journeys
beyond the outermost sphere of this universe and behold
all things as they really are ; and those who have once
attained to this vision of eternal truth are free spirits,
safe for ever from the bonds of the mortal world.   Thus
Milton closes on the Platonic theme with which he
opened—the free immortal life awaiting the virtuous
soul, the lover of wisdom.

*Lycidas* (1637)

" Lycidas " was composed in November 1637.
Edward King, the subject of the elegy, was a younger
contemporary of Milton's at Christ's ; he had been
made a fellow of the college and was consequently
preparing for holy orders.   Milton had no doubt liked
and respected King, who was a man of cultivation, a
promising scholar and a poet, and one who was popular
with all who knew him.   The news that he had been
drowned while crossing to his home in Ireland may not
have reached Milton until he was invited to contribute
to a volume of memorial poems to be published at
Cambridge by King's friends.   The volume, which
appeared early the next year, contained twenty-three
poems in Latin and Greek and thirteen in English, of
which " Lycidas " was the last.

" Lycidas " is a poetical tribute in the most artificial
of all literary forms.   But it is also the most personal
of Milton's early poems, being in effect an expression
of the poet's thoughts and sentiments evoked by the
occasion on which he is writing.   In order to follow
the argument of the poem it is therefore necessary to
understand first how Milton's mind reacted to the death
of King ;  and here we are helped by a particular
knowledge of what he was thinking and doing at the
time.   In September 1637 it was three years since
Milton had written any English verse, and we know the
reason to have been that he was entirely engaged in
preparing for the major poetic task ahead.   At the
moment he had no thought of turning aside from this
main purpose.   Our information comes from two Latin
letters to his friend Diodati, dated respectively September 2 and 23, 1637 ; there is no mention of King's

death in these letters, which therefore tell us Milton's thoughts and employments just before he received the news. In the first letter he speaks of the long time since he and Diodati were in communication, and excuses himself by saying that he has been immersed in his studies ; for his intellectual temper is such that when he has entered on some course of reading, " no delay, no rest, no care or thought for anything else, can divert me from my purpose, until I reach the end I am making for and complete some great period of my studies." In the second letter he gives an account of the historical studies that have especially occupied him (see " Life ") ; while the immediately preceding sentences clearly indicate their relation to his poetic ambition : " You ask me what I am meditating. By the help of Heaven, an immortality of fame. And what I am doing ? Growing wings and learning to fly ; but as yet my Pegasus can only rise on tender pinions, so let me be lowly wise."

It is evident that the poetic flight he contemplated was not a poem on Edward King, to whom he does not so much as refer. He has indeed no immediate intention of breaking the poetic silence of the last three years ; so that when soon afterwards he began to compose " Lycidas " he was aware of turning aside from his main purpose. This is the meaning of the opening lines of the poem : intent only on the heroic poetry he has long been preparing for, he finds himself compelled by "sad occasion dear " to resume the humbler pastoral style of the novice. In the concluding lines he reverts to this attitude of literary self-consciousness : looking back critically on what he has written, he dismisses the work in the final line,

" Tomorrow to fresh woods and pastures new."

Such literary self-consciousness may appear strange in an elegy, but that is a question that can be left for later comment ; the immediate point is that it indicates the personal attitude which is the clue to the argument of the poem. These opening and closing lines show Milton's mind, as the letters have shown it, preoccupied with his poetic ambition ; and we watch his mind react as he meditates the fate of one not unlike himself in youthful hope and promise. The opening movement of the poem, the lament for the young poet and fellow student, rises to its climax in the great passage on fame,

that immortality of fame Milton had lately been
dreaming of for himself. Is all such ambition and high
endeavour a vanity and a delusion ?—

> " But the fair guerdon when we hope to find,
> And think to burst out into sudden blaze,
> Comes the blind Fury with the abhorred shears
> And slits the thin-spun life. ' But not the praise,'
> Phoebus replied, and touched my trembling ears ;
> ' Fame is no plant that grows on mortal soil.' . . ."

That unmistakably is Milton answering the personal
problem that confronts him. Equally personal is the
invective on the English clergy, which provides the
next climax of the poem. Most critics, regarding the
poem simply as a lament for Edward King, censure
this passage as a digression ; but if the real theme is
the poet's own thoughts and sentiments evoked by the
occasion on which he is writing, the passage falls into
place in the argument.

So far we have been considering the obviously personal passages in the poem that reveal Milton's attitude
to his subject ; but there is more in the argument of
the poem than these matters of his literary and political
interests, which some critics indeed are inclined to treat
as extraneous to the real theme. The main burden
of " Lycidas " is, after all, a passionate lament for a
dead friend. How are we to reconcile this with that
other self-conscious attitude to his subject ? Are we
to regard the sentiment as insincere or fictitious,
responding merely to the conventional requirements of
the elegy ? The answer is to be found once more in
the letters to Diodati. Speaking of his feeling for his
friend, Milton sets forth an ideal of friendship in terms
of the Platonic doctrine of love and beauty which we
know to have been a dominant influence on his mind ;
and the sentences, like those on poetic fame, reveal his
deepest thoughts and experiences :—

> " I assure you that I cannot but love such men as
> yourself ; for whatever God has bestowed on me in
> other respects He has certainly inspired me, if any
> were ever so inspired, with a passion for beauty.
> Ceres did not seek her daughter Proserpine (as the
> legend goes) with greater ardour than I do the Idea
> of Beauty, like some image of loveliness, ever pur-
> suing it by day and night through all the forms and
> appearances of things (" for many are the shapes of

things divine ") and following close on its footsteps
as it leads. And so wherever I find one who,
despising the base conceptions of common men, dares
to be in thought and word and deed that which the
wisest minds throughout the ages have approved as
the best, to that man, wherever found, I cleave as
by necessity."

This ideal of friendship, as a communion of minds in
love with the good and fair, inspires his poetic tribute
to Lycidas. Whether in addressing King as the object
of such a friendship he may have idealised their relationship, is a question of historical rather than poetic
relevance ; enough that it leaves the poet free to express
his deepest convictions.

We find then that " Lycidas " is indeed the most
personal of poems ; the centre of treatment, which
gives unity to the work, is the poet's own mind reacting
to the event on which he writes. Nor is there anything
surprising in this when we consider the real purpose
and function of an elegy. The elegy is not, as often
thought, merely a lament for an individual, but an
elaborate literary memorial intended to perpetuate his
memory. The duty or practical job of the elegist, as
of the sculptor in similar circumstances, is to commemorate the dead by creating a worthy and enduring
work of art ; only if the work endures as literature has
the intention of the elegy been fulfilled. Consequently
the predominant motive of the elegist, however sincere
his personal grief, must be an artistic one, implying a
literary detachment such as is evident in the opening
and closing lines of " Lycidas." Milton chose to work
in a form of the elegy sanctioned by long tradition and
by the outstanding names of Theocritus, Vergil, and
Spenser ; and the poem is partly inspired, as all Milton's
greatest work is, by a literary ambition—the ambition
to produce in English a consummate example of the
pastoral elegy. His success in this literary ambition
measures his success as an elegist ; but for " Lycidas "
the name of Edward King would long ago have been
forgotten.

This literary attitude of the elegist further implies
that he will follow, as Milton does, his normal process
of imaginative creation. The poet's sorrow necessarily
resolves itself into a general theme and receives ideal
expression in accordance with his ruling ideas ; the

individual whom he mourns becomes a typical figure, representative of the loss of all he holds most dear. So Milton represents Lycidas as the scholar and poet and friend, and as the servant of God ; and the passion that informs the poem comes from his attachment, not merely to an individual, but to all he admires and values in life.

P. 85, ll. 1–3. The laurel was sacred to Apollo, the myrtle to Venus, the ivy to Bacchus ; of the leaves of these three plants the poet's garland was woven ; by plucking the berries Milton symbolises his return to poetry.

*Brown :* dark.

*Sere :* withered.

*Crude :* unripe (Milton is referring to his own want of " inward ripeness " as in the sonnet " On His Being Arrived at the Age of Twenty-three ").

l. 4. *Rude :* unskilled.

l. 5. *Before the mellowing year :* before their " season due."

l. 6. *Dear :* of intimate concern, touching one nearly.

l. 8. *Lycidas :* a shepherd in Theocritus, Idyl VII, and in Vergil, Eclogue IX.

l. 9. *Peer :* equal.

ll. 10–11. These are direct translations of Latin phrases (cp. " Comus," l. 87).

*Rhyme :* verse.

l. 13. *Parching :* withering.

l. 14. *Meed :* tribute.

*Melodious tear :* poetic lament. " Tear " was a common word for " elegy " (Spenser, *e.g.*, entitles his elegies " The Tears of the Muses ").

ll. 15–16. The nine Muses, whose shrine was the Pierian Spring at the foot of Olympus.

l. 19. *Muse :* poet.

l. 20. *Lucky words :* words of good omen (perhaps also in the literary sense of " felicitous " words).

ll. 23–36. These lines describe under pastoral imagery the common life of Milton and King at Cambridge, their studies and poetic pursuits.

P. 86, l. 25. *High lawns :* grassy uplands.

l. 28. *What time the gray-fly :* the gray-fly at that time when.

*Winds :* blows.

*Sultry :* expresses the noonday heat when the " horn " is heard.

l. 29. *Battening :* fattening.

ll. 30–31. *I.e.* the evening star " that bids the shepherd fold " (" Comus," l. 93).

l. 32. *Ditties :* words of a song.

l. 33. *Temper'd :* attuned.

*Oaten :* cp. " Comus," l. 345, note.

l. 34. *Fauns :* were Roman country divinities, identified with the Greek Satyrs ; both were partly human and partly bestial in form, satyrs being represented with a shaggy hide, and fauns with the feet of goats.

l. 36. *Damoetas :* a common name in pastoral poetry, no doubt representing some figure in Milton's Cambridge.

l. 38. *Never must :* are forbidden ever.

l. 39. *Desert :* deserted.

l. 40. *Gadding :* straggling.

l. 46. *Taint-worm :* a worm causing disease in cattle.

*Weanling :* lately weaned.

l. 47. *Wardrope :* wardrobe.

l. 48. *White-thorn :* hawthorn.

*Blows :* blooms.

ll. 50–55. These lines are modelled on Theocritus, " Idylls," i. 66–69, and Vergil, " Eclogues," x. 9–12. The places mentioned are near the scene of the shipwreck in which King was drowned.

l. 52. *Steep :* either Penmaenmawr or the mountain Kerig-y-Druidion in Denbighshire, the ancient burying-place of the Druids.

l. 53. *Bards :* an ancient Celtic order of minstrels who preserved in their verse the traditions, laws, and religious precepts of their nation. Caesar ascribes these functions to the Druids, and the two classes were certainly closely connected.

l. 54. *Mona :* Isle of Anglesey, a centre of druidism.

*Shaggy :* Anglesey was once thickly wooded.

l. 55. *Deva :* river Dee.

*Wisard :* many British legends and superstitions are associated with the river Dee, partly because it was the ancient boundary between England and North Wales (the shifting of its fords, for instance, was supposed to foretell good and evil fortune to either country) ; it is commonly referred to by the poets as holy or hallowed Dee, and by Spenser as the haunt of magicians. Milton delighted in the old British legends and fables (compare " Comus "), and at one time intended to write an epic on the Arthurian romances.

l. 57. The expression is broken and elliptical, answering

the emotion, and it is uncertain how *for* should be
construed.

l. 58–63. *The Muse :* Calliope, the muse of epic song,
was the mother of Orpheus, the mythical poet (cp.
" L'Allegro," ll. 145–150, note) ; Orpheus was torn
to pieces by the Thracian Maenads, and his head,
thrown into the Hebrus, was borne down to the sea
and across to Lesbos, the isle of poets (cp. " Paradise
Lost," vii. 32 *seq.*, where Milton retells the story,
identifying himself with Orpheus).

    *Enchanting :* alluding to the magic power of Orpheus'
song.

    *Rout :* rabble (used of either a pack of animals or
disorderly crowd of people).

P. 87, l. 64. *What boots it :* of what avail is it ?

l. 65. *Shepherd's trade :* poetry.

l. 66. *Meditate :* cp. " Comus," l. 547, note.

l. 67. *Use :* are wont (now confined to the preterite,
" used to ") ; cp. l. 136.

l. 69. *Neaera :* " De Neaera " is the title of one of
Buchanan's Latin love elegies, which Milton had
imitated in his own " Elegies," v. and vii.

ll. 70–71. The best gloss on these lines is " Paradise
Regained," ii. 227–228 :—

" Of worth, of honour, glory and popular fame,
  Rocks whereon greatest men have oftest wrecked " ;
and iii. 25–28 :—

" Fame and glory, glory the reward
  That sole excites to high attempts the flame
  Of most erected spirits, most temper'd pure
  Etherial, who all other pleasures else despise."

    *Clear :* pure, illustrious, exalted (Latin, *clarus*).

    *Raise :* rouse, elevate.

l. 73. *Guerdon :* reward, prize.

l. 74. *Blaze :* renown (in the sense of the verb " to
blaze abroad," which means " to proclaim as with a
trumpet ").

l. 75. *I.e.* Atropos (cp. " An Epitaph on the Marchioness
of Winchester," l. 28).

l. 76. *But not the praise :* The verb is supplied, by zeugma,
from " slits."

l. 77. *Phoebus :* Apollo, introduced as the god of prophecy and of poetry. Touching the ear was in classical
times a gesture of admonishment ; Vergil (" Eclogues,"
vi. 3–4) says that when he was venturing out of his

pastoral strains into heroic song Apollo twitched his ear to remind him of the humbler nature of his poetic gift.

ll. 79–80. *Nor . . . nor :* co-ordinate clauses with the common verb " lies."

*Foil :* thin sheet of metal placed behind a gem to throw it into relief.

*Set off : i.e.* in which it is set off.

ll. 81–84. As ruler of gods and men Jupiter sees and judges all things, watches over truth and justice, and is invoked as witness to all oaths.

*By :* near, before.

*Witness :* the root meaning of the word is " knowledge."

l. 85. *Arethuse :* Arethusa (cp. " Arcades," ll. 29–31), the Sicilian spring to which Theocritus refers in his first Idyll and which thus typifies Theocritean pastoral poetry.

l. 86. *Mincius :* the river near which Vergil was born and which he describes in his seventh Eclogue.

l. 88. *I.e.* but now I resume the humbler pastoral style.

*Oat :* cp. " Comus," l. 345, note.

l. 89. *Herald of the sea :* Triton (cp. " Comus," l. 873, note).

l. 90. *In Neptune's plea :* in Neptune's defence (against the charge of being responsible for the death of Lycidas).

l. 91. *Felon :* cruel, murderous.

l. 96. *Hippotades :* Aeolus, son of Hippotes, who kept the winds in a cavern of his island.

P. 88, l. 99. *Panope :* one of the Nereids, who befriended sailors (cp. " Comus," l. 835, note).

l. 101. An eclipse was of evil omen.

l. 103. *Camus :* river god of the Cam, representing Cambridge University.

l. 105. *Figures dim :* mysterious symbolical figures.

l. 106. *I.e.* the hyacinth (cp. " Death of a Fair Infant," ll. 23–27, note). Ovid, telling the story (" Metamorphoses," x. 162 *seq.*), adds that Apollo " inscribed his very groans on the leaves, and the flower bore the marks, AI, AI, letters of lamentation, written thereon."

l. 107. *Pledge :* something valuable and dear, especially a child (cp. Latin, *pignus*).

l. 109. *I.e.* St. Peter (see Luke v.).

ll. 110–111. Matt. xvi. 19. That there were two keys was a tradition of the Church.

*Amain :* with force, violently.

l. 112. *Mitred :* as first bishop of the Church.

l. 113. *King* had entered into holy orders, or was preparing to.

l. 114. *Milton* himself had declined to enter the Church merely for a living or other worldly reason.

l. 115. " He that entereth not by the door into the sheepfold, but climbeth up by some other way, the same is a thief and a robber " (John x.). Milton distinguishes three types of worldly clergy : the low-minded who *creep* into the church for the sake of a comfortable living ; the bold and confident persons who thrust (*intrude*) into the church ; and the ambitious who *climb* into it (see Ruskin, " Sesame and Lilies ").

l. 116. Cp. " Comus," l. 642, note. *Care :* charge, duty.

l. 117. *I.e.* grab ecclesiastical emoluments. The shearing feast was an agricultural festival like harvest home.

l. 119. *Blind mouths :* so completely sensual as to be mentally and spiritually blind, as though rudimentary forms of life moving without intelligence ; the passionate contempt expressed throughout the passage culminates in this singularly violent figure. Ruskin (" Sesame and Lilies ") observes, " those two monosyllables express the precisely accurate contraries of right character in the two great offices of the Church—those of bishop and pastor. A 'Bishop' means 'a person who sees.' A 'Pastor' means 'a person who feeds.' The most un-bishoply character a man can have is therefore to be Blind. The most unpastoral is, instead of feeding, to want to be fed,—to be a Mouth.''

l. 120. *Sheep-hook :* emblem of the pastoral charge.

ll. 120–121. Milton in his prose writings often animadverts on the ignorance of the clergy.

l. 122. *What recks it them ? :* what does it matter to them ? (cp. " Comus," l. 404).

*Are sped :* have succeeded, prospered.

l. 123. *When they list :* implying that they preached when it pleased them.

*Lean :* thin-toned.

*Flashy :* tasteless.

l. 124. *Scrannel :* thin, meagre.

l. 126. *Rank :* corrupt, poisonous (doctrine).

l. 128. *Grim wolf :* Church of Rome.

l. 129. *And nothing said :* One of the charges made against Laud and his party was that they were in sympathy

178

with or at best indifferent to the increase in England of Romish practices and beliefs.

P. 89, l. 130. *Engine :* weapon.

ll. 130–131. Milton in the note prefixed to the poem in 1645 remarks that he had foretold " the ruine of our corrupted Clergy then in their height," but he would not have claimed foreknowledge of exactly how this was to be brought about ; those who find in these two long-suffering lines of " Lycidas " a prediction of the doings of the Long Parliament (the *two-handed engine* being the two Houses), or the execution of Laud or the King, or other events of the Civil War, forget that Milton regarded himself as a poetic prophet and not as an Old Moore. Of the innumerable interpretations the best is that the two-handed engine is the sword of justice or vengeance of God, its merit being that it tells us no more than Milton's verse.

l. 132. Once again, as at l. 85 *seq.*, Milton indicates his return to the gentler mood and manner of the Theocritean elegy. He invokes Alpheus as the lover of Arethusa (cp. " Arcades," ll. 29–31). ~~See 143.~~

l. 136. *Use :* frequent, haunt.

l. 137. *Shades :* tree-shaded places.
*Wanton :* unrestrained.

l. 138. *Swart star :* swarthy star, viz. Sirius or Dog Star, which was associated with the burning heat of August.
*Looks :* used in an astrological sense to express the influence exercised by the aspects of the stars (cp. " Nativity Ode," l. 71 ; " Arcades," l. 51).

l. 139. *Quaint :* daintily made (cp. " Nativity Ode," l. 198, note).

l. 141. *Purple :* empurple ; " purple " for Milton has the classical sense of " any splendid colouring."

ll. 142–150. The catalogue of flowers is a regular feature of the pastoral ; a much-revised passage in Milton's manuscript.

l. 142. *Rathe :* early.
*Forsaken :* neglected, both because the primrose lives in the shade and because it appears before the sun has gained in strength ; the cancelled version in the Trinity MS. is—

" Bring the rathe primrose that unwedded dies
Colouring the pale cheeke of uninjoyd love,"
lines inspired by " The Winter's Tale," IV. III. 122–124 :—

“ pale primroses
That die unmarried, ere they can behold
Bright Phœbus in his strength.”

l. 143.  *Crow-toe :* wild hyacinth or bluebell.

l. 144.  *Freakt :* freckled.

l. 146.  *Woodbine :* was the name for both the wild con-volvulus and the honeysuckle.

*Well-attir'd :* as Keightley observes, Cowper's line is the best comment : “ Copious of flowers, the wood-bine ” (“ Task,” vi. 162).

l. 148.  *Sad :* sober. The original Trinity MS. reading is, “ And every bud that sorrow's liverie weares.”

l. 149.  *Amaranthus :* (i) a legendary flower reputed never to fade, and so an emblem of immortality (cp. “ Paradise Lost,” iii. 353–355) ; (ii) a genus including prince's feather and love-lies-bleeding.

l. 151.  *Laureate :* crowned with the poetic laurel.

*Hearse :* bier.

l. 154.  *Shores :* substituted in Trinity MS. for “ floods.” Shores cannot be said to “ wash far away.”  Taken in connection with “ sounding seas ” (deep seas) and in the light of the original reading, the word clearly means the “ shallow water of the shore,” a sense that was then current (cp. *shore,* l. 183, and “ Il Penseroso,” l. 75, note). The idea is carried on in the contrast between being sunk in the seas beyond the stormy Hebrides and sleeping beside St. Michael's Mount.

l. 157.  *Whelming :* overturning, engulfing, ruining. Chaucer uses the word for the downward turning of Fortune's wheel (“ Troilus and Criseyde,” i. 139). Original reading, “ humming.”

l. 158.  *Monstrous world :* world of monsters (cp. “ Comus,” l. 533).

l. 159.  *Moist vows :* votive offerings to Neptune (cp. “ Trans. Fifth Ode of Horace,” ll. 13–16 and note). The meaning is that Lycidas has not been preserved by our prayers and votive offerings for his safety at sea.

l. 160.  *Sleep'st :* contrasting with “ where'er thy bones are hurled.”

*By the fable of Bellerus old :  i.e.* beside the scene of the fabulous history of Bellerus. In the Trinity MS. Bellerus is substituted for Corineus (see “ Comus,” l. 824, note), after whom Cornwall was said to have been named. Bellerus does not figure in British legend ;

## NOTES

perhaps Milton invented the name from Bellerium, the
Roman name for Cornwall.

l. 161. *Guarded mount :* St. Michael's Mount, a large rock
in Mount's Bay near Land's End, which is connected
with the shore at low water : it was originally the site
of a monastery and later of a fortress.

*Great Vision :* the apparition of St. Michael, once
seen at a point on the rock where a stone seat is still
called St. Michael's Chair.

l. 162. *Namancos and Bayona's hold :* fortresses (holds) on
the north coast of Spain and in a direct line with Land's
End across the open sea. Camden notes what was
commonly remarked during the long national struggle
with Spain, " there is no other place in this island
(except Land's End) that looks towards Spain."

l. 163. *Angel :* St. Michael.

l. 164. *Ye dolphins :* Referring to the story of Arion, the
Greek poet and musician. His life being threatened
by the crew of the ship on which he was sailing, Arion
threw himself into the sea and was brought safely to
shore on the back of a dolphin that had been charmed
by his song.

*Waft :* convey either through the air or, as here, over
water.

l. 166. *Your sorrow :* cause of your sorrow.

P. 90, l. 168. *Day-star :* sun.

l. 170. *Tricks :* a metaphor from " dressing " the hair
(cp. " Il Penseroso," l. 123, note).

*Ore :* gold.

*Spangled :* glittering (cp. " Nativity Ode," l. 21).

l. 176. *Unexpressive :* inexpressible.

l. 183. *Genius :* local god (" Nativity Ode," st. xx.,
note).

l. 184. *Thy large recompense :* generous recompense to
you.

*Good :* propitious (Latin, *bonus*).

l. 186. *Uncouth swain :* unknown and unskilled poet.

l. 188. *Tender :* delicate.

*Various quills :* various musical pipes (referring perhaps to the various moods and styles of the poem).

l. 189. *Doric :* Theocritus and his fellow pastoralists
wrote in the Doric dialect.

l. 190. *Stretch'd out all the hills :* Explained by the last
line of Vergil's first Eclogue,' ' And the shadows fall
larger from the high hills."

**l.** 192. *twitch'd :* pulled together.

*Sonnets.*

(Any editor of Milton's sonnets must be indebted to J. S. Smart's edition. My introductory note is founded on his masterly treatment of the topics discussed, and much of my commentary on the text derives from his.)

In nothing was Milton more individual and at the same time more scholarly than in his use of the sonnet. The sonnet was a popular form with Elizabethan writers, but this literary fashion had ceased in the early years of the new century as abruptly as it had begun ; by Milton's day the form had come to be entirely neglected. As Smart says, " Milton almost alone cultivated the sonnet in the middle of the seventeenth century." Yet in doing this he was not resuming a broken tradition but starting a fresh one in English literature ; for he was prompted and taught not by the Elizabethan but by the Italian sonnet writers. The difference shows, when Milton's sonnets are compared with those of his Elizabethan predecessors, in the wider range of subjects and the more exacting metrical structure.

The sonnet is designed to convey a single idea, mood or experience that can be perfectly expressed within the compass of fourteen lines. It is an intimate and subjective form of poetry, the poet speaking in his own person and confiding his thoughts and feelings to the reader. From the beginning it was the favourite medium of love poetry, frequently in a series of sonnets that told the story, real or imaginary, of a particular experience in love ; Dante had so used it to commemorate his love for Beatrice, and Petrarch his love for Laura. It was Petrarch whom succeeding love poets followed as their master, and it is Petrarch whom Milton imitates in his youthful sequence of love sonnets in Italian. The sonnet, however, was not confined by Italian writers to this one theme, but was put to many other similar social uses : to express friendship and admiration as well as love ; sometimes to express personal enmity and scorn ; for the exchange of literary compliments, or to convey a social invitation as in Milton's sonnets to Laurence and Skinner ; for the praise of public men, as in Milton's sonnets to Fairfax, Cromwell, and Vane ; to express opinion on some political event, as in Milton's sonnet " On the Late Massacre in Piedmont," or simply to record the poet's more private meditations. There was in fact no occasion in public or private life that might not be commemorated or commented on, whether in a single sonnet or in a connected series.

The form had been used on occasion for one or other of these varied purposes by individual Elizabethan poets, but the Elizabethans generally regarded the sonnet as a love poem and love is the theme of the bulk of their productions in this kind. Milton with his knowledge of Italian literature was the first English poet fully to appreciate the scope of the medium and to avail himself of all its uses ; the consequent range and variety of subjects in his sonnets is not surprising when we remember that during the period most of them were written he was mainly occupied with other tasks, and the sonnet provided the one form in which his poetical energy might conveniently find an outlet. Although he was more learned in the history of the sonnet than his English predecessors, or perhaps for this very reason, his sonnets are far less " literary," less prone than theirs to the conventional phrases, images, and ideas of the genre ; each one is a personal and characteristic utterance, arising from a real occasion and perfectly adapted in manner to the particular topic or the person addressed. Various and familiar, they reveal his character and personality more intimately and completely than any other lines written either by himself or his friends ; which means that they perform the proper function of the sonnet.

The metrical structure of Milton's sonnets equally distinguishes them from those of the Elizabethans, and proves the impulse and direction to have come from Italian poetry. The regular Italian sonnet contains two quatrains and two tercets, the main break or division coming after the second quatrain. The eight lines forming the quatrains have two rhymes only between them, and so are bound together to form the first half of the poem ; in the arrangement of these two rhymes Petrarch preferred the _enclosed_ order (*a b b a, a b b a*), which is the scheme always followed by Milton, but Italian poets also used the _alternate_ order (*a b a b*) and other variations. The tercets are similarly linked together by rhyme ; but there is much

more variety in the rhyme schemes, since these six
concluding lines may contain either two or three rhymes
between them. One point especially to note is that
it is rare, though by no means unknown, for a poem to
end in a couplet ; when this occurs in a Petrarchan
sonnet the couplet is linked by rhyme to a preceding
line, the invariable rhyme scheme for the tercets then
being *c d d, d c c*. Sometimes, but this is even rarer
in Italian verse, we find a concluding couplet that is
separated from the rest of the poem by a fresh rhyme
and preceded by a distinct metrical pause ; this device
is employed where the poet aims at an emphatic conclusion to the poem, and a good example is to be seen
in Milton's sonnet to Cromwell. Yet even when this
occurs, the main allotment of rhymes is the same—two
for the first eight lines and three for the remaining
lines ; the rhyme scheme in Milton's sonnet to Cromwell, for instance, is *a b b a, a b b a, c d d c, e e*. Turning
now to the form chiefly favoured by Elizabethan
sonneteers and adopted by Shakespeare, we find not
only that the concluding couplet is the invariable and
distinctive feature but that it is combined with a
metrical scheme unknown to Italian poetry. It consists of three pairs of alternate rhymes and a concluding
rhyming couplet (*a b a b, c d c d, e f e f, g g*) ; not only
are there seven rhymes as against the four or five o
the Italian sonnet, but the poem falls into three
quatrains and a couplet instead of two quatrains and
two tercets. This is something quite different from the
Italian sonnet or from anything to be found in Milton.

The importance of this question of structure lies in
the relation between the form and content of the poem.
In the regular Petrarchan sonnet the single idea to be
expressed is unfolded by stages that correspond to the
fixed metrical divisions of the poem. Grammatically
this meant that a sentence or main clause was concluded
with the end of each quatrain, and a new sentence
began with the tercets (a further rule was that all minor
pauses required by the sense should occur at the end
of a line, as in Pope's verse, and never inside a line) ;
the main pause or division in the poem naturally
came at the end of the eighth line, between quatrains
and tercets. The effect of this strict metrical and
grammatical arrangement was to force the poet to
organise his thought in a certain manner, which fre-

quently produced one logical form in particular ; the idea was stated in the first quatrain, and more completely developed in the second ; then the first tercet introduced a " turn or suspense," an unexpected change in the thought or mood ; and the final tercet summed up the intellectual or emotional movement of the whole poem, bringing it to a quiet close. This procedure, particularly the sudden change of direction in the middle of the poem, was not a prescribed rule or law of the Italian sonnet, as critics in the nineteenth century made it out to be ; many Italian sonnets unfold the idea in a straightforward manner, without any " turn or suspense." Nevertheless this frequent type serves admirably to illustrate the way in which the strict Petrarchan form determines the whole character of the poem.

In Sonnets II, III, V, XI and XVII Milton adheres strictly to the form established by Petrarch. But in other sonnets (e.g. XII, XIII, XIV, XVI) he departs from these rules : the divisions of the metrical form and of the thought are not brought into strict agreement ; pauses and breaks occur in any part of the line instead of only at the end ; and a sentence is sometimes carried over from the second quatrain into the first tercet, ignoring the customary break at the end of the eighth line. By these practices Milton was not, however, departing from Italian tradition ; still less was he reverting to the methods of the Elizabethan sonneteers. At all points he was following Italian poets of the sixteenth century, particularly Giovanni della Casa, who had reacted against the strict uniformity imposed on the sonnet by Petrarch ; these innovators aimed to make the sonnet more of a single unit, concealing rather than emphasising the metrical divisions and " drawing quatrains and tercets closer together in one fabric." It was a reform of a similar kind to that of English poets at the Romantic Revival who, reacting against the enclosed couplet of the eighteenth century, introduced the *enjambement* or run-on line and wrote their verse in continuous paragraphs. Milton's imitation of these methods is one further example of the important effect of Italian poetry on the development of his art ; for the metrical variations and general handling of the verse in the sonnets composed on the model of Della Casa, especially the method of carrying sentences freely from one line into another, are characteristic of Milton's epic manner and illustrate the transition from the earlier to the mature style of " Paradise Lost."

### Sonnet I (1629)

The symbolism of this sonnet has a long poetic tradition in mediaeval literature, Milton's immediate source being " The Cuckoo and the Nightingale," once attributed to Chaucer : the nightingale is the friend of love and the cuckoo the enemy, and those lovers who hear the nightingale at the beginning of May (the season of love) will have good fortune, but those who first hear the cuckoo will suffer disappointment.

P. 91, l. 4.   *The jolly hours :* cp. " Comus," l. 986, note.

l. 6.   *Shallow :*   thin in sound, unmusical (Bacon's " Sylva " :  " It must needs make the sound perfecter, and not so shallow and jarring ").

### Sonnet II (December 9, 1631)

This sonnet was written in the winter before Milton left Cambridge.  It appears in the Trinity MS. along with two drafts of the letter to an unknown friend (see " Life "), who had apparently accused him of an idle love of learning and advised him to adopt a profession. The letter concludes, " Yet that you may see that I am something suspicious of myself and do take notice of a certain belatedness in me, I am bolder to send you some of my nightward thoughts some while since, because they come in not altogether unfitly, made up in a Petrarchian stanza."

P. 91, l. 3.   *Career :* speed.

l. 4.   And yet, besides his Latin poems, Milton had written the " Nativity Ode " and other English poems.

ll. 5–6.   Milton had a very youthful appearance, which may have been one reason why he was known at Cambridge as " The Lady of Christ's."  Long after, in the " Defensio Secunda," he wrote, " Though I am more than forty years old, there is scarcely any one to whom I do not appear ten years younger than I am."

l. 7.   Cp. " Lycidas," ll. 3–5.

l. 8.   *More timely-happy spirits :*  minds maturing earlier.

l. 13.   *Grace :*  in the theological sense of the favour of God, giving inspiration and strength.

## *Sonnet III* (1642)

In the Trinity MS. there is an alternative deleted title, "On his door when the city expected an assault." After the first battle of the Civil War at Edgehill, the King marched from Oxford on London, his cavalry under Rupert pillaging as they went ; on November 12th a Parliamentary force was defeated at Brentford, which was taken and sacked ; everyone expected that London would now fall into the Royalists' hands and suffer a like fate. The next day, however, the King retreated before a Parliamentary army drawn up at Turnham Green, and the city was saved. Whether the sonnet was written, as is generally assumed, during the actual days of alarm and suspense in London, or whether from "emotion recollected in tranquillity," the mere writing of it shows, as Smart says, that Milton "remained calm and detached . . . the suggestion that the sonnet was actually placed on the door of his dwelling, to placate some Royalist commander, need not be taken seriously : we are in the presence of a poetical situation, not of a practical expedient." The poem is indeed a "witty" poem in the old and fuller sense of the word, and that is what a sonnet should be.

P. 92, l. 1. *Colonel :* trisyllabic.

l. 2. *Chance :* personification of the person's fortune.

    *Seize :* cp. "The Passion," l. 10, note.

l. 3. *Honour :* chivalry (cp. "Comus," l. 27, note).

l. 5. *Charms :* Used with a characteristic play on the etymological meaning of the word, "verses having occult power, spells."

l. 6. *Gentle :* pertaining to a gentleman in the old sense of a man of birth and breeding (cp. "Arcades," l. 26).

l. 8. *Clime :* cp. "Arcades," l. 24, note.

l. 10. *The great Emathian conqueror :* Alexander the Great. Emathia was the name of a district of Macedon, used for Macedon itself. When the Thebans rose in revolt in 335 B.C. Alexander took Thebes by storm, slaughtered the inhabitants, and razed the city to the ground. Tradition said that he spared only the house once occupied by the poet Pindar.

l. 12. *The repeated air :* the repetition of the song (a Latin passive participle construction similar to "Comus," l. 48).

l. 13. Plutarch in his "Life of Lysander" says that when, in 404 B.C., the Spartans and their allies had captured

Athens and were discussing whether to " pull down
the city and turn the country into a sheep-run," one
of them began singing the first chorus in Euripides'
" Electra " ; " they were all melted with compassion,
and it seemed to be a cruel deed to destroy and pull
down a city which had been so famous and produced
such men."

## Sonnet IV (1642–1645)

The girl to whom this sonnet is addressed is not
mentioned by Milton's biographers and it is idle to
speculate about her identity in the absence of all
evidence.

P. 93, l. 5. *Mary :* Luke x. 38–42.
 *Ruth :* Ruth i.

l. 6. *Overween :* are wise in their own conceit.

l. 7. *Fret their spleen :* are spitefully vexed. The girl was
evidently thought precocious and priggish by her
" elders and betters," and duly disapproved of.

l. 8. *Ruth :* there was plenty of precedent for thus
rhyming words of the same sound but different
meaning.

l. 9. *Care :* dutiful purpose.
 *Attends :* is heedful.

ll. 10–14. There is of course allusion to the parable of
the ten virgins (Matt. xxv.).

ll. 13–14. *Passes . . . hast gain'd :* vivid present for
future tense.

## Sonnet V (1643–1645)

Lady Margaret Lee was the eldest daughter of Sir
James Lee, who had been Lord Chief Justice, had been
created Earl of Marlborough by Charles I, and had
held for brief periods towards the end of his life the
successive posts of Lord High Treasurer and Lord
President of the Council. He retired from the latter
office in December 1628, whilst the Parliament was
still in being that had presented Charles with the
Petition of Right and defined the political issues on
which the Civil War was later to be fought. Edward
Phillips tells us that, after Mary Powell had left Milton
in the summer of 1642, " Our author, now as it were a
single man again, made it his chief diversion now and
then in an evening to visit the Lady Margaret Lee. . . .
This lady being a woman of great wit and ingenuity,

had a particular honour for him, and took much delight in his company, as likewise her husband Captain Hobson." Hobson and his wife were living at this time in Aldersgate Street, near to Milton. Lady Margaret must have been faced, as so many others at that time, with the problem of divided loyalties ; for whereas her family adopted the Royalist cause, her husband enlisted in the Parliamentary army, rising to the rank of colonel. Since it is as her father's daughter that Milton gracefully pays his tribute to the Lady Margaret, we are led to suppose that her political sympathies were similar to his ; and Milton makes it appear that the Earl had been among those who would have had the King resolve all dissensions by a wiser and more liberal policy, meeting the just demands of his subjects. In construction the sonnet is a model of its kind—the octet presenting the noble portrait of the father, the sestet bringing home the compliment to the daughter.

P. 93, l. 3. *Unstain'd with gold or fee :* It is of interest that Sir James Lee, as Lord Chief Justice, presided over the House of Lords during the trial of the Lord Chancellor Francis Bacon on charges of taking bribes in the administration of justice.

ll. 5–6. The Earl died on March 14th, 1629, four days after the dissolution of the Parliament that had first brought Charles to task. The dissolution, which occurred amid tumultuous scenes, marked a complete break between Charles and the Parliamentary leaders and was the beginning of the eleven years of personal government leading up to the Civil War. It would appear that Milton was told by Lady Margaret herself, in those reminiscences referred to in the sonnet, that the news of these ominous events had hastened her father's end.

l. 6. *Dishonest :* shameful, inglorious (Latin, *inhonestus*).

l. 7. *At Chaeronea :* In 338 B.C. the Macedonians under Philip, father of Alexander the Great, utterly defeated the allied armies of Athens and Thebes. This was the end of Greek liberty.

l. 8. Isocrates, the Athenian rhetorician, had exhorted the Athenians to get rid of the corruptions and defects in their political system by re-establishing the former democracy, and had appealed to Philip of Macedon to reconcile the differences of the Greek states in order to lead their united forces against the barbarian Persians. In 338 B.C. he was in his ninety-eighth year and still vigorous, but the battle of Chaeronea destroyed all his political hopes, and tradition said that he died four days later from voluntary starvation. It will be seen how much appropriate meaning, both personal and political, Milton has packed into this historical parallel.

### Sonnet VI (c. 1645)

"Tetrachordon," published on March 4th, 1645, was the fourth of Milton's tracts on divorce. The angry hostility aroused among ordinary men by his views on marriage is summed up by James Howell in his "Familiar Letters": "But that opinion of a poor shallow-brained puppy, who upon any cause of disaffection would have men to have a privilege to change their wives or repudiate them, deserves to be hissed at rather than confuted; for nothing can tend more to usher in all confusion and beggary throughout the world." What Milton, however, took harder than such common contempt was the denouncing of his views by leaders of Puritan thought. Herbert Palmer, a member of the Assembly of Divines, declared in a sermon before the Houses of Parliament that among the doctrines which should not be tolerated by the State was that new theory of divorce, "of which a wicked book is abroad and uncensured, though deserving to be burnt, whose author has been so impudent as to set his name to it and dedicate it to yourselves."

P. 94, l. 1. *Tetrachord:* A tetrachord is a scale-series of four notes, a half-octave; the point of Milton's title was to suggest that he had harmonised the four authoritative biblical passages on the question of divorce—in Genesis, Deuteronomy, St. Matthew, and First Corinthians.

l. 7. *Spelling false:* cp. "Il Penseroso," l. 170.
*Mile-End Green:* Mile End was at the eastern limit of London.

ll. 8–9. Englishmen had become acquainted during the Civil War with many Scotch names that seemed to them harsh and uncouth.
*Colkitto:* a lieutenant to the Duke of Montrose.
*Galasp:* George Gillespie, a Covenanter and member of the Assembly of Divines, may be intended. (For the feeling behind these references to the Scotch, cp. Sonnet X.)

l. 10. *Rugged :* a deleted MS. reading is " barbarous."

*Like mouths :* equally barbarous mouths.

*Sleek :* smooth.

l. 11. *Quintilian :* the classical authority on style, which he examines exhaustively as one aspect of the art of oratory ; he has much to say on elegance and the choice of words for reasons of euphony. It was a commonplace among classical writers that foreign names were to be avoided on account of their harsh sounds.

l. 12. *Thy age, like ours :* thy age did not, like ours.

*Sir John Cheek :* first Professor of Greek at Cambridge, and afterwards tutor to Edward VI. He played a distinguished part in the introduction of the New Learning into England.

### Sonnet VII

The four divorce tracts belong to the group of tracts on what Milton called " domestic " liberty, which were all written during the period 1643–1645 and include the " Tractate on Education " and the " Areopagitica." He describes their purpose in the Second Defence :—

" When, therefore, I perceived that there are three species of liberty which are essential to the happiness of social life—religious, domestic, and civil ; and as I had already written concerning the first, and the magistrates were strenuously active in obtaining the third, I determined to turn my attention to the second or the domestic species. As this seemed to involve three material questions, the conditions of the conjugal tie, the education of children, and the free publication of thoughts, I made them objects of distinct consideration."

P. 95, ll. 5–7. Ovid (" Metamorphoses," vi. 331 *seq.*) relates that when Latona, with her new-born twins Apollo and Diana, was fleeing from the wrath of Juno, she came into the country of Lycia, and suffering from thirst went to drink from a lake ; but some peasants prevented her, and reviled both her and her children. As a punishment Jove transformed them into frogs.

*In fee :* as a fief.

l. 11. This distinction is a commonplace with those Latin writers from whom Milton, as a good son of the

Renaissance, learned "the known rules of ancient liberty."

l. 12. This is the lesson that Milton perpetually draws from the fact that the Puritans failed to establish the liberty for which they fought.

### Sonnet VIII (1646)

The position of Henry Lawes in the musical world of the time and his early friendship with Milton have already been explained (see Introduction to " Arcades " and " Comus "). The Civil War put an end to masques and to the musical life of the Court in which Lawes had taken so large a part ; but Lawes continued his work as a teacher of music, and his reputation as a composer steadily grew. Throughout he remained a steadfast Royalist. In 1648 he published a volume of " Choice Psalms," which opens with a loyal dedication to the King, then a prisoner. His publications also include three volumes of " Airs and Dialogues," the first of which appeared in 1653 ; among the poets whose songs are set to music in this volume are Waller, Herrick, Lovelace, Carew, Randolph, and Davenant.

Milton's sonnet was first published among other poetic tributes prefixed to the " Choice Psalms." In the Trinity MS. are two drafts in Milton's own hand : the first (a rough draft, deleted) has the title " To my Friend, Mr. Henry Lawes," and the date " February 9, 1646 " ; the second, a fair copy, has the title " To Mr. Henry Lawes on the publishing of his Airs." But the " Airs " were in fact not published until 1653 ; it has therefore been conjectured that there was a proposal to publish the " Airs " in 1646, which was allowed to drop and remained in abeyance for seven years. Meanwhile Milton allowed Lawes to use his lines on publishing the " Choice Psalms." Whatever the explanation of this particular puzzle, it remains clear that political differences did not touch the lifelong friendship between Milton and Lawes—although Milton was soon to publish two violent attacks on the King, to whom Lawes had boldly declared his loyalty and devotion.

P. 95, l. 1. *Measur'd :* cp. " Arcades," l. 71, note.

l. 2. *Span :* measure.

l. 4. *Midas' ears :* Ovid (" Metamorphoses," xi. 146 *seq.*) relates how when Midas, King of Phrygia, preferred

NOTES

the piping of Pan to the music of Apollo, the god
punished him by giving him an ass's ears.

*Committing :* combining (a Latinism) ; marginal MS.
reading, " misjoining."

*Short and long :* metrical quantities.

l. 5. *Exempts :* singles out.

l. 8. *Air :* melody.

l. 10. *Priest of Phoebus' quire :* ministering to poets.

l. 11. *Their : i.e.* the poets'.

*Story :* a marginal note appended to the sonnet as
published in the " Choice Psalms " says, " The story
of Ariadne set by him to music." A poem by Cart-
wright entitled " Complaint of Ariadne " was set to
music by Lawes.

l. 13. *His Casella :* Dante tells (Purgatorio," ii. 76–117)
that among the souls he met on the Mount of Purgatory
was his friend Casella, a musician who had set some of
Dante's canzoni to music. The poet asks his friend to
sing, " if a new law take not from thee memory or
skill in the song of love," and the spirit responds by
singing one of Dante's songs. Dante addresses him as
" My Casella."

*Sonnet IX*

Catherine Thomason was the wife of George
Thomason, a bookseller and publisher, and a man of
knowledge and cultivation. He is remembered for his
great collection of some 22,000 pamphlets printed in
London during the Civil War and the Commonwealth,
which is now in the British Museum and is one of the
chief sources of our knowledge of the period. This
collection contains several of Milton's tracts, inscribed
as given him by the author ; and there is other evidence
of the friendly association of the two men. Thomason's
wife, Catherine, was the niece of Henry Fetherstone,
also a well-known bookseller and publisher, to whom
Thomason had been originally apprenticed. She was
brought up by her uncle, acquiring from him a love
of literature and becoming a woman of considerable
learning. Thomason's devotion to his wife is proved
by the reference to her in his will, written twenty years
after her death ; and no doubt Milton's sonnet was as
much an act of friendship to Thomason as a tribute to
his wife.

The chief Scripture texts in Milton's mind in writing

the sonnet were Romans vii. 24 ; Revelation xiv. 13
and xxii. 1, 17 ; Acts x. 4 ; Psalms xxxvi. 8, 9.

*Sonnet X* (? 1646)

This is a form of the Italian sonnet known as the
*sonetto caudato* or *tailed sonnet.* The tail or coda consists
of a half-line and a couplet, and an indefinite number
of tails might be appended to the normal fourteen lines.
The form is generally reserved for humorous and
satirical subjects.

Milton as an Independent is here satirising the
Presbyterian members of the Westminster Assembly of
Divines, whom he considered responsible for the new
religious tyranny the country was in danger of being
subjected to. When the Long Parliament in 1643
resolved to abolish the episcopal form of Church government it set up the Assembly of Divines to prepare a new
constitution for a State Church which should be nearer
that of the Church of Scotland and other Reformed
Churches. A large majority, led by the four Scotch
divines appointed to the Assembly, proved to be in
favour of establishing a Presbyterian Church, to which
all persons should be made to conform. This proposal,
however, was fought tooth and nail by the group of
five Independent ministers in the Assembly, led by
Thomas Goodwin, who saw that a uniform Presbyterian rule would be even more tyrannous than the
rule of the bishops they had just rid themselves of ;
they insisted on the rights of the individual conscience
and on a certain measure of religious toleration. The
struggle, which went on during the years 1644–1646,
was not confined to the Assembly debates but became
a press warfare. Of the numerous pamphlets that
appeared, the most important on the Independent side
was a joint manifesto, the " Apologetical Narration,"
signed by Goodwin and his four fellow ministers ; of
the Presbyterian champions four are named by Milton
in the sonnet.

P. 96, l. 1. *Prelate Lord :* bishops.

l. 2. *Liturgy :* the Anglican liturgy was prohibited under
penalties in 1644.

l. 3. *Plurality :* the practice of holding more than one
ecclesiastical living or benefice. In the " History of
Britain " Milton says that the Presbyterians, " those
great rebukers of non-residence . . . were not ashamed

194

to be seen quickly pluralists and non-residents themselves."

l. 5. The Presbyterians demanded that those found
guilty of heresy by the Church courts should be
punished by the civil magistrate. For blasphemy the
penalty was death.

l. 7. *Classic hierarchy :* *Classis* was the word used in
England for presbytery, the ruling body of ministers
and elders for an ecclesiastical district. Thus when
London was formally presbyterianised at the end of
1645 it was divided into twelve *classes.* "Hierarchy"
means government by priests organised in grades, and
suggests once more the similarity of the presbyterian
to the episcopal system.

l. 8. *Mere A. S. :* Adam Stuart, a Scotch divine, who was
not a member of the Assembly but published several
pamphlets against the Independents during 1644, one
of which is signed only by his initials.

*Rotherford :* Samuel Rutherford, Professor of Divinity
at St. Andrews, was one of the Scotch members of the
Assembly ; he had published two tracts in the general
warfare, "The Due Right of Presbyteries " and " The
Divine Right of Church Government." In 1649 he
was to publish his " Free Disputation against Pretended
Liberty of Conscience," which proposes nothing less
than a Presbyterian Inquisition to deal with heretics.

P. 97, ll. 9–11. These lines refer to the five Independents
in the Assembly.

l. 12. *Edwards :* Thomas Edwards was a preacher in
London, well known as the author of several popular
treatises on behalf of strict Presbyterianism and against
religious toleration. He replied to the " Apologetical
Narration " of the five Independents in a work entitled
" Antapologia," disparaging his opponents as heretics.
In 1645–1646 he also published " Gangraena : or a
Catalogue of many of the Errors, Heresies, Blasphemies,
and pernicious Practises of the Sectaries of this Time,"
a scurrilous work in which Milton appears as the author
of the divorce tracts.

*Scotch What-d'ye-call :* has been identified as Robert
Baillie, Professor of Divinity at Glasgow University and
the most bitter opponent of the Independents among
the Scotch commissioners in the Assembly. In his
pamphlet " A Dissuasive from the Errors of the Times,"
published in 1645, he freely speaks of Goodwin and his

party as heretics—and Milton incidentally is stigmatised for his divorce pamphlets as in Edwards's " Gangraena."

l. 14. The Council of Trent (1545–1563), which had redefined Roman Catholic doctrine after the Reformation, was a byword amongst Protestants for intrigue and sharp practice. *Packing :* fraudulent, underhand dealing.

l. 15. *Parliament :* Although Presbyterian opinion was also in the ascendant in Parliament, there was an anti-clerical group as well as an influential group of Independents in the House of Commons, and Parliament had more than once rebuked the Assembly of Divines for arrogating too much power and authority to themselves ; however, Milton's appeal to Parliament, like his appeal in the " Areopagitica," is made in hope rather than in confidence, and it was in fact the army that was to decide the issue. If the Scotch Covenanting army had proved indispensable to their English allies, the Presbyterians would have dictated religious terms to the Parliament ; but it was Cromwell who triumphed and with him the cause of the Independents.

l. 17. *Baulk :* spare. Milton at first wrote " Clip ye as close as marginal P——'s ears," the allusion being to William Prynne, who had twice had his ears cropped for publishing anti-prelatical tracts under Laud's régime. Since the beginning of the Long Parliament he had been an ardent pamphleteer in the cause of Presbyterianism, and at the time Milton wrote this line, was engaged in a violent polemic against the Independents. His works were always overloaded with marginal references. On second thoughts Milton decided that Prynne's former sufferings in the cause of freedom were no matter for jest.

l. 18. *Succour :* relieve.

l. 19. *Charge :* accusation.

l. 20. *Presbyter* and *Priest* are both derived from the Greek word *Presbyteros.*

### Sonnet XI (1648)

Sir Thomas Fairfax, commander-in-chief of the Parliamentary forces, was a brave and capable soldier but not, as Milton hoped, a great statesman. By his victories at Marston Moor (1644) and Naseby (1645) he decided the issue of the Civil War, and by the next year he had crushed the Royalist power in every part of England. For two years there was peace, but in 1648 Royalist rebellions broke out simultaneously in several parts of the country, and the Scots, in violation of the Solemn League and Covenant, invaded England in support of Charles. All these risings were quickly suppressed by Fairfax and Cromwell. Fairfax defeated the southern Royalist forces in Kent, and, when they crossed the Thames and seized the fortified town of Colchester, he established a blockade. Colchester surrendered on August 27, 1648, and the rebellion was over. Milton's sonnet appears to have been written during the siege of Colchester and before the Scots were defeated by Cromwell at Preston, August 17th. With the suppression of this rebellion the career of Fairfax was practically ended ; the leadership passed to Cromwell, and it was he who undertook the task, to which Milton points, of reorganising and settling the country for peace.

l. 5. *Virtue :* in the Latin sense of " valour," which is the reading in the text printed by Phillips in his " Life of Milton."

l. 7. *Hydra :* cp. " Comus," l. 605, note.

l. 8. *Imp :* to graft new feathers on the broken feathers of a falcon.

ll. 12–14. The public finances had fallen into a state of utter confusion under the Long Parliament, and charges of mismanagement and fraud were freely made against the Government. In order to raise money, Royalist estates were declared forfeit, and either redeemed by the owner on payment of a proportion of the value, or sold. These transactions naturally resulted in mis-appropriations, extortions, bribery and corruption, and all the evils proper to a wholesale confiscation carried through by a horde of temporary officials and informers. Milton again denounces this period of misrule in the " History of Britain," where he speaks of councils and committees that " fell to huckster the commonwealth ; men for the most part of insatiable hands and noted disloyalty ; the ravening seizure of innumerable thieves in office."

## Sonnet XII (1652)

In the spring of 1652 Parliament appointed a Committee for the Propagation of the Gospel, with instructions to draw up a plan of religious settlement.

The Committee proceeded to examine a scheme laid before it by fifteen ministers, who included three of the Independent ministers praised by Milton in Sonnet X. The most difficult question was the extent of toleration to be allowed Independent preachers and teachers not belonging to the clergy appointed by the State. It was proposed that such teaching should be permitted only in public places after notice given to the magistrates ; and that none should be allowed to speak against the common principles of the Christian religion, which were defined in a list of fifteen fundamental points. In a pamphlet setting forth these proposals the fifteen ministers further recommended that no one should be permitted to speak in public on a religious matter without a certificate from two orthodox ministers; and it was perhaps this last proposal, threatening all liberty of conscience, that specially aroused Milton's indignation. He addressed his protest to Cromwell as the head of the State and as one known to favour the utmost religious freedom. At one of the meetings of the Committee Cromwell had declared " that he had rather that Mahometism were permitted among us than that one of God's children should be persecuted." The sonnet was probably sent to Cromwell personally. It is to be noted that this is the only one of Milton's sonnets that ends in a rhyming couplet.

P. 98, ll. 5–6. The idea is that the servant of the true God has triumphed over the pagan goddess of Fortune.

l. 7. The battle of Preston, in which Cromwell routed the invading Scotch army in 1648 (see Sonnet XI), was fought on the banks of the river Darwen.

l. 8. At Dunbar, September 3, 1650, Cromwell routed the Scots, after which Scotland was practically annexed to the English Commonwealth.

l. 9. *Worcester's laureate wreath :* Cromwell's crowning victory at Worcester, September 3, 1651, when he defeated the Scotch army led by Charles II.

l. 14. Cp. " Lycidas," ll. 114–122. *Maw :* belly.

### Sonnet XIII (July 1652)

Sir Henry Vane was one of the ablest members of the Parliament, and of the Council of State which at this time constituted the Government. He interested himself particularly in foreign affairs and the navy, and at the time the sonnet was written had been particularly engaged in dealing with a crisis in the relations between England and Holland. The two countries had for some time been on the verge of war, and on May 19, 1652, fighting began between the English and Dutch fleets. The Dutch ambassadors, however, still remained in London with a show of negotiating peace. Their conduct was puzzling, and they were suspected of playing for time and of lingering in London as spies. On June 4th the Council of State appointed Vane the first member of a Committee to deal with the situation. On June 30th the ambassadors had received their passports and departed. These events are referred to by Milton in the first half of his sonnet, a copy of which he sent to Vane three days after the ambassadors were dismissed. The latter part of the poem presents Vane as a champion of Milton's own views on religious toleration. Vane was a member of the Westminster Assembly of Divines, and both in that body and in the House of Commons had been a strenuous and consistent advocate of complete freedom of conscience.

P. 98, l. 1. *Young in years :* Vane was forty. He was commonly called Young Sir Henry Vane to distinguish him from his father.

ll. 2–3. To Milton, whose republicanism was inspired and sustained by classical example, the comparison of the English Parliament and Council of State with the Roman Senate was obvious.

*Gowns :* cp. Cicero's dictum, "Arms yield to the toga." Livy makes clear how much was due to the firmness and courage of the Roman Senate in finally repelling the invasions of Pyrrhus, King of Epirus (280–272 B.C.), and of Hannibal (220–182 B.C.).

l. 6. *Drift :* aim, designs.
*Hollow :* false.
*Spell'd :* interpreted.

l. 7. *Upheld :* once decided on.

l. 8. *Nerves :* sinews.

P. 99, l. 9. *Equipage :* equipment, a word used then as " armament," is now for " the whole apparatus of war."

ll. 10–11. In discussing the free State, Milton always emphasises the fundamental distinction between civil and ecclesiastical authority. Each religious congregation has the right to discipline or expel members of its own communion for religious reasons, and the State has the right to punish subjects for offending against the civil laws ; but the magistrate has no authority in affairs of religion, nor should the Church call on the civil power to enforce its judgments ; the confusion of these separate functions has been the cause of endless wars.

l. 12. *Either sword :* civil and spiritual authority. The " civil and spiritual swords " was a common expression, " sword " being used as a symbol of authority and not as a symbol of destruction.

## Sonnet XIV (1655)

During the time Milton was Secretary for Foreign Tongues, one of the most dramatic incidents in foreign affairs was the massacre of the Vaudois and the action taken by Cromwell on their behalf. The Vaudois or Valdenses were regarded as the earliest Protestants. Their founder, Pierre Valdes, taught the simple faith that the Christian life was one of self-denial and charity similar to Christ's. In 1215 the sect was excommunicated, but their doctrines spread in France, Germany, and Bohemia. By the time of the Reformation the movement had declined, but its adherents were still numerous in certain valleys of the Alps, on the borders of France and Italy ; and they were finally organised as a Protestant Church. The sect still exists in its ancient home above the plain of Piedmont. The Dukes of Savoy had done their utmost at the time of the Reformation to extirpate this heretical sect from their territory, but in 1561 freedom of worship was granted to the Vaudois living within a certain restricted area in the upper valleys. By the middle of the following century it was found that the Vaudois had spread outside these limits into the lower valleys, and the Duke of Savoy resolved to attempt once more to deal with this menace to authority and to orthodoxy. In January 1655 an edict was issued commanding all those Vaudois living outside the prescribed limits to withdraw ; in April an army was sent to enforce the order, whereupon the Vaudois in these districts fled to their fellow religionists in the hills. The district was now cleared of the offending Vaudois and the treaty of 1651 vindicated ; but the Duke had evidently resolved to exterminate the sect. On April 24th his army attacked the villages in the tolerated area, laying

them waste ; men, women, and children were all put
to the sword, and many of those who escaped over the
Alps towards the French frontier perished in the snow.
The news of this massacre came as a great shock to
Protestant Europe, and Cromwell in his rôle of Protestant champion at once took up the cause of the
Vaudois with energy. A protest, composed by Milton,
was sent to the Duke of Savoy ; letters, also composed
by Milton, were sent to the kings of Sweden and Denmark, the Dutch Republic, and the Protestant cantons
of Switzerland, urging them as Protestant powers to join
in making representations to the Court of Savoy ; and
appeals were made to the King of France and Cardinal
Mazarin. A special envoy was also sent to Savoy to
demand redress. Cromwell was prepared, if necessary,
to go to war on behalf of the Vaudois. Meanwhile the
Vaudois had rallied and taken to arms in their own
defence ; they recaptured their territory and defeated
the Piedmontese in two decisive engagements. On
August 18th peace was signed and the former rights of
the Vaudois were restored.

P. 99, l. 4. Puritans regarded the statues and images in
churches as idolatry.

ll. 7–8. Sir Samuel Morland, Cromwell's envoy to the
Duke of Savoy, reported an instance of this barbarity.

l. 12. *The triple Tyrant :* the Pope, with his three-tiered
crown.

l. 14. *The Babylonian woe :* a reminiscence of one of
Petrarch's sonnets with which Milton is known to have
been familiar. Petrarch inveighs against the Papal
Court as " a fountain of woe " and " a false and wicked
Babylon." The Church of Rome was commonly
identified by its enemies with the mystical Babylon
whose doom is foretold in the Apocalypse (Revelation
xvii., xviii.).

## Sonnet XV (? 1655)

This sonnet reflects the agony of the first years of
Milton's blindness. Milton lost the sight of his left
eye by the beginning of 1650. In January of that year
he was requested by the Council of State to reply to
the attack of Salmasius on the English republicans, and
began his " Defence of the English People." His
physicians warned him that he ran the risk of losing the
sight of his remaining eye if he continued with the

work, but he chose the risk rather than abandon what he regarded as a sacred duty. By 1652 he was totally blind. The present sonnet, in which Milton's blindness is mentioned for the first time in his poetry, was placed after that " On the Late Massacre " in the 1673 edition, suggesting that it was written not earlier than 1655 ; but it has been argued that the mood of mere resignation expressed in the poem points rather to the period 1652–1653, after he had accepted his fate and schooled himself in patience, yet before he had come to realise that he was far from being disabled. It is certainly true that from 1654 onwards Milton did not by any means " only stand and wait." In that year he resumed his public work with " The Second Defence of the English People " ; and there he writes of his blindness in a very different strain, answering a taunt of his opponent that God had visited him with blindness as a punishment for his sins : " My blindness, with which you reproach me, deprives things of their colour and surface, but it does not take away the mind's contemplation of whatever is real and permanent in them. . . . There is a way through weakness to strength. May I be of the weakest, provided only in my weakness that immortal and better vigour be put forth with greater effect . . . thus through this infirmity I shall be consummated, perfected ; and through this darkness I shall be enlightened." In this passage, which is the prose counterpart to the famous lines on his blindness in the prologue to Book III of " Paradise Lost," Milton is claiming that his physical disability has turned to intellectual and spiritual strength ; and it was in this consciousness of renewed power that he went on not only to do further service in the cause of liberty, but to write the great poems of the final years. Yet to argue on these general grounds that the mood of passive fortitude expressed in the present sonnet was impossible to Milton in 1655 is to fail to appreciate the awful nature of the disaster that had overtaken him : who is to say what recurring crises of misery and rebellious despair he had to face and overcome, fighting again each time for the mental safety and peace that came only from patient submission to the will of God ? Milton was to make the vanquished Satan speak of " the unconquerable will . . . and courage never to submit or yield," knowing from experience that such rebellious pride was the deadly sin. It was because he himself had the courage to submit and yield that he found the courage and strength to triumph over adversity : but that was a lesson not easily learned once and for all, or to be nicely assigned to a period of so many months.

P. 99, l. 3. See Matt. vi.

P. 100, l. 12. *Thousands : i.e.* of angels.

l. 14. *Stand :* stand firm, endure.

*Wait :* Smart observes that in many passages of the Old and New Testament the word " wait " has the significance here given it by Milton. " Wait on the Lord ; be of good courage, and he shall strengthen thine heart ; wait, I say, on the Lord " (Psalms, xxxvii. 7).

### Sonnet XVI (c. 1655)

Edward Phillips gives a particular account of Milton's social life for the eight years from 1652 to 1660 during which he was living in the " pretty garden-house in Petty-France in Westminster " : " all the time of his abode there . . . he was frequently visited by persons of quality . . . all learned foreigners of note, who could not part out of the city without giving a visit to a person so eminent ; and lastly by particular friends that had a high esteem for him, *viz.* Mr. Andrew Marvel ; young Laurence (the son of him that was President of Oliver's Council) to whom there is a sonnet among the rest in his printed poems ; Mr. Marchamont Needham, the writer of ' Politicus ' ; but above all, Mr. Cyriack Skinner whom he honoured with two sonnets." The young Laurence mentioned by Phillips as the person addressed in the present sonnet was Edward Lawrence, eldest son of Henry Lawrence, who was conspicuous among Commonwealth statesmen and Lord President of the Council. Edward Lawrence was born in 1633, in 1656 became a Member of Parliament, and died in 1657 at the age of twenty-four. He appears to have been a young man of brilliant and attractive personality whose abilities gave promise of high achievements. Among the works of William Davenant is a poem " To Mr. Edward Laurence," which was probably composed on the occasion of his election to Parliament and which concludes by predicting for him an illustrious future. A similar confidence in his worth and abilities is revealed in four letters addressed to Lawrence by Henry Oldenburg, a German of some note in the philosophical and scientific world who was settled in England and later became the first secretary of the Royal Society, and who was also a friend of Milton's. These letters show clearly the affection and esteem in which Oldenburg held his young friend. In one of Milton's own letters to Oldenburg, dated August 1, 1657, he says, " To our Lawrence, as you bade me, I have given greetings in your name."

P. 100, l. 1. *Virtuous :* used in the larger Latin sense of unusual ability and merit, both mental and moral.

l. 6. *Favonius :* the west wind, harbinger of spring.

l. 8. Matt. vi. 28.

l. 9. *Neat :* dainty, elegant.

l. 10. *Attic :* marked by Athenian simplicity and refinement.

l. 13. *Spare :* forbear (an idiom in literary English derived from the similar use of Latin, *parcere*).

## Sonnet XVII (c. 1655)

Cyriack Skinner was the grandson on his mother's side of Sir Edward Coke, Chief Justice of the King's Bench from 1613 to 1616, the rival of Francis Bacon, and the leading jurist of his day. Cyriack, born in 1627, was one of the students who came to live with Milton in the house in Aldersgate, and the close friendship that then developed between them was lifelong. Smart says that the poet Marvell, in a letter written in 1654, " congratulates Milton on the fact that Mr. Skinner has taken a dwelling near his, and may now be more frequently in his society " ; and in the passage quoted in the introductory note to the preceding sonnet Phillips suggests that Skinner was the closest of all Milton's companions. He had adopted the law as a profession, being admitted a member of Lincoln's Inn in 1647. It would appear that he had imbibed Milton's political views and Milton's interest in political theory. Aubrey in his biography of Harrington, the political philosopher and author of " Oceana," tells of the club of republicans, known as the Rota Club, which in the disturbed months preceding the Restoration met every night in a coffee-house in Westminster to discuss political Utopias. Harrington was the leading spirit, but " Mr. Cyriack Skinner, an ingenious young gentleman, scholar to John Milton, was chairman." At the Restoration, when Milton's life was in danger, Skinner was one of the loyal friends who came to his assistance.

This sonnet, like the preceding one to Lawrence, imitates the Horatian manner.

l. 2. *Themis :* goddess of Justice.

P. 101, l. 3. *Volumes :* Coke's " Reports " and " Institutes of the Law of England " are legal classics.

l. 7. This line suggests that Skinner was interested in the new mathematical sciences.

l. 8. Between 1654 and 1660 Charles X of Sweden was conducting his brilliant campaigns, first in Poland and then in Denmark. At the same time France, under the astute direction of Mazarin, was pursuing her war against Spain in the Netherlands. There is a recollection of Horace's advice to his friend (" Odes," II. xi.) " to cease from enquiring what the warlike Cantabrian and the Scythians intend " and to enjoy the happiness of the moment.

## Sonnet XVIII (1655)

P. 101, l. 1. *This three years' day :* for three years (an idiom of the time). Since Milton became totally blind in the spring of 1652, we may date the sonnet 1655.

ll. 1–2. Milton is equally explicit on this point in the " Second Defence " : " so little do [my eyes] betray any external appearance of injury that they are as unclouded and bright as the eyes of those who have the keenest of sight."

l. 10. *Conscience :* consciousness.

ll. 10–13. *I.e.* in writing his " Defence of the English People." See introductory note to Sonnet XV.

## Sonnet XIX (1658)

The last of Milton's sonnets was written after the death of his second and best beloved wife. Katharine Woodcock was twenty-eight years of age when Milton married her in 1656. It appears from the sonnet that they did not meet until after Milton had become blind. In October 1657 Mrs. Milton gave birth to a daughter. The following February she died, her child surviving her only a few weeks.

P. 102, l. 1. *Saint :* Used in the double sense of " a good woman " and " a soul in heaven."

l. 2. In the tragedy of Euripides, Alcestis gives her life as a ransom for that of her husband ; but Hercules, " the son of Zeus," wrestles with death and brings Alcestis back from the grave.

ll. 5–6. The Mosaic law pronounced a woman " unclean " after childbirth and ordained a ritual of purification (Leviticus xii.).

l. 9. *Vested all in white :* cp. Revelation vii. 13–14.

ll. 10–12. *Her face was veil'd :* is usually taken to imply that Milton had never seen his wife and therefore, although he " sees " the vision, the face remains indistinct.

*Fancied sight :* the sense of seeing experienced in the dream. The blind enjoy sight in their dreams inasmuch as they are able to visualise the scenes. Both the following words of the sonnet and the fact that Milton knew that his wife's face was veiled imply that he *saw* her. Sir Arthur Pearson has said : " In my dreams I am never blind. Then I see as I used to ; and if I dream of something bringing in people whom I have only known since I lost my sight, they are, unless I have become very intimately acquainted with them, people whose faces are indistinct, though somehow I know who they are." And Mr. Booth Tarkington, who was totally blind for more than a year, has said : " It is difficult for me to realise now . . . that I have never seen several of the nurses. . . . It seemed to me that I saw everything, and so it still seems now ; my memory of those months is all in mental pictures." (These quotations are from Miss E. G. Brown's interesting book, " Milton's Blindness.")

l. 14. *Day brought back my night :* These words also clearly indicate that Milton had enjoyed sight in his dream.

# APPENDIX

## MILTON'S COSMOLOGY

MILTON's imagination took all time and space for its province and his poetry is full of cosmic imagery. It will save much commentary on the particular poems if we explain here some of the main ideas on which this imagery is based.

Milton imagines the universe in accordance with what is known as the Ptolemaic astronomy, although he was acquainted with the Copernican or modern theory. In the Ptolemaic system the earth, not the sun, was regarded as the centre of our universe. To account for the apparent movements of the stars and planets it assumed a succession of spheres wheeling at various distances and with various motions round the earth as their stationary centre. The sphere of the moon was nearest the earth, and then came in order the other planetary spheres of Mercury, Venus, the Sun, Mars, Jupiter, and Saturn ; the eighth sphere was the firmament of fixed stars. The eighth sphere was supposed to wheel from east to west, completing the revolution in twenty-four hours and carrying with it not only its own fixed stars but also the seven interior spheres of the planets ; this accounted for the alternation of night and day. The seven planetary spheres also had their separate motions, which accounted for the alterations of their positions relative to each other and to the fixed stars. Later a ninth sphere was added to account for the fact that the equinoxes occur at slightly different times each year ; and finally a tenth sphere was added. In " Paradise Lost " Milton recognises all ten spheres, but in the early poems he speaks only of nine.

There was one special doctrine or fancy grafted on to this astronomical system that was a favourite theme with Milton and is given particular expression in the " Nativity Ode," " At a Solemn Music," and " Arcades." It is fully

set forth in his Second Prolusion, " On the Harmony of the
Spheres " : " Now I beg you, my hearers, not to take this
theory too solemnly. . . . If Pythagoras taught the doctrine
of the harmony of the spheres and that the heavens turn
under the charm of a melody, surely he meant only to
suggest allegorically the mutual enfolding of their orbits
and their eternally uniform revolutions in accordance with
the fixed laws of fate. In this he followed the example of
the poets or, what is almost the same thing, the divine
oracles, by whom no holy and secret mystery is shown to
the public unless in some way veiled and cloaked. Pythagoras was followed by Plato, that best interpreter of Mother
Nature ; he relates that on each of the celestial orbs is seated
a siren, and that gods and men are rapt in wonder by their
sweet song. And finally, this universal concord and loving
agreement of all things, which Pythagoras figures in poetical
manner as harmony, Homer in turn represents by the
striking and apt metaphor of the golden chain suspended
by Jove from heaven. But Aristotle, the rival and constant
calumniator o. Pythagoras and Plato, wishing to make a
road to fame out of the ruins of these great men's opinions,
imputed to Pythagoras the literal doctrine of the unheard
symphony of the heavens and the melody of the spheres. . . .
Yet why should not the celestial bodies, in those perennial
circuits, give forth musical tones ? . . . What though no
one on earth has ever heard this symphony of the stars ?
Does it therefore follow that everything above the moon is
mute and sunk in a torpid silence ? Let us rather blame
our own weak ears which are unable or unworthy to receive
those songs and so sweet sounds. . . . But if our hearts
were pure and chaste and white as snow, as was Pythagoras'
of old, then indeed our ears would ring and be filled with
that lovely music of the circling stars ; then our world
would at once return to that golden age ; and we ourselves,
free at last from evils, would pass our lives in a blessed peace
that even the gods might envy."

# QUESTIONS

1. WRITE a summary of the "Nativity Ode."

2. In what respects is the "Nativity Ode" the first distinctively Miltonic poem?

3. What qualities does Milton most admire in Shakespeare? Do you know of any passages in Milton's poetry that reveal the influence of Shakespeare?

4. What was Milton's view of the poetic life and character?

5. Summarise the contrasted traits of L'Allegro and Il Penseroso. Does Milton seem to be presenting two distinct characters?

6. Discuss "L'Allegro" and "Il Penseroso" as nature poems. Compare them with any nature poetry of (a) the eighteenth century, (b) the nineteenth century.

7. Summarise the argument of "Comus."

8. Discuss "Comus" as a dramatic poem.

9. Compare the character of Comus with that of Satan in "Paradise Lost."

10. Compare the styles of "Comus" and "Lycidas."

11. Analyse the metrical structure of Lycidas.

12. Write down in their order the topics treated in "Lycidas," noting where the main divisions come in the movement of the poem. Has the poem unity?

13. State the effect on your mind of the pastoral conventions in "Lycidas."

14. Compare "Lycidas" with Shelley's "Adonais" and Arnold's "Thyrsis."

15. Johnson says of Lycidas: "It is not to be considered as the effusion of real passion; for passion runs not after remote allusions and obscure opinions." Discuss.

16. Write a sonnet in the form of (a) Milton's Sonnet II, (b) Sonnet XIV, (c) Sonnet XII, (d) a Shakespeare sonnet.

17. Write a character sketch of Milton based on the evidence of the Sonnets.

18. What do the Sonnets tell of Milton's political opinions?

19. Give examples of Milton's use of classical mythology to express Christian beliefs. Do you think the form of expression in these examples has an effect on the sentiment and thought ?

20. Quote examples from the present poems of what seem to you distinctive devices of Milton's style.

**THE END**

PRINTED BY R. & R. CLARK, LTD., EDINBURGH

# THE SCHOLAR'S LIBRARY

## SELECT LIST OF TITLES

### Selections : Prose

DR. JOHNSON : A SELECTION FROM BOSWELL'S BIOGRAPHY. Edited by M. ALDERTON PINK.

EIGHT ESSAYISTS. Edited by A. S. CAIRNCROSS.

MODERN ESSAYS IN CRITICISM. Edited by A. S. CAIRNCROSS.

FACT AND FICTION : AN ANTHOLOGY. Edited by A. S. CAIRNCROSS.

ADVENTURE SOUGHT AND UNSOUGHT. Edited by P. D. CUMMINS.

GREECE AND ROME : A SELECTION FROM THE WORKS OF SIR JAMES GEORGE FRAZER. Edited by S. G. OWEN.

HOMER : THE ILIAD AND THE ODYSSEY. Extracts from the Translations by LANG, LEAF and MYERS, and BUTCHER and LANG. Edited by H. M. KING and H. SPOONER.

MODERN AUTOBIOGRAPHY : AN ANTHOLOGY. Edited by FREDERICK T. WOOD.

ESSAYS AND SKETCHES. By CHARLES DICKENS. Selected and Edited by M. A. PINK.

MODERN ESSAYS. First Series, 1939-1941. Selected and Edited by A. F. SCOTT.

MODERN ESSAYS. Second Series, 1941-1943. Selected and Edited by A. F. SCOTT.

MODERN PORTRAIT ESSAYS. Edited by M. A. PINK.

POINTS OF VIEW. Edited by M. A. PINK.

MODERN ENGLISH PROSE. First Series. Edited by GUY BOAS.

MODERN ENGLISH PROSE. Second Series. Edited by GUY BOAS.

MODERN ENGLISH PROSE. Third Series. Edited by GUY BOAS.

MODERN SHORT STORIES. Edited by A. J. MERSON.

MODERN SHORT STORIES. Second Series. Edited by A. J. MERSON.

MODERN TRAVEL : AN ANTHOLOGY. Edited by F. T. WOOD.

THE DIARY OF SAMUEL PEPYS. Edited by N. V. MEERES.

PROSE OF YESTERDAY : DICKENS TO GALSWORTHY. Edited by GUY BOAS.

QUEST AND CONQUEST : AN ANTHOLOGY OF PERSONAL ADVENTURES. Compiled by E. V. ODLE.

READINGS FROM THE SCIENTISTS. Edited by EDWARD MASON.

READINGS FROM RICHARD JEFFERIES : AN ANTHOLOGY OF THE COUNTRYSIDE. Chosen by R. HOOK, M.A.

THE SCHOOLBOY IN FICTION: An Anthology. Selected by F. T. Wood.

SHORT MODERN PLAYS. First Series. Edited by Guy Boas.

SHORT MODERN PLAYS. Second Series. Edited by S. R. Littlewood.

"THE TIMES": An Anthology. Edited by M. A. Pink.

SHORT STORIES BY OSCAR WILDE. Edited by G. C. Andrews.

SHORT HISTORICAL PLAYS. By Modern Authors. Edited by E. R. Wood.

ENGLISH LIFE IN THE EIGHTEENTH CENTURY: A Prose Anthology. Selected by G. A. Sambrook.

ENGLISH LIFE IN THE NINETEENTH CENTURY. Selected by G. A. Sambrook.

SEA VOYAGES OF EXPLORATION. Edited and Selected by G. A. Sambrook.

*Selections: Poetry*

SHELLEY, SELECTIONS FROM HIS POETRY. Edited by F. B. Pinion.

BROWNING: THE RING AND THE BOOK. Edited by F. B. Pinion.

MODERN POETRY, 1922–1934. Edited by M. Wollman.

POEMS OF TWENTY YEARS: An Anthology, 1918–1938. Edited by M. Wollman.

POEMS OF THE WAR YEARS. Edited by M. Wollman.

POEMS OLD AND NEW. Edited by A. S. Cairncross.

MORE POEMS OLD AND NEW. Edited by A. S. Cairncross.

LONGER POEMS OLD AND NEW. Edited by A. S. Cairncross.

POEMS FOR YOUTH. Edited by A. S. Cairncross.

THE AENEID OF VIRGIL. Translated by John Dryden. Selections. Edited by Bruce Pattison.

THE INGOLDSBY LEGENDS. Selected and Edited by J. Tanfield.

*Selections: Prose and Poetry*

A "PUNCH" ANTHOLOGY. Edited by Guy Boas.

SELECTIONS FROM SIR W. S. GILBERT. Edited by H. A. Treble, M.A.

STORIES AND POEMS OF THOMAS HARDY. Edited by N. V. Meeres.

COUNTRY LIFE. Selected and Edited by A. F. Scott.

There are also Complete Texts by Jane Austen, John Bunyan, Charles Dickens, Thomas Hardy, A. W. Kinglake, John Milton, Sean O'Casey, R. L. Stevenson, Jonathan Swift.

MACMILLAN & CO. LTD., LONDON